P9-EDT-034

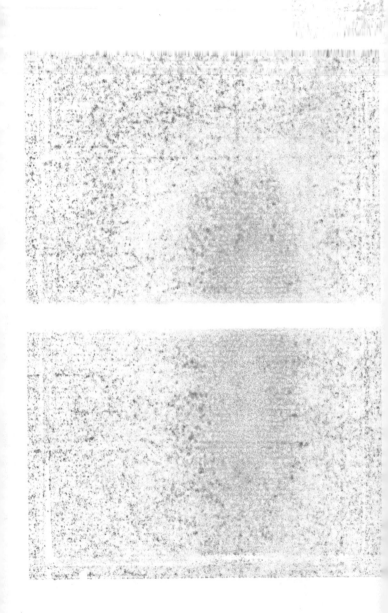

ENGLISH RECUSANT LITERATURE
1558–1640

Selected and Edited by
D. M. ROGERS

Volume 353

THOMAS A KEMPIS
The Folowing of Christ
1585

THOMAS A KEMPIS

The Folowing of Christ

1585

The Scolar Press

1977

ISBN 0 85967 398 7

Published and printed in Great Britain by
The Scolar Press Limited, 59-61 East Parade,
Ilkley, Yorkshire and
39 Great Russell Street,
London WC1

NOTE

Reproduced (original size) from a copy in the library of Stonyhurst College, by permission of the Rector.

References: Allison and Rogers 814; STC 23968/23960a

THE FOLOVVING OF

CHRIST, TRANSLATED OVT
of Latin into Englishe, newlie cor-
rected and amended.

*VVhervnto alfo is added the golden Epiftle
of Sainct Bernarde.*

And nowe laftelie the rules of a Chriftian lyfe,
made by Iohn Picus the elder earle of mirädula.

Anno. 1585.

Cum Priuilegio.

Ereafter foloweth a booke called in Latin *Imitatio Christi*, that is in Englishe, the folowing of Christe, wherein be cõteyned foure litle bookes. VVhich booke, as some men affirme, was firste made and compyled in Latin by the famous Clerke master Iohn Gerson, Chauncellour of Paris. And the sayed foure bookes be nowe of late newly tranflated into Englifh in fuch maner as hereafter appeareth. And though three of the firft bookes of the fayd foure bookes haue bene before this time right well and deuoutlie trãflated into Englifhe by a famous Clerke called mafter VVilliam Atkinfon which was a doctour of diuinitie, Yet for as muche as the fayde tranflatour (for fome caufe him mouinge) in diuers places left out muche parte of fome of the Chapters, and fometime varied from the letter, as in the thirde chapter, and in the.18 and.19.chapters of the firft booke, and alfo in diuers other chapiters of the fayde three bookes will appeare to them that will examine the Latin and the fayd firft tranflation together: Therefore the fayed. 3. bookes be eftfones trãflated into Englifh, in fuch maner as hereafter foloweth, to the intent that they that lift maye at their pleafure be occupied with the one or the other, after as their deuotion fhall ftirre them when they haue feene the both. And after the fayde three bookes foloweth the fourth booke, which was firft tranflated out of Frenche into Englifhe, by the right noble and excellent Princes Margaret late Counteffe of Richmonde and Darbye, mother vnto the noble Prince of bleffed memorie Kynge Henry the. 7.

father

father vnto our late foueraine Lord Kinge Henry
the. 8. And for as muche as it was tranflated by
the fayed noble Princes out of Frenche, it coulde
not folowe the Latin fo nigh nor fo directlie as
if it had bene tranflated out of Latin. And therefore it is nowe tranflated out of Latin, and yet
neuertheleſſe it keepeth the fubftaunce and the
effect of the firft tranflation out of Frenche,
though fometime it varie in wordes, as to the
Reader will appeare. And in the latter ende, after
the fourth booke, is a ſhort morall doctrine,
which is called The fpirituall glaſſe of the foule.
And it is right good and profitable to euery perfon ofte tymes to looke vpon it.

A preface to the booke folovvinge.

Monge manye Treatifes, which haue
bene put out both in Latin and Englifhe, in this perillous worlde, to
feduce the fimple people, & to bring
them from the vnitie of the Catho-
like Churche into peruers and abbominable errours, there hath bene alfo in ty ne paft before
made by'diuers learned and vertuous men many
good Treatifes, which yf men woulde be fo diligent to looke vpon, as they are curious to looke
on the other, they fhou!de not fo foone fall from
the true knowledge of Chriftes doctrine, and the
right fenfe of holie Scripture, whiche euer hath
bene taught by continuall fucceſsion in his holie
Churche, of the holie ghoft, the fpirite of truth,
who fhall euer remayne with it. And amonge many of thefe good Treatifes, there is one called,
the Imitation or folowinge of Chrifte, whiche in
my iudgement is excellent: and the more it is fe-
A 2   riouflye

riouflie and aduifedllie reade and looked vpon, the more it fhall like euery Chriftian Reader, who will fet his minde earneftlie to folow Chrift his fteppes. Let them proue by reading euery day a chapter whē they haue beft leafure, and I doubt not, but they fhall finde my fayinges true. I haue reade it ouer very many times, and the more I reade, the more I like it and finde profite to my foule health. It teacheth the true mortification of the flefhe to the fpirite, accordinge to the right fenfe of holie Scripture, and the doctrine of S. Paul. VVhich I confideringe defired the Queenes highnes printer to take the paynes eftfones to imprint it, feeinge the other is worne awaye, whiche was verie faultie in many places. And in this he hath done his diligence in correction thereof, as you fhall well perceyue in conferring them together. Thus fare you well in Chrift, and praye for them that haue taken paynes in this behalfe.

Hereafter folovveth the chapters. of this prefent booke.

That

                         A 3   The

The chapters of the thirde booke.

A

That

cap

The

Here endeth the Table.

Of the Imitation or folovving of Chriſte,
and of the deſpiſing of all vanities
of the vvorlde.

The firſte Chapter.

E that foloweth me (ſay=
eth Chriſte our Sauiour)
walketh not in darknes,
but he ſhall haue the light
of life. Theſe be the wordes
of our Lorde Ieſus Chriſt,
whereby we be admoniſhed and warned,
that we ſhall folowe his teachinges, and
his maner of lyuing, if wee will truely be
illumined, & be deliuered from all blind=
nes of hearte. Let all the ſtudy of our
heart be therfore from hēceforth, to haue
our meditation wholly fixed in the lyfe,
& in the holy teachinges of Ieſus Chriſte:
for his teachinges are of more vertue, &
of more ghoſtlye ſtrength , then are the
teachinges of all Angels and Saintes.
And he that thorough grace might haue
the inner eye of his ſoule opened into the
ſoothfaſt beholdinge of the Goſpels of
Chriſte, ſhould finde in thē Manna, that
is to ſay, ſpirituall foode of the ſoule: but

B   it

it is often times ſeene, that ſome perſons which ofte heare the Goſpelles of Chꝛiſt, haue litle ſweetenes therein, and that is, foꝛ that they haue not the ſpirite of Chꝛiſte. Wherefoꝛe, if we will haue the true vnderſtanding of Chꝛiſtes Goſpels, we muſt ſtudy to confoꝛme our life to his life as nigh as we can. What auaileth it a man to reaſon high ſecrete miſteries of the Trinitie, if he lack meekenes, wherby he diſpleaſeth the Trinitie? Truely no-thinge. Foꝛ high curious reaſons make not a man holie noꝛ rightwiſe, but a good lyfe maketh hym beloued with God. I had rather feele compunction of hearte foꝛ my ſinnes, then onely to knowe the diffinitiō of compunctiō. If thou couldeſt all the Bible without the booke, and alſo the ſayinges of all Philoſophers by hart, what ſhould it pꝛofite thee without gra-ce and charitie? All that is in this woꝛlde is vanitie, but to loue God, and onely to ſerue him. This is the moſt noble and the moſte excellent wiſdome that may be in any creature, by deſpiſinge of this woꝛld to dꝛawe daylie neerer and neerer to the kingedome of heauen. It is therefoꝛe a great vanitie to labour inoꝛdinatlie foꝛ woꝛldly riches, which ſhoꝛtlye ſhall pe-riſhe, and to couet honoꝛ, oꝛ any other inoꝛdinate pleaſures oꝛ fleſhlie delightes in this lyfe, wherby a man after this lyfe
ſhall

ſhall be ſore and greeuouſlye puniſhed.
Howe great a vanitie is it alſo to deſire
a longe life, and litle to care for a good
life:to heede thinges preſent, and not to
prouide for thinges that are to come:
to loue thinges that ſhortlie ſhall paſſe
away, and not to haſte thither where is
ioy euerlaſtinge. Alſo haue this common
prouerbe ofte in thy minde,That the eye
is not ſatiſfied nor fullye pleaſed with
the ſight of any bodilye thinge, ne the
eare with hearing:and therfore ſtudye to
withdrawe the loue of thy ſoule from all
thinges that be viſible, and turne it to
thinges that be inuiſible. For they that
folowe their ſenſualitie,hurt their owne
conſcience,and leeſe the grace of God.

Againſt vayne ſeculer cunning,and of a
meeke knowinge of our ſelfe.

The 2.Chapter.

Uery man naturallye deſi-
teth to knowe : but what
auaileth knowledge without
the dreade of God? A meeke
huſband man that ſerueth god,
is muche more acceptable to
him,thē is a curious Philoſopher, which
conſideringe the courſe of heauen, wilfully forgetteth him ſelfe: He that wel
                    B ij   kno

knoweth him selfe, is vile and abiect in
his owne sight, and hath no delight in
the vaine praisinges of man. If I knewe
all thinges that be in this world without
charitie, what should it auaile me before
God, that iudgeth euery man after his
deedes? Let vs therfore cease from the
desire of suche vaine knowledge: for ofte
times is founde therin great distraction
and deceipt of the enemy, wherby the
soule is muche hindred and let from the
perfect and true loue of God. They that
haue great cunninge, desire commonly to
be seene, and to be holden wyse in the
worlde, and there be many thinges, that
the knowledge of them bringe but litle
profite and fruit to the soule, and he is
verye vnwyse that taketh heede to any
other thinge, then to that which shall
profite hym to the health of his soule.
Wordes feede not the soule, but a good
life refresheth the minde, and a cleane
conscience bringeth a man to a firme and
stable trust in God. The more cunninge
thou haste, if thou liue not therafter, the
more greeuouslie shalte thou therefore be
iudged, for the misusinge thereof. Therefore raise not thy selfe into pride, for any
crafte or cunninge that is geuen vnto
thee, but haue therefore the more feare
and dreade in thy heart: for certayne it
is, that thou must hereafter yeelde therefore

foze the ſtrayter accompt. If thou thinke
that thou knoweſt many thinges, and
haſt great cunninge, yet knowe it foz cer=
taine, that there be many mo things that
thou knoweſt not: and ſo thou mayeſt
not rightwiſely thinke thy ſelfe cunning,
but oughteſt rather to cõſeſſe thine igno=
raunce and vncunninge. Why wilt thou
preferre thy ſelfe in cũning befoze other,
ſith there be many other moze excellent
and moze cunning then thou, and better
learned in the law? If thou wilt any
thinge learne and knowe, profitably to
the health of thy ſoule, learne to be vn=
knowen, and be glad to be holden vile &
nought, & vncunninge as thou art. The
moſt high and the moſte profitable cun=
ninge is this, a man to haue a ſoothfaſt
knowledge, and a full deſpiſinge of him
ſelfe. Alſo a man not to preſume of him=
ſelfe, but alwaye to iudge and thinke wel
and bleſſedly of other, is a ſigne & a token
of great wiſdome, and of great perfectiõ
and ſinguler grace. If thou ſee any perſõ
ſinne, oz commit any great crime openly
befoze thee, yet iudge not thy ſelfe to be
better then he, foz thou knoweſt not how
longe thou ſhalt perſeuer in goodnes.
We be all frayle: but thou ſhalt iudge no
man moze frayle then thy ſelfe.

B iij   Of

The. 3. Chapter.

Appye and bleſſed is that perſon whom truth teacheth and
enformeth, not by figures, oʒ
by deceitful voyces, but as
the truth is: our opinion and
our wit many times deceiueth vs, foʒ
we ſee not the truth. What auayleth vs
the knowledge of ſuche thinges as ſhal
neyther helpe vs at the daye of iudgement if we knowe them, noʒ hurt vs if
we know them not. It is therfoʒe great
folly to be negligent in ſuche things as
be pʒofitable and neceſſary to vs, and to
labour foʒ ſuch thinges that be but curious and damnable. Truely if we doo
ſo, we haue eyes but we ſee not. And
what auayleth vs the knowledge of the
kinde and woʒking of creatures? truely
nothing. He to whom the euerlaſting
woʒde (that is Ieſus) ſpeaketh, is diſcharged of many vayne opinions, and
of that woʒde al thinges pʒoceede, and
all thinges openlye ſhewe and crye, that
he is God. No man without him vn-
derſtädeth the truth, ne rightfully iudgeth, but he to whom al thinges is one,
and he that all thinges dʒaweth into
one, and all thinges ſetteth in one,
and.

and deſireth nothinge but one, may
quickly be eſtabliſhed in heart, and be
fully pacifyed in God. O truth that
God art, make me one with thee in perfect charitie, for all that I reade, heare,
or ſee without thee, is greeuous to me,
for in thee is all that I wil or maye deſire. Let all Doctours be ſtil in thy preſence, and let all creatures keepe them
in ſilence, and thou only Lord ſpeake to
my ſoule. The more that man is ioyned
to thee, and the more that he is gathered
together in thee, the more he vnderſtan-
deth without labour high ſecrete miſteries: for he hath recepued from aboue
the light of vnderſtanding. A cleane,
pure, and a ſtable hart is not broken ne
lightly ouercome with ghoſtely labours,
for he doeth al thing to the honour of
God: and for that he is cleerely mortifyed to him ſelf, therfore he coueteth
to be free from folowing his owne wil.
What hindereth thee more then thy
affections not fully mortifyed to the wil
of the ſpirite? truelye nothing more. A
good deuout man ſo ordereth his outwarde buſines, that it draweth not him
to the loue of it, but that he compell it
to be obedient to the wil of the ſpirite,
& to the right iudgemēt of reaſon. Who
hath a ſtronger battayle then he that
laboureth for to ouercome him ſelfe? and
that

that shoulde be our dayly labour & our dayly desire to ouercome our selfe, that we may be made stronger in spirite, and increase daily frō better to better. Euery perfectiō in this life hath some imperfection annexed vnto it, and there is no knowledge in this worlde but that it is mixt with some blindnes of ignorance. And therfore a meeke knowing of our selfe is a more surer way to God, then is the searching for highnes of cunning. Cunning wel ordred is not to be blamed, for it is good and cōmeth of God: but a clean conscience and a vertuous life is muche better, & more to be desired. Because some men studye to haue cunning rather then to liue well, therfore they erre many times, and bring forth litle good fruite or none. O if they woulde be as busye to auoyde sinne, and to plante vertues in their soules as they be to moue questions, there shoulde not be so many euill thinges seene in the worlde, ne so much euil example geuen to the people, ne yet so much dissolute liuing in religiō. At the daye of iudgement it shall not be asked of vs, what we haue read, but what we haue done, nor howe well we haue sayde, but howe religiously we haue liued. Tell me nowe, where be all the great clerkes and famous doctors, whom thou haste wel-
kno-

knowen?when they liued,they flourish=
ed greatly in their learning, and now
other men occupy their prebendes & pro=
motiōs,and I can not tell whether they
think any thing on thē:in their life they
were holden great in the world, & nowe
is litle speaking of thē. O howe shortly
passeth away the glorye of this world,
with al the false deceauable plesures of
it?would to God their life had accorded
well with their learning, for then had
they well studied and read. How many
perishe dayly in this worlde by vayne
cunning, that care litle for a good life,
ne for the seruice of God. And because
they desire rather to be great in the
worlde then to be meeke, therfore they
banishe awaye in their learninges as
smoke in the ayre. Truely he is great
that hath great charitie:and he is great
that is litle in his owne sight,and that
setteth at nought all worldly honour.
And he is very wise,that accompteth all
worldly pleasures as vile dounge, so
that he maye winne Christe. And that
person is very wel taught,that forsaketh
his owne will, and foloweth the will of
God.

B iij

The.4.Chapter.

 T is not good lightly to be=
leeue euery worde o₂ inſtinct
that commeth, but the thing
is aduiſedly and leaſurely to
be cōſidered & pondered, that
almightie God be not offended through
our lightnes. But alas fo₂ ſo₂owe,
we be ſo fraile, that we anone beleeue
of other euil, ſoner then good. But ne=
uertheles, perfect men be not ſo light of
credence, fo₂ they know well, that the
frayltie of man is mo₂e p₂one to euil thē
to good, and that it is in wo₂des very
bnſtable. Jt is therefo₂e great wiſdome,
not to be haſtie in our deeds, ne to truſt
much in our own wits, no₂ lightly to
beleeue euery tale, no₂ to ſhewe anone
to other al that we heare o₂ beleeue. Take
alway counſel of a wiſe man, and couet
rather to be inſtructed and o₂d₂ed by
other, then to folowe thine owne in=
uention. A good life maketh a man wiſe
to God, and inſtructeth him in many
things, that a ſinful man ſhal neuer
feele ne knowe. The mo₂e meeke that a
man is in him ſelfe, & the mo₂e obedient
that he is to God, the mo₂e wiſe & the
mo₂e peaceful ſhall he be in euery thing
that he ſhal haue to do.

Of

Of the readinge of holy Scripture.

The. 5 .Chapter.

Charitie is to be sought in holye
Scripture, and not eloquence,
and it should be read with the
same spirite that it was firste
made. We ought also to seeke
in holy Scriture , ghostlye profite rather
then curiositie of stile, and as gladly shall
we reade simple and deuoute bookes, as
bookes of high learninge and cunninge.
Let not the authoritie of thine authour
mislike thee, whether he were of greate
cunning or litle : but that the loue of the
verye pure truth styr thee to reade. Aske
not who sayde this, but take heede what
is sayde. Men passe lightlye awaye, but
the truth of God euer abideth. Almightie God speaketh to vs in his Scripture
in diuers maners, without acceptinge of
persons: but our curiositie ofte letteth vs
in reading of Scripture , when we will
reason and argue thinges that we should
meekely and simply passe ouer. If thou
wilt profite by readinge of Scripture,
reade meekely, simply, and faithfullye, &
neuer desire to haue thereby the name of
cunning. Aske gladlye, and heare meekely the sayinges of Saintes , & mislike not
the parables of ancient fathers , for they
were not spoken without great cause.

Of

The 6.Chapter.

When a man deſireth any thinge inordinatelye, forth=with he is vnquiet in him ſelfe. The proude man, & the couetous man neuer haue reſt: but thee meeke man, and the poore in ſpirite liueth in greate aboundance of reſt & peace. A man that is not yet morti=fied to himſelfe, is lightly tempted and ouercome in litle and ſmall temptations. And he that is weake in ſpirite, and is yet ſome what carnall, and inclined to ſenſible thinges, maye hardly withdrawe himſelfe from worldly deſires: And ther=fore he hath oft greate griefe & heauines in heart, when he withdraweth him from them, and he diſdayneth anone, if any man reſiſt him, and if he obteyne that he deſireth, yet is he vnquieted with grudge of conſcience, for he hath folowed his paſſion which nothinge helpeth to the getting of that peace he deſired. Then by reſiſting of paſſions is gotten the very true peace of heart, and not by folowing of them There is therfore no peace in the heart of a carnall man, nor in the hearte of a man that geueth him ſelfe all to out=ward thinges: but in the heart of a ghoſtli man

man or woman which haue their delite in
God,is founde great peace and inwarde
quietnes.

*That vayne hope and elation of mynde are
to be fled and auoyded.*

The.7.Chapter.

E is vayne that putteth his
trust in man,or in any creature. Be not ashamed to serue
other for the loue of Iesu
Christe,and to be poore in this
worlde for his sake:trust not thy selfe,but
all thy trust set in God:doo that in the is
to please him , & he shall well helpe forth
thy good will. Trust not in thine owne
cunning,neither in the cunning or pollicie of any creature liuinge, but rather in
the grace of God , which helpeth meeke
persons,and those that presume of them
selues , he suffereth to fall till they be
meeke.Glorify not thy selfe in thy riches,
nor in thy worldlie freends,for that they
be mightie,but let all thy glorie be in god
onelie that geueth all thinges , and that
desireth to geue himselfe aboue all thin-
ges.Exalt not thy selfe for the largenes
or fayrenes of bodie,for with a litle sickenes it may be soone defouled. Ioy not in
thy selfe for thy habilitie or readines of
wit,

wit, least thou displease God, of whose gifte it is all that thou hast. Holde not thy selfe better then other, least happlye thou be thereby impaired in the sight of God, who knoweth all that is in man. Be not proude of thy good deedes, for the iudgementes of God be other then the iudgementes of man, to whom it displeaseth ofte times, that pleaseth man. If thou haue any goodnes or vertue in thee, beleeue yet that there is much more goodnes & vertue in other, so that thou maiest alwaye keepe thee in meeknes. It hurteth not though thou holde thy selfe worse then any other, though it be not so in deede, but it hurteth much if thou preferre thy selfe aboue any other, be he neuer so great a sinner. Great peace is with the meeke mā, but in the heart of a proud man is alwaye enuye and indignation.

That muche familiaritie is to be auoyded.

The.8.Chapter.

Pen not thy heart to euery person, but to him that is wise, secrete, and dreadinge God. Be seldome with yonge folkes and straūgers: flatter not riche men, and afore great men do not lightly appeare. Accompanie thy selfe with

with meeke persons and simple in heart, who be deuoute & of good gouernaunce, and treate with them of things that may edify and strength the soule. Be not famillier to any woman, but all good women commend to God. Couete to be familier onelie with God and with his Angels: but the familiaritie of man, as much as thou mayest, looke thou eschewe. Charitie is to be had to all: but familiaritie is not expedient. Sometime it happeneth, that a person vnknowen thorough his good fame is much commendable, whose presence after liketh vs not so muche. We weene sometyme with our presence to please other, when we rather displease them, through the euill maners and euill conditions that they see and will consider in vs.

Of meeke subiection and obedience, and that vve shall gladly folovve the counsayle of others.

The 9. Chapter.

It is a great thing to be obedient, to lyue vnder a prelate, and in nothing to seeke our owne libertie. It is much more surer waye, to stande in the state of obedience, then in the state of prelacie

prelacie.Many be vnder obedience moze
of necessitie then of charitie, and they
haue great paine, and lightlye murmure
and grudge:and they shall neuer haue li=
bertie and freedome of spirite, till they
whollye submit them selues vnto their
superiour.Go here and there where thou
wilt, and thou shall neuer finde perfect
rest, but in meeke obedience vnder the
gouernance of thy prelate. The imagi=
ning and chaunging of place hath decea=
ued many a religious person:Truth it is,
that euery man is disposed to doo after
his owne will, and best can agree with
them that folowe his wayes. But if we
will that God be amonge vs , we must
sometime leue our owne will, though it
seeme good, that we may haue loue and
peace with other.Who is so wise that he
can fully knowe all thinges?truely none.
Therefoze trust not to muche to thyne
owne witt, but heare gladlye the coun=
sayle of other. And if percase the thinge
which thou wouldest haue done be good
and profitable,and yet neuertheleffe thou
leauest thine owne will therein, and fo=
lowest other,thou shalt finde much pzo=
fite therby. I haue often times heare say,
that it is the moze surer waye to heare
and take counsell,then it is to geue it.It
is good to heare euerie mans counsel,but
not to agree,when reason requireth,it is

a

a figne of a great fingularitie of minde,
and of much inward pride.

That vve fhoulde auoyde fuperfluitie of vvor-
des,and the company of vvorldly
liuinge people.

The.10.Chapter.

Lee the company of wordly
liuinge people as much as
thou maieſt : for the trea-
tinge of wordlie matters
letteth greatlie the feruour
of ſpirite:though it be done
with a good intent,we be anone deceiued
with vanitie of the world , and in maner
are made as thral vnto it, if we take not
good heede. I would I had helde my
peace many times when I haue ſpoken,
and that I had not beene ſo much amōge
wordly company as I haue beene. But
why are we ſo glad to ſpeake and com-
men together , ſith we ſo ſeldome depart
without ſome hurt of conſcience?This is
the cauſe, By our comminge together we
thinke to comforte eche other,and to re-
freſhe our hearts when we be troubled
with vaine imaginations,and we ſpeake
moſte gladly of ſuch thinges as we moſte
loue , or els of thinges that be moſte contrarious vnto vs.But alas for ſorowe,
all

all is vaine that we doo: for this out=
ward comfort is no litle hinderance of
the true inward comfort that commeth
of God. Therfore it is neceſſarie, that we
watche and pray, that the time paſſe not
away from vs in ydlenes. If it be lawfull
and expedient to ſpeake, ſpeake then of
God, and of ſuche thinges as are to the
edifyinge of thy ſoule, or of thy neigh=
bours. An euill vſe, and a negligence of
our ghoſtly profite, maketh vs ofte times
to take litle heede how we ſhould ſpeake.
Neuertheleſſe, ſometime it helpeth right
much to the health of the ſoule, a deuout
commoning of ſpirituall thinges, ſpecial=
ly when men of one minde and ſpirite in
God, doo meete, and ſpeake and common
together.

The meanes to get peace, and of deſire to
profite in vertues.

The. 11. Chapter.

We might haue much pea=
ce, if we would not meddle
with other mens ſayinges
and doeinges that belong
not vnto vs. How may he
longe liue in peace, that
wilfully will medle with other mens bu=
ſines, and that ſeeketh occaſions abroade
in

in the worlde, and seldome or neuer ga-
thereth him selfe together in God. Bleffed be the true, simple and meeke persons, for they shal haue great plentie of
peace. Why haue many saintes bene so
perfectly contemplatiue, for they alway
studied to mortifie thē selues fro worldly desires, that they might freely with
al the power of their hart tend to our
lord. But we be occupied with our paf-
fions, and be muche busied with transitory thinges, & it is very seldome that
we may fully ouercome any one vice:
And we be nothing quicke to our due-
ties, wherfore we remayne colde & slowe
to deuotion. If we were perfectly mortifyed to the world and to the fleshe, and
were inwardly purifyed in soule, we
shoulde anone sauour heauēly thinges,
and somewhat shoulde we haue experience of heauenly contemplation. The
greatest hinderance of the heauenly cō-
templation is, for we are not yet cleerly
deliuered from al passions and concupiscence, ne we enforce not our self to
folowe the way that holy Saints haue
gone before vs: but when any litle aduersitie commeth to vs, we be anone cast
downe therin, and turne vs ouer soone
to seeke mans cōfort. But if we woulde,
as strong men, and as mightie champiōs
fight strongly in this ghostlye battayle,

we.

we ſhoulde vndoubtedlye ſee the helpe
of God come in our neede: for ho is al=
way redy to helpe al them that truſt in
him, and he procureth occaſions of ſuche
battayle, to thende we ſhould ouercome
and haue the victorye, and in the ende
to haue the greater reward therfore. If
we ſet the ende and perfection of our re=
ligion in theſe outward obſeruaunces,
our deuotiō ſhal ſoone be ended. Wher=
fore we muſt ſet our axe depe to the
roote of the tree, that we (purged frō al
paſſiōs,) may haue a quiet minde. If we
wold euery yeare ouercome one vice, we
ſhould anone come to perfection: But I
feare rather, that contrariwiſe we were
better and more pure in the beginning
of our conuerſiō, then we be many yeres
after we were cōuerted. Our feruor and
deſire to vertue ſhould dayly increaſe in
vs, as we increaſe in age: But it is now
thought a great thing, if we may holde a
litle ſparcle of the feruor that we had
fyrſt: but if we would at the beginning
break the euil inclination that we haue
to our ſelfe and to our owne wil, we
ſhould after doo vertuous workes eaſily,
and with great gladnes of heart. It is
an harde thing to leaue euil cuſtomes,
but it is more hard to breake our owne
wil, but it is moſt harde, euermore to lye
in payne, and endleſlye to loſe the ioyes
of

of heauen If thou ouercome not small
thinges and light, howe shalt thou then
ouercome the greater? Resist therefore
quickelie in the beginninge thy euill in-
clinations, and leaue of whollie all thine
euill customes, least happlie by litle and
litle they bringe the after to greater dif-
ficultie. O if thou wouldest consider how
great inwarde peace thou shouldest haue
thy selfe, and how great gladnes thou
shouldest cause in other, in behauinge of
thy selfe well, I suppose verilye thou
wouldest be much more diligent to profite in vertue, then thou haste bene before this time.

Of the profite of aduersitie.

The. 12. Chapter.

T is good, that we haue sometime griefes and aduersities:
for they driue a man to beholde
him selfe, and to see, that he is
here but as in an exile, and be
learned therby to know, that he ought
not to put his trust in any worldly thing.
It is good also, that we suffer sometime
contradiction, and that we be holden of
other as euill and wretched, and sinfull,
though we doo well and intend well:
for such thinges helpe vs to meekenes,
and

and mightilye defende vs from vayne glorie & pride. We take God the better to be our iudge and witnes , when we be outwardlis despiſed in the worlde, and that the worlde iudgeth not well of vs. Therefore a man ought to settle himselfe so fullie in God , that what aduersitie so euer befall vnto him, he ſhall not nede to seke any outward cōfort. When a good mā is troubled or tēpted, or is inquieted with euill thoughtes , then he vnderſtā: deth & knoweth that God is moſt neceſ: ſarie to him,& that he may nothinge doo that is good without him,Then he soro: weth , waileth & prayeth for the miseries that he rightfully ſuffereth:Thē it yrketh him also the wretchednes of this life,& he coueteth to be diſſolued frō this bodie of death),& to be with Chriſt.And thē also he ſeeth well,that there may be no ful peace nor perfect quietnes here in this worlde.

Of temptations to be reſiſted.

The 13. Chapter.

A S longe as we liue i this worlde we may not be fully without temptation.For as Iob ſayth, temptation is the life of mā vpon earth , therefore euery man ſhould beware well againſt his tēp:
ta:

tations , and watche in prayers that
the ghostly enemy finde not time & place
to deceiue him, which neuer sleepeth, but
alwaye goeth about , seekinge whom he
may deuoure. There is no man so perfect
nor so holye in this worlde, that he sometime hath not temptations. And we may
not fully be without the: for though they
be for the time verye greeuous and painfull, yet if they be resisted, they be verye
profitable : for a man by experiēce of such
temptations is made more meeke, and is
also purged & informed in diuers maner,
which he should neuer haue knowen, but
by experience of suche temptations. All
blessed Sainctes that nowe be crowned
in heauē, grewe and profited by temptations and tribulations , and those that
coulde not well beare temptations , but
were finallye ouercome, be taken perpetuall prisoners in hell. There is no order
so holy, ne no place so secrete, that is fully
without temptatiō, and there is no man
that is fully free from it here in this life:
for in our corrupt body we beare the matter whereby we be tempted, that is, our
inordinate concupiscence , wherein we
were borne. As one temptation goeth,
another commeth, and so we shall alway
haue somewhat to suffer: and the cause
is, for we haue lost our innocencie. Many
folke seeke to flee temptation, and they
fall

fall the more greeuouslie into it : For by
onely fleeing we may not haue victory,
but by meekenes & patience we be made
stronger then al our enemies. He that
only flieth the outward occasions , and
cutteth not away the inordinate desires
hid inwardly in the heart, shal litle profite , and temptations shal lightly come
to him againe,and greeue him more then
they did fyrste, by litle and litle with patience and sufferaunce , & with the helpe
of God, thou shal sooner ouercome temptations then with thine owne strength
and importunitie. In thy temptation it
is good that thou ofte aske counsayle , &
that thou be not rigorous to no person
that is tempted : but be glad to comfort
him, as thou wouldest be comforted.The
beginning of all euil temptatiõs is incõ-
stancie of mind , & to litle a trust in God.
For as a ship without guide is driuen
hither and thither with euery storme , so
an vnstable man that anone leaueth his
good purpose in God, is diuerslye tem-
pted.The fyre proueth gold, and temptation proueth the righteous man. We
know not many times what we can
suffer, but temptation sheweth plainely
what we are , and what vertue is in vs.
It is necessary in the beginning of euery
temptation to be wel ware , for then
the enemy is soone ouercome, if he be
not

not suffered to enter into the heart, but
that he be resisted and shut out assoone as
he profferech to enter: For as a bodily medicine is verie late ministred, when the
sickenes hath bene suffred to increase by
longe continuance: so is it of temptation.
Firste commeth to the minde an vncleane
thought, and after foloweth a stronge
imagination, and then delectation and
diuers euill motions, and in the ende foloweth a full assent, and so by litle & litle
the enemy hath ful entrie, for he was not
wisely resisted in the beginninge: and the
more slowe that a man is in resisting, the
more weake he is to resist, & the enemye
is daylie the more stronger against him.
Some persons haue their greatest temptations in the beginninge of their conuersion, some in the ende, and some in
maner all their lyfe tyme be troubled
therewith, and there be many that be but
lightlie tempted, and all this commeth of
the great wisedome and righteousnes of
God, which knoweth the state & merite
of euery person, & ordeineth all thinges
for the best, and to the euerlastinge health
and saluation of his elect & chosen people. Therefore we shal not dispayre when
we be tempted, but shall the more feruet-
lye praye vnto God, that he of his infinite goodnes and fatherlie pitie vouchesafe to helpe vs in euery ende, and that
he, (according to the sayinge of S. Paule)

C		so

to preuent vs with his grace in euerye temptation, that we may be able to suſtayne. Let vs then meeken our ſoules vnder the ſtronge hand of allmyghtie God, for he will ſaue all them, and exalt all them that be here meeke and lowly in ſpirite. In temptations and tribulatiõs a man is proued howe much he hath profited, and his merite is thereby the greater before God, and his vertues are the more openlie ſhewed. It is no great meruaile if a man be feruent and deuoute when he feeleth no griefe: but if he can ſuffer patientlie in time of temptation or other aduerſitie, and therewithall can also ſtirre himſelfe to feruour of ſpirite, it is a token, that he ſhall greatly profite hereafter in vertue and grace. Some perſons be kept from many great temptations, and yet daylie they be ouercome through litle and ſmall occaſions, and that is of the great goodnes and ſufferance of God to keepe them in meeknes, that they ſhall not truſt ne preſume of them ſelues, that ſee them ſelues ſo lightlye, and in ſo lytle thinges daylie ouercome.

That

That vve shall not iudge lightly other mens deedes, nor cleaue much to our ovvne vvill.

The 14. Chapter.

Aue alwaye a good eye to thy selfe, and beware thou iudge not lightlye other men. In iudging other men a man ofte laboureth in vaine, ofte erreth, and lightly offendeth God: but in iudging him selfe and his owne deedes, he alwayes laboreth fruitfully, and to his ghostly profite. We iudge oftentimes after our owne hart and affections, & not after the truth: for we ofte lose the true iudgment through our priuate loue. But if God were alwaye the whole intent of our desire, we should not so lightly erre in our iudgementes, nor so lightly be troubled, for that we be resisted of our will. But commonly there is in vs some inward inclinatiō, or some outward affection, that draweth our heart with them from the true iudgmēt. Many persōs through a secrete loue that they haue to their selfe, worke vndiscretlye after their owne will, & not after the will of God, and yet they weene not so: and they seeme to stand in great inwarde peace when thinges folowe after their minde; but if it folowe otherwise then they would, anone they be moued with

C v impa·

impatience, and be right heauy and pen-
sife. By diuersities of opinions be sprong
many times dissentions betwene frendes and neighboures, and also betweene
religious and deuoute persons. An olde
custome is hardly broken, & no man will
lightly be remoued from his owne will:
but yf thou cleaue more to thine owne
will or to thine owne reason, then to the
meeke obedience of Iesus Christe, it will
be long or thou be a man illumined with
grace. For almightie God will, that we be
perfectlie subiect and obedient to him, &
that we ascend and rise high aboue our
owne will, and aboue our owne reason,
by a greate brenning loue, and a whole
desire to him.

Of vvorkes done in charitie.

The 15. Chapter.

F
Or nothing in the world, nor
for the loue of any creature, is
euill to be done, but sometime
for the neede and comfort of
our neighbour a good deede
may be deferred, or be turned into another good deede, for thereby the good
deede is not destroyed, but is chaunged
into better. Without charitie the outwarde deede is litle to be praysed: but
whatsoeuer is done of charitie, be it neuer

uer so litle, o2 neuer so despisable in sight
of the wo2lde, it is right p2ofitable befo2e
God, who iudgeth all thing after the intent of the doer, & not after the greatnes
o2 wo2thines of the deede. He doth much
that much loueth God, & he doth much
that doeth his deede well, and he doeth
his deede well, that doth it rather fo2 the
comminaitie then fo2 his owne will. A
deede sometime seemeth to be done of
charitie and of loue to God, when it is
rather done of carnalitie, and of a fleshly
loue, then of a charitable loue: fo2 comon-
lie some carnall inclinatio to our fredes,
o2 some ino2dinate loue to our selfe, o2
some hope of a tempo2all reward, o2 a desire of some other p2ofite, moueth vs to
doe the deede, and not the pure loue of
charitie. Charitie seeketh not him selfe in
that he doth, but he desireth to doe onlie
that, which shalbe honour and p2aysinge
to God. He enuieth no man, fo2 he loueth
no p2iuate loue, neither wil he ioy in him
selfe, but he coueteth aboue all thinges to
be blessed in God. He knoweth well, that
no goodnes beginneth o2iginallie of ma,
and therefo2e he referreth all goodnes to
God, of whom all thinges p2oceede, and
in whom all blessed Saintes doe rest in
euerlasting fruition. Oh, he that had but
a lytle sparkle of this perfect charitie,
should feele soothfastlie in his soule, that
all earthlie thinges be full of vanitie.

       C iij

The. 16. Chapter.

Uche defaultes as we can not amende in our selues nor in other, we must patientlye suffer, til our Lord of his goodnes wil otherwise dispose. And we shall thinke, that happlye it is so best for to be for prouinge of our patience, without which our merites are but litle to be pondred. Neuertheleffe, thou shalte pray hartilye for suche impedimentes, that our Lorde of his great mercye and goodnes vouchsafe to helpe vs, that we may patientlye beare them. If thou admonishe any person once or twise, and he will not take it, striue not ouermuche with him, but commit al to God, that his wil be Done, and his honour in al his seruauntes, for he can wel by his goodnes turne euil into good. Study alway, that thou maiest be patient in suffering of other mens defaultes, for thou haste many thinges in thee, that other doe suffer of thee: and if thou canste not make thy selfe to be as thou wouldest, how mayest thou then looke to haue another to be ordered in al thinges after thy wil? We woulde gladlye haue other perfect, but wil not amēde our owne defaultes. We would that other should be straitly corrected

rected for their offences , but we will
not be corrected. It misliketh vs , that
other haue libertie , but we will not
be denyed of that we aske. We wolde
also,that other should be restrained accor
ding to the statutes , but we in no wise
wilbe restrayned.Thus it appeareth eui
dentlye , that we seldome ponder our
neighbour,as we doe our selfe. If al men
were perfect,what had we then to suffer
of our neighbours for God? Therfore
God hath so ordeyned , that one of vs
shal learne to beare anothers burden:for
in this world no man is without default, no man without burden , no man
sufficiente to him selfe,nor no man wise
ynough of him selfe. Wherefore it behoueth eche one of vs to beare the bur
den of other , to comfort other , to helpe
other , to enforme other , and to instruct
and admonish other in all charitie : who
is of most vertue, appeareth beste in time
of aduersitie. Occasions make not a man
frayle,but they shewe openly what he is.

VVhat sholde be the life of a true religious
person.

The. 17. Chapter.

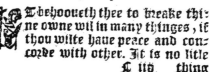
T behooueth thee to breake thi-
ne owne wil in many thinges , if
thou wilte haue peace and con-
corde with other. It is no litle

thing to be in monasteries or in congre-
gations, and to continue there without
complayning or missaying, & faithfully
to perseuer there vnto the ende: Blessed
are they that there liue well, and make a
good ende. If thou wilt stand surely in
grace, and muche profite in vertue, holde
thy selfe as an outlaw, and as a pilgrime
here in this life, and be glad (for the
loue of God) to be holden as a foole, and
as a vile person in the worlde, as thou
art. The habite and tonsure helpe litle,
but the chaunging of life, and the mortifying of passiōs make a person perfect
and true religious. He that seeketh any
other thing in religion, then purely god,
and the health of his soule, shal finde
nothing there but trouble and sorowe,
and he may not lōg stand there in peace
and quietnes that laboreth not to be
least and subiect to all. It is good therfore that thou remember ofte, that thou
camste to religion to serue, and not to be
serued, and that thou art called thither
to suffer and to labour, & not to be ydle,
or to tel vayn tales. In religion a man
shal be proued as gold in a fornace,
and no man may stand long
there in grace and vertue,
but he wil with al his
heart meeke him selfe
for the loue
of God.

Of the examples of holy fathers.

The. 18. Chapter.

Eholde the liuely examples of holy fathers and blessed Saintes, in whom flourished and shined all true perfection of life and perfecte religion. And thou shalt see howe litle it is , and welnigh as nothing , that we doe nowe in these dayes, in comparison of them: O what is our life, if it be to them compared? They serued our Lorde in hunger and thirste, in heate & in colde , in nakednes, in laboure and in werines, in vigiles and fastinges, in prayers , & in holy meditations , in persecutions, and in many reproufes. O how manye, and howe greeuous tribulations suffered the Apostles, Martyrs, Confessours , virgins , & other holy Saintes , that would folowe the steppes of Christe? They refused honours and all bodily pleasures here in this life, that they might alway haue the euerlasting life. O howe straite and abiecte a life led the holy fathers in wildernes? how greeuous temptatios suffred they, howe fiersly were they with their ghostly enemies assailed, and how feruent prayer offered they dailye to God? What rigorous abstinence vsed they , howe great zeale and feruour had they to spirituall proffit : how strong battayle helde they againſt all ſinne, and howe pure & whole intent had they to God in all their deedes? On the day they labored, & in the night they prayed. And though they labored on the day bodily, yet they prayed in minde, and ſo they ſpent their time alway fruitfullye, and thought euery houre ſhorte for the ſeruice of God : and for the great ſweetenes that they had in heauenly contemplatiō, they forgot ofte times their bodily refection. All riches, honour, dignities, kinſemen and frendes they renounced for the loue of god. They coueted to haue nothing in the worlde, & ſcarſely they would take that was neceſſary for the bodily kinde. They were poore in worldly goodes, but they were riche in grace & vertue. They were needy outwardly, but inwardly in their ſoules they were repleniſhed with grace and ghoſtly cōfortes. To the world they were alienes and ſtrangers, but to God they were right deere and familier frendes. In the ſight of the world, and in their owne ſight they weare vile & abiecte, but in the ſight of God and his Saintes they were precious, & ſingulerlye electe. In thē ſhined all perfection of vertue, true meekenes, ſimple obedience, charitie & patiēce, with other like vertues & gracious giftes of God: Wherefore they profited dayly in ſpirit, & obteyned great grace of God.

They

They be lefte as an exāple to al religious
persons: and more ought their examples
to stirre them to deuotiō, and to profite
more and more in vertue and grace, then
the great multitude of dissolute & ydle
persons shoulde anye thing drawe them
abacke. O what feruour was in religious persons at the beginning of their
religion? what deuotion in prayers?
what zeale to vertue? what loue to ghostlye discipline? and what reuerence and
meeke obedience flourished in thē vnder
the rule of their superiour? Truely their
deedes yet beare witnes, that they were
holy and perfect, & so, mightily subdued
the world, and thruste it vnder foote.
Nowe a dayes he is accōpted vertuous,
that is no offender, and that may with
patience keepe some litle sparcle of that
vertue and feruor that he had firste. But
alas for sorowe, it is through our owne
slouth and negligence, and through lo-
sing of time, that we be so soone fallen
from our first feruour into suche a ghostly weaknes and dulnes of spirite, that
in maner it is to tedious to vs for to
liue. But woulde to God, that the
desire to profite in vertue slepte
not so vtterly in thee, that so
ofte haste seene the holy
examples of blessed
Saintes.

D

The 19. Chapter.

He lyfe of a good religious man should shine in all vertue, and be inward, as it appereth outwarde, and that much more inwarde: for almightie God beholdeth the heart. Whom we should alwaye honour and reuerence, as if we were euer in his bodilye presence, and appere afore him as Angels clene and pure, shining in all vertue: we ought euery daye to renewe our purpose in God, and to stirre our heart to feruor and deuotiō, as though it were the firste daye of our conuersion, & dayly we shall pray and say thus: Helpe me my Lorde Jesu, that I may perseuer in good purpose, and in thy holy seruice vnto my death, & that I may nowe this present daye perfectly beginne, for it is nothinge that I haue done in time past. After our purpose, and after our intent shalbe our reward: And though our intent be neuer so good, yet it is necessarie, that we put therto a good will, and a great diligence. For if he that often times purposeth to doe well and to profite in vertue, yet fayleth in his doing, what shall he doe then, who seldome or neuer taketh such purpose? Let vs intend to doe the best

we

we can, and yet our good purpose may
happē to be hindred and letted in diuers
maners.And our speciall hinderaunce is
this,that we so lightly leaue of our good
exercises that we haue vsed to doe before
time:for it is seldome seene, that a good
purpose wilfully broken may be recouered agayne without great spirituall hin-
derance.The purpose of righteous men
dependeth in the grace of God more then
in thēselues,or in their owne wisedome:
for man purposeth,but God disposeth:ne
the waye that man shall walke in this
worlde,is not in himselfe,but in the grace
of God. If a good custome be sometime
left of for helpe of our neighbour,it may
soone be recouered : but if it be left of
through slouth , or through our owne
negligence,it will greatlie hinder vs,and
hardly will it be recouered agayne.Thus
it appereth,that though we incorage our
selues all that we can to doe well, yet it
is good that we alwaye take such good
purpose,especiallie against such thinges
as hinder vs moste.We must also make
diligent searche both within vs & without vs,that we leaue nothing inordinate
vnreformed in vs,as nigh as our frailtie
may suffer. And if thou can not for fraylt-
tie of thy selfe doe thus continuallie, yet
at the least , that thou doe it once on the
day,euening or morning.In the morning
thou shalt take a good purpose for that
Day

daye folowinge, and at night thou shalte
discusse diligentlie, how thou hast beha-
ued thee the daye before, in worde, in
deede, and in thought: for in them we
doe oft offend God and our neighbour.
Arme thee as Christes true knyght with
meeknes and charitie, against all the malice of the enemie: Refraine glotonie, and
thou shalt the more lightlie refrayne all
carnall desires. Let not the ghostly enemy
finde thee all ydle, but that thou be readinge, writing, prayinge deuoutlie, thin-
kinge, or some other good labour doinge,
for the comminaltie. Bodily exercises are
to be done discretelie: for that that is profitable to one, is sometime hurtfull to
another: and also spirituall labours done
of deuotion, are more sure, done in priui-
tie, then in open place. And thou must
beware, that thou be not more readie to
priuate deuotiōs, then to them, that thou
arte bounde to by duetie of thy religion.
But whē thy duetie is fulfilled, thē adde
thereto, after as thy deuotion gyueth. All
may not vse one maner of exercise, but
one in one maner, another in another
maner, as they shall feele to be most profitable to thē. Also, as the time requireth,
so diuers exercises are to be vsed, for one
maner of exercise is necessary on the holy
daye, another on the ferial daye: one in
time of temptation, another in time of
peace and cōsolation: one when we haue
sweete-

sweetenes in deuotion, another, when
deuotion withdraweth. Also againſt prin=
cipall feaſtes we ought to be more diligēt
in good workes, and deuoutlie to call for
halpe to the bleſſed Saintes, that then be
worſhipped in the Churche of God, then
in other times, and to diſpoſe out ſelues
in like maner, as if we ſhoulde then be
taken out of this world, and be brought
into the euerlaſtinge feaſt in heauen. And
ſith that bliſſe is yet differred from vs for
a time, we may well thinke, that we be
not yet readye nor worthye to come
therto. And therefore we ought to pre=
pare our ſelues to be more readie another
time. For as S. Luke ſaith, Bleſſed is that
ſeruaunt, whom our Lorde, when he ſhall
come at the hour of death, ſhall finde
readie: for he ſhall take him, and lifte him
vp high aboue all earthlie thinges, into
the euerlaſtinge ioye and bliſſe in the
kingdome of heauen. Amen.

Of the loue of onelines and ſilence.

The. 2 o. Chapter.

Eeke for a conuenient time
to ſearche thine owne cō=
ſcience, and thinke ofte on
the benefites of god. Leaue
of all curious thinges, and
reade ſuch matters as ſhal
ſtirre thee to compunctiō
of

of heart for thy sinnes, rather then to reade onelie for occupyinge of the time. If thou wilt withdrawe thy selfe from superfluous wordes, and from vnprofitable runninges about, and from the hearinge of rumours and vayne tales, thou shalt finde time conuenient to be occupied in holy meditations. The moste holie men and women that euer were, fled the company of worldlie liuing men with all their power, & chose to serue god in secrete of their heart: And one holye mā sayde: As ofte as I haue beene amōge worldlie cōpanie, I haue departed with lesse feruour of spirite then I came: and that we know well when we talke long, for it is not so harde to keepe allwaye silence, as it is, not to exceede in wordes when we speake much. It is also more light to be alwaye solitarie at home, then to go forth into the world, and not offēd. Therefore he that intendeth to come to an inwarde setting of his heart in God, and to haue the grace of deuotion, must with our Sauiour Christe withdrawe him from the people. No man maye surelie appeare amōge the people, but he that woulde gladlie be solitarie if he might: nor no man is sure in prelacie, but he that would gladlie be a subiect: no, none maye surelie commaunde, but he that hath learned gladlie to obey: and none ioyeth trulie, but he, whose heart witnes-

seth

feth,that he hath a cleane conscience: ne
none speaketh surelie,but he that would
gladlie keepe silence, if he might. And alwaye the suretie of good men and blessed men hath beene in meekenes & dreade
of God.And though such blessed men shined in all vertue,yet they were not therfore lifte vp into pride,but were therfore
the more diligent in the seruice of God,
and the more meeke in all their doeings.
And on the contrarywise, the suretie of
euill men riseth of pride,and of presumption, and in the ende it deceaueth them.
Therefore thinke thy selfe neuer sure in
this life, whether thou be religious or
seculer : for ofte times they that haue
beene holden in the sight of the people
moste perfecte, haue beene suffered to
fall more greeuouslye for their presumption. Also it is muche more profitable
to many persons that they haue some-
times temptations (least happlye they
thinke them selues ouermuch safe,and be
thereby lift vp into pride, or run to see-
king of outward consolation) then that
they be alwayes without temptations.
O how pure a conscience should he haue,
that would despise all transitorie ioye, &
neuer would meddle with worldlie busines. And what peace & inward quietnes
should he haue,that would cut away fró
him all business of minde, and onelye to
thinke on heauenlye thinges. No man is
woor-

worthy to haue ghostlye cōfortes, vnleſſe
he haue ſicк deene well exercised in yoly
cōpunctiō. And if thou wilt haue cōpunctiō, goe into a ſecret place, ⁊ put frō thee
all the clamorous noyſe of the worlde: for
the prophete Dauid ſaith, Let the ſorowe
for thy ſinnes be done in thy ſecrete chā-
ber: ī thy celle thou ſhalt finde great grace
which thou maieſt lightlye loſe without.
Thy Celle wel cōtinued, ſhal waxe ſweete
⁊ pleaſaunt to thee, ⁊ ſhall be to thee hereafter a right deere frende: ⁊ if it be but
euill kept, it ſhall growe verie tedious ⁊
yrkeſome to thee. But if in the beginning
thou be ofte therein, and keepe it well in
good prayers ⁊ holy meditations, it ſhall
be after to thee a ſpeciall frende, a ndone
of thy moſte ſpeciall comfortes, in ſilence
and quietnes of hearte. A deuout ſoule
profiteth much, and learneth the hidde
ſentēces of Scripture, and findeth there
alſo manye ſweete teares in deuotion,
wherewith euery night ſhe waſheth her
mightilie from all filth of ſinne, that ſhe
may be ſo much the more familiar with
God, as ſhe is diſleuered from the clamorous noyſe of wordly buſines. Therefore, they that for the loue of vertue
withdrawe them from their acquaintāce,
and frō their worldlie frendes, our Lord
with his aungels ſhall drawe nigh to
them, and ſhall abide with them. It is
better, that a man be ſolitarie, and well
take

take heede of him selfe , then that he doe
miracles in the world forgettinge himselfe. It is also a laudable thinge in a religious person, seldome to goe forth,sel-
dome to see other , & seldome to be seene
of other. Why wilt thou see that , the
which it is not lawefull for thee to haue?
The worlde passeth awaye with all his
concupiscence and deceuable pleasures.
Thy sensuall appetite moueth thee to go
abrode, but when the time is past , what
bearest thou home againe,but remorse of
conscience,and vnquietnes of hart?It is
ofte seene,that after a mery goinge forth
foloweth a heauy returninge, and that a
glad euentide causeth a heauie morning:
and so all fleshly ioy entreth pleasantlie,
but in the ende it biteth & slayeth.What
maiest thou see without thy Celle, that
thou maiest not see within? Lo, heauen &
earth,and all the elementes, whereof all
earthly thinges be made:and what maiest
thou elsewhere see vnder the sunne that
may long endure? And if thou might see
all earthly thinges, and also haue all bodilie pleasures preset at once before thee,
what were it but a vaine sight? Lyfte vp
thine eyes therfore to God in heaué, and
praye hartily,that thou maiest haue forgeuenes of thine offences. Leaue vayne
thinges to them that wilbe vaine, & take
thou heede onelye to those thinges that
our Lorde commaundeth thee. Shet fast

the doore of thy soule, that is to saye, thy
ymagination, and keepe it warilye from
beholding of any bodilie thing as muche
as thou maiest: and then lift vp thy mind
to thy Lorde Iesu, and open thy heart
faithfullie to him, and abide with him in
thy Celle, for thou shalt not finde so much
peace without. If thou haddest not gone
forth so muche as thou haste done, nor
haddest geuen hearinge to vaine tales,
thou shouldest haue beene in muche more
inward peace then thou art: but forasmuch
as it delighteth thee to heare newe thinges, it behoueth thee therefore to suffer
sometime both trouble of heart, and vnquietnes of minde.

Of compunction of the heart.

The. 2 1. Chapter.

IF thou wilt any thinge profite to the health of thy soule
keepe thee alwaye in the
dreade of God, and neuer
desire to be fullie at libertie,
but keepe thee alwaye vnder
some wholsome discipline. Neuer geue
thy selfe to vndiscrete mirth for no maner
of thinge, as nigh as thou mayest. Haue
perfect compunction, and sorowe for thy
sinnes, and thou shalt finde therby great
inwarde deuotio. Compunction openeth
to the syght of the soule manye good
thinges

thinges,which lightnes of heart,& vaine
mirth soone driueth awaye. It is mer=
uaile, that any man can be merye in this
life,if he consider well, howe farre he is
exiled out of his coūtrey, and how great
perill his soule daylie standeth in: but
through lightnes of heart,and negligēce
of our defaultes, we feele not , nor we
will not feele the sorowe of our owne
soule : but often times we laugh, when
we ought rather to weepe and mourne:
for there is no perfect libertie, nor true
ioye, but in the dreade of God, and in a
good conscience. That person is right
happie, that hath grace to auoyde from
him all thinges that letteth him from
beholdinge of his owne sinnes, and that
can turne him selfe to God by inward
compunction: and he is happie also that
auoideth from him all thinges that may
offend or greeue his conscience. Fight
stonglie therefore against all sinnes,and
dreade not ouermuch, although thou be
incumbred by an euill custome, for that
euill custome may be ouercome, with a
good custome.And excuse thee not , that
thou art let by other men,for if thou wilt
leaue the familiaritie with other, they
will suffer thee to doe thy deedes with=
out impediment. Meddle thee not with
other mens goodes,neither busie thee in
great mens causes:haue alwaye an eye to
thy selfe,and diligentlie informe and ad=
monishe

mollifye thy selfe before all other. If thou
haue not the fauour of worldlie liuinge
people, sorowe not therfore: but let this
be thy daylie sorowe, that thou behauest
not thy selfe in thy conuersation, as it
beseemeth a good religious person for to
doe. It is more expedient, and more profitable, that a man sometime lacke consola-
lations in this life, then that he haue them
alwayes after his owne will, namelye,
fleshlie consolations. Neuerthlesse, that
we haue not sometime heauenly consolations, or that we so seldome feele them as
we doe, it is through our owne defaulte:
for we seeke not to haue the true compunction of harte, nor we caste not fullie
awaye from vs the false outwarde consolatios. Holde thy selfe therfore vnworthy
to haue any consolation, and worthye
to haue much tribulation. When a man
soroweth perfectlye for his sinnes, then
all wordly comfortes be painefull to him. A
good man findeth alway matter ynough,
why he ought iustlie so sorowe & weepe:
for if he beholde him selfe, or if he thinke
on his neighbour, he seeth well, that
none liueth here without great miserie,
& the more throughlie that he may con-
der him selfe, the more sorow he hath. And
alwaye the matter of true sorowe, and of
true inwarde copunction, is the remembraunce of our sinnes, wherein we be so
wrapped on euery side, that seldome we
may

may beholde any ghostly thinges. But if
we would moꝛe ofte thinke on our death,
then we doe on long lyfe, no doubt but
we ſhould moꝛe feruentlie apply our ſelfe
to amendment : and I beeleue alſo, that
if we woulde hartily remember the paines of hell, and of purgatoꝛie, that we
ſhoulde moꝛe gladlye ſuſtayne all laboꝛs
and ſoꝛowes, and that we ſhoulde not
dꝛeade anye paine in this woꝛld, wherby
we myght auoyde the paynes that are to
come. But foꝛaſmuch as theſe things goe
not to the heart, and we yet loue the flattering and falſe pleaſures of this woꝛlde,
therefoꝛe we remaine colde, and voide of
deuotiõ, and ofte it is through the weakenes of the ſpirite , that the wretched
bodie ſo lightlie complaineth. pꝛay ther-
foꝛe meekelie to our Loꝛde, that he of his
great goodnes geue thee the ſpirite of
compunction, and ſaye with the
pꝛophete thus: Feede me (Loꝛd)
with the bꝛeade of compunction, and geue me to
dꝛinke water of tea-
res in great
abundance.

Of

Of the conſideringe of the miſerie of mankinde, and vvherein the felicitie of
man ſtandeth.

The. 2 2. Chapter.

Wretch thou art, whoſoeuer
thou be, witherſoeuer thou
turne thee, but if thou turne
thee to God. Why arte thou
ſo lightlie troubled, for that it
faileth not to thee as thou wouldeſt and
deſireſt. What is he that hath all thinge
after his wil? neither thou nor I, nor any
man liuinge: for none liue here without
ſome trouble or anguiſhe, be he kyng. Or
who thinkeſt thou, is in moſte fauour
with God? truelie he that ſuffreth gladlie
moſte for God. But many perſons weake
and feeble in ſpirite, ſaye thus in their
heartes: Lo, howe good a life that man
leadeth, howe riche he is, howe mightie
he is, how high in authoritie, how great
in ſight of the people, and how faire and
beautifull in his bodily kinde: but if thou
take heede to the goodnes euerlaſtinge,
thou ſhalt well ſee, that theſe worldlye
goodes and worldly likinges are but litle
worth, and that they be more rather greuous then pleaſaunt, for they may not
be had ne kept, but by great labour and
buſines of minde. The felicitie of man
ſtandeth not in abundance of worldlie
goodes

goodes, for the meane is best. And verilie,
to liue in this world is but miserie: and
the more ghostlie that a man would be,
the more painfull it is to him for to liue,
for he feeleth more plainely the defaultes
of mans corruption. For why, to eate, to
drinke, to sleepe, to wake, to rest, to labour, and to serue all other necessities of
the bodie, is great miserie, and great affliction to a deuout soule, which woulde
gladly be free from the bondage of sinne,
that it might without let serue our Lord
in puritie of conscience, and in cleannes
of heart. The inwarde man is greatlie
greeued through the bodilie necessities
in this world. Wherefore the prophete
Dauid desired, that he might be deliuered from such necessities. But woe be to
them that knowe not their owne misery,
& woe be to them that loue this wretched
and this corruptible life: for some loue it
so muche, that yf they might euer lyue
here, though they myght poorelye get
their liuinge with labour & begginge, yet
they would neuer care for the kingdome
of heauē. O madde and vnfaithfull creatures are they, that so deepelie set their
loue in earthly things, that they haue no
feeling nor taste but in fleshlie pleasures.
Truelie in the hour of death they shall
knowe, howe vile and howe naughtie it
was, that they so much loued. But holie
Saintes, and deuout folowers of Christ,

D.   they

they did not what pleased the fleshe, ne
what was pleasaunt in the sight of the
world, but all their whole intent and desire they helde to thinges inuisible, and
feared, least by sight of thinges visible
they might be drawen downe to the loue
of them. My welbeloued brother, lose not
the desire to profite in spirituall thinges,
for thou hast yet good time and space.
Why wilt thou any longer deferre the
time? Arise, and now this same instant
beginne, and saye thus, Nowe is time to
laboure in good workes, nowe is time to
fight in ghostlie battaile, and nowe is
time to make amēdes for trespasse passed.
When thou art troubled, then is best
time to merite and get rewardes of God.
It behoueth thee to go through fire and
water, before thou come to the place of
recreation, and but if thou can fullie haue
the mastry ouer thy selfe, thou shalt neuer
ouercome sinne, nor liue without great
tediousnes and sorow. We would gladlie be deliuered frō all miserie and sinne:
but because we haue through sinne lost
our innocencie, we haue lost also the
verie ioye and felicitie. Wherefore, we
must holde vs in patience, and with good
hope abide the mercie of God, till wretchednes and miserie be ouerpassed, and
that this bodilie lyfe be chaunged into
the life euerlastinge. O how great is the
frailtie of man, that he is euer readie and

proue

prone to sinne. This daye thou art con=
fessed, and to morow thou fallest againe.
Now thou purposest to beware, and in=
tendest to go forth stronglie in good wor=
kes, and shortlie after thou doest as thou
neuer haddest taken such purpose.Right=
fullie therefore we ought to meeke our
selfe, and neuer to thinke in vs any ver=
tue or goodnes, for that we be so fraile
& vnstable: Soone may it be lost through
negligence, that with much labour and
speciall grace was hardlie gotten. But
what shall become of vs in the ende, whē
we so soone waxe dull and slow? Sothlie
sorowe and woe shall be to vs, if we fail
to bodilie rest nowe, as though we were
in ghostly sikernes, whē there appeareth
not as yet, neither signe nor token of
vertue nor of good liuing in our conuer=
sation. Wherfore it were expedient to
vs, that we were yet againe instructed
(as Nouices) to learne good maners, if
happly there might by that meanes
be founde hereafter any trust of
amendment and spirituall
profite in our conuer=
sation.

D ij   Di

The.23.Chapter.

He hour of death wil shortly
come, & therefore take heede
how thou orderest thy selfe:
for the common prouerbe is
true, To daye a man, to mo=
rowe none. And when thou
arte out of sight, thou arte anone out of
minde, and soone shalt thou be forgotte.
O the great dulnes and hardnes of mans
heart, that only thinketh on thinges pre=
sent, & litle prouideth for the life to come.
If thou diddest well, thou shouldest so
behaue thy selfe in euery deede, and in
euery thought, as thou shouldest in this
instant dye. If thou haddest a good con=
science, thou shouldest not muche feare
death. It were better for thee to leaue
sinne, then feare death. O my deere bro=
ther, if thou be not readie this daye, how
shalt thou be readie to morow? To mo=
rowe is a daye vncertaine, and thou canste
not tel, whether thou shalt liue so longe.
What profite is it to vs to liue longe,
when we therby so litle amende our life?
Longe life doth not alwaye bringe vs to
amendment, but ofte times increaseth
more sinne. Woulde to God that we
might be one daye well conuersant in this
worlb? Manie recken their yeares of con=
uersion, and yet there is but litle fruite
of

of amendment, nor of any good example
seene in their conuersation. If it be fearefull to die, peraduenture it is more perillous to liue long. Blessed be tho e persons, that euer haue the houre of death
before their eyes, and that euerie daye
dispose themselues to die. If thou euer
sawest anye man die, remember that thou
must needelie goe the same waye. In the
morninge doubt whether thou shalt liue
to night, & at night thinke not thy selfe
sure to liue till to morowe. Be alwaye
readie, and liue in such maner, that death
finde thee not vnprouided. Remember
howe many haue died sodenlie and vnprouided, for our Lorde hath called them
in such an houre as they leaste thought.
And when that last hour shall come, thou
shalt begin to feele all otherwise of thy
life passed, then thou haste done before:
and thou shalt then sorowe greatlie, that
thou hast bene so flowe and negligent
in the seruice of God as thou haste bene.
O how happie and wise is he therfore,
that laboreth nowe to stand in such state
in this lyfe, as he would be founde in at
his death. Truely, a perfect despising of
the worlde, and a feruent desire to profite in vertue, a loue to be taught, a fruitfull labour in workes of penaunce, a readie will to obey, a forsaking of our selfe,
and a willing suffering of all aduersities
for the loue of God, shall geue vs a great
D ij   truste

truſte, that we ſhall die wel. Now, whileſt
thou art in health, thou mayeſt doo many
good deedes, but if thou be ſicke, I can
not tell, what thou mayeſt doe: For why,
fewe be amended through ſicknes. And
likewiſe, they that go muche on pilgri-
mage, be ſeldome thereby made perfect
& holye. But not thy truſt in thy frendes
and thy neighbours, neither deſerue thy
good deedes till after thy death: for thou
ſhalt ſooner be forgotten then thou wee-
neſt. Better it is to prouide for thy ſelfe
betime, and to ſend ſome good deedes before thee, then to truſt to other, who per-
aduēture will lightly forget thee: if thou
be not nowe buſie for thy ſelfe, & for thine
owne ſoule health, who ſhall be buſie for
thee after thy death? Nowe is the time
very precious, but alas for ſorowe, that
thou ſpēdeſt the time ſo vnprofitablie, in
the which thou ſhouldeſt winne the life
euerlaſting. The time ſhal come, whē thou
ſhalt deſire one daye or one houre to
amende thee, but I wot not whether it
ſhalbe graunted vnto thee. O my deere
brother, from how great perill & dreade
mighteſt thou now deliuer thy ſelfe, yf
thou wouldeſt alwaye in this lyfe dreade
to offend God, and alwaye haue the comminge of death ſuſpect. Therefore ſtudye
nowe to liue ſo, that at the houre of death
thou mayeſt rather ioye then dreade.
Learne nowe to dye to the worlde, that
thou

thou mayeſt then liue with Chꝛiſt.Learne
alſo to deſpiſe all woꝛldlie thinges , that
thou mayeſt then freelye go to Chꝛiſte.
Chaſtiſe nowe thy bodye with penance,
that thou mayeſt then haue a ſure and a
ſtedfaſt hope of ſaluatiō.Thou art a toole,
if thou thinke to liue longe,ſith thou art
not ſure to lyue one daye to the ende.
How many haue beene deceaued thꝛough
truſt of longe life , & ſodenlie haue beene
taken out of this woꝛlde oꝛ they had
thought. Howe ofte haſt thou heard ſay,
that ſuche a man was ſlayne, and ſuche a
man was dꝛowned, and ſuche a man fell
and bꝛake his necke?This man as he eate
his meat was ſtrangled,and this man as
he played tooke his death, one with fyꝛe,
another with yꝛon,another with ſicknes,
and ſome by theft haue ſodenly periſhed?
And ſo the ende of all men is death, foꝛ
the life of man as a ſhadowe ſodenly ſli-
deth and paſſeth away.Thinke ofte,who
ſhall remember thee after thy death, and
who ſhall pꝛaye foꝛ thee ? Doe nowe foꝛ
thy ſelfe all that thou canſt , foꝛ thou
wotteſt not when thou ſhalt dye , noꝛ
what ſhall folowe after thy death.Whi-
leſt thou haſt time , gather thee riches
immoꝛtall,thinke nothing abidingly,but
on thy ghoſtly health.Set thy ſtudy onely
on thinges that be of God, and that belonge to his honoꝛ.Make thee frendes
againſt that time , woꝛſhip his Saintes,
                    D iij   and

and folowe their steppes, that when thou
shalt go out of this worlde, they may re=
ceaue thee into the euerlasting tabernac=
cles. Keepe thee as a pilgrime, & as a strã=
ger here in this world, to whom nothing
belongeth of worldlye busines. Keepe
thy hearte alwaye free, and lifted vp to
God, for thou hast no cittie here long abi=
ding. Sende thy desires, and thy daylie
prayers alwaye vpwarde to God, and
praye perseuerantly, that thy soule at the
houre of death, may blessedly depart out
of this world, and goe to Christe.

Of the last iudgement, and of the payne
that is ordeyned for sinne.

The 24. Chapter.

IN all thinges beholde the ende
and ofte remember, howe thou
shalt stande before the high
Iudge, to whom nothing is
hidde: who will not be pleased
with rewardes, nor receaue any maner
excuses, but in all thinges will iudge that
is righteous and true. O moste vnwise &
moste wretched sinner, what shalt thou
then answere to God, who knoweth all
thy sinnes and wretchednes, sith thou
dreadest here sometime the face of a mor=
tal man? Why doest thou not nowe pro=
uide for thy selfe against that daye, sith
thou mayest not then be excused nor de=
fended

fended by none other? But euery man
ſhall then haue ynough to doe , to anſwere for him ſelfe. Nowe thy labor is
fruitfull, and weeping is acceptable,thy
mourning is worthye to be hearde , and
thy ſorowe alſo is ſatiſfactory & purging
of ſinnes.The patiēt man,who ſuffereth
iniuryes and wronges of other, and yet
neuertheleſſe ſoroweth more for their
malice, then for the wrong done to him
ſelfe , hath a wholſome and bleſſed purgatory in this worlde, and ſo haue they
that gladly can praye for their enemies,
and for them that be contrarious vnto
them,and that in their heart can forgeue
thoſe that offend them,and tary not lōge
to aſke forgeuenes. And ſo haue they
alſo , that more lightly be ſtirred to mercye then to vengeance, and that can , as
it were,by a violēce breake downe their
owne will,and ſtrongly reſiſt ſinne, and
labour alway to ſubdue their body to the
ſpirite.It is better nowe to purge ſinne,
and to put away vice , then to reſerue it
to be purged hereafter. Bnt verilye , we
deceaue our ſelues by inordinate loue
that we haue to our bodily kinde.What
ſhall the fyre of purgatorye deuoure,but
thy ſinne? truelye nothing. Therefore,
the more thou ſpareſt thy ſelfe nowe,and
the more thou foloweſt thy fleſhly liking
the more greeuouſlye ſhalt thou wayle
hereafter, and the more matter thou re-

D v ſerueſt

serued for the fice of purgatory. In suche thinges as a man moste hath offended, shall he moste be punished. The slouthful persons shall be there pricked with burning prickes of yron, and gluttons shall be tormented with great hunger & thirste. The lecherous persons, and louers of voluptuous pleasures shal be filled ful with brenning pitche and brimstone: and enuious persons shall wayle and howle, as doe madde dogges. There shal no sinne be without his proper torment. The proude man shal be filled full with all shame and confusion, and the couetous man shall be pined with penurie & neede. One houre there in paine shall be more greuous then here a hundred yere in moste sharpest penaunce. There shall be no rest nor consolation to the damned soules: but here sometime we feele reliefe of our paynes, and haue sometime consolation of our frendes. Be now sorowful for thy sinnes, that at the day of iudgemét thou mayest be saued with blessed Saintes. Then shall righteous men stande in great constancie against them that haue wronged them, and oppressed them here. Then shall he stande as a Iudge that here submitted himselfe meekelye to the iudgement of man. Then shall the meeke poore man haue great confidence and trust in God, & the obstinate proude man shal quake & dreade. Thé shall it appeere, that he was

wise

wise in this worlde, that for the loue of
God was content to be taken as a foole,
and to be despised, and set at nought.
Then shall it also please him muche the
tribulation that he suffereth patiently in
this world, and all wickednes shall stop
his mouth. Then euery deuout person
shall be ioyful and glad, and the vnreli-
gious persons shall wayle and dreade.
Then shall the fleshe, that hath beene
with discretion chastised ioy more, then
if it had beene nourished with all delectation and pleasure. Then shall the vile
habite shine cleere in the sight of God,
and the precious garmentes shall waxe
foule and lothsome to beholde. Then the
poore cottage shall be more allowed, thē
the pallace ouer gilted with golde. Then
shall more helpe a constant patience, thē
all worldly power and riches. Then shall
meeke obedience be exalted more high,
then all worldly wisedome and pollicie
and then shall a good cleane conscience
make vs more gladsome and mery, then
the cunning of all philsophye. Then the
despising of worldly goodes shalbe more
of balure then all worldly riches & treasure. Then shalt thou haue more comfort
for thy deuout prayinge, then for all thy
delicate feedinge. Then shalt thou also
ioye more for thy silence keepinge, then
for thy long talkinge and iangling. Then
good deedes shall plenteouslie be rewar-
ded

bed, and faire wordes shall litle be regar
ded. Then shall it please more a straite life
and hard penance here, then all worldlie
delectation and pleasure. Learne nowe
therefore to suffer the small tribulations
in this worlde, that thou mayest then be
deliuered from the greater there ordeyned for sinne. Firste proue here, what
thou mayest suffer hereafter. And yf thou
mayest not nowe suffer so lytle a payne,
howe shalt thou then suffer the euerlastinge tormentes? And yf nowe so litle a
passion make thee impatient, what shall
then doe the intolerable fire of purgato-
rie or of hell? Thou mayest not haue two
heauens, that is to saye, to ioye here, and
to haue delectation here, and after to
ioye also with Christe in heauen. Moreouer, if thou haddest lyued alwaye
vnto this daye in honours, and fleshlye
delectations, what should it profite thee
nowe, if thou shouldest this present instant departe the worlde. Therefore all
thing is vanitie, but to loue God, and to
serue him. He that loueth God with all
his heart, dreadeth neither death, torment, iudgement nor hell, for a perfect
loue maketh a sure passage to God: but if
a man yet delite in sinne, it is no meruaile
though he dreade both death and hell.
And though suche a dreade be but a thral
dread, yet neuerthelesse it is good, that if
the loue of God withdrawe vs not from
sinne

sinne, that the drede of hell constraine vs
therto. He that setteth apart the drede of
God, may not longe stand in the state of
grace, but soone shall he run into the
snare of the deuill, and lightlye shall he
therewith be deceaued.

*Of the feruent amendinge of all our life, and
that vve shall speciallie take heede of
our ovvne soule health, before
all other.*

The. 25. Chapter.

M y sonne, be wakinge and
diligent in the seruice of
God, and thinke ofte wher=
fore thou art come, and why
thou haste forsake the world:
was it not that thou shoul=
dest liue to God, and be made a spirituall
man? yes truelie. Therefore stirre thy selfe
to perfection, for in short time thou shalt
receaue the full rewarde of all thy la=
boures, and from thenceforth shall neuer
come to thee neither sorowe nor dreade.
Thy labour shalbe litle and short, and
thou shalt receaue therefore againe euer=
lastinge rest and comfort. If thou abide
faythfull and feruent in good deedes,
without doubt our Lorde will be fayth=
full and liberall to thee in his rewardes.
Thou shalt alwaye haue a good trust,
that thou shalt come to the palme of vi=
ctorie

ctorie, but thou shalt not set thee in a full suretie thereof, least happlie thou ware dul and proude in heart. A certaine person, which often times doubted whether he where in the state of grace or not, on a time fell prostrate in the Churche, and sayde thus: O that I might knowe, whether I shoulde perseuer in vertue to the ende of my life. And anone he hearde inwardlie in his soule the answere of our Lord, sayinge: What wouldest thou doe yf thou knewest thou shouldest perseuer? Doe nowe, as thou wouldest doe then, and thou shalt be safe, and so anone he was comforted, and committed himselfe whollie to the will of God, and all his doubtfulnes ceassed, and neuer after would he curiouslie search to know what should become of him, but rather he studied to knowe, what was the will of god against him, and how he might begin and ende all his deedes that he should doe to the pleasure of God, and to his honour. Trust in God, and do good deedes, sayth the prophete Dauid, inhabite the earth, and thou shalt be fedde with the riches of thy good deedes. But one thing withdraweth manie from profitinge in vertue, and from amendment of life, that is an horrour, and a false worldlie dreade, that they may not abide the paine and labour that is needefull for the gettinge thereof. Therefore they shall most profite

in

in vertue before all other, that enforce
them selues mightilie to ouercome those
thinges that be moste greeuous and con=
trarious to them. For a man profiteth
there moste, & there winneth moste grace,
where he moste ouercommeth him selfe,
and wherin he moste mortifieth his bodye
to the soule. But all men haue not in lyke
much to mortifie and ouercome, for some
haue mo passions then some haue. Ne=
uerthelesse, a feruent louer of god, though
he haue more greater passions the other,
yet shall he be more stronger to profite in
vertue, then another that is better ma=
nered, and that hath fewer passions, but
is lesse feruent to vertue. Two thinges
helpe a man much to amendment of lyfe,
that is, a mightie withdrawinge of him=
selfe from those thinges that the bodye
moste inclineth him to, and a feruent la=
bour for suche vertues as he hath moste
neede of. Studie also to ouercome in thy
selfe those thinges that most mislike thee
in other men; and take alwaye some spe=
ciall profite in euerie place wheresoeuer
thou become, as, yf thou see any good
example, enforce thee to folowe it: and yf
thou see any euill example, looke thou
eschewe it. As thy eye considereth the
workes of other, right so, and in the same
wise thy workes be considered of other.
O howe ioyous and howe delectable is
it, to see religious men deuoute and fer=
uent

uent in the loue of God, well manered,
and well taught in ghostlie learning: and
on the contrarye part, howe heauye and
sorowfull is it to see them liue inordinat=
lie, not vsinge those thinges that they
haue chosen and taken them to. Also, how
inconuenient a thinge is it, a man to be
negligent in the purpose of his firste cal=
linge, and to set his mynde to thinges
that be not committed to hym. Thinke
ofte therefore on the purpose that thou
haste taken, and set before the eye of thy
soule the memorie of Christes passion:
and if thou beholde well, and diligentlie
his blessed life, thou mayest well be asha=
med, that thou haste no more conformed
thee to him then thou haste done. He that
will inwardly and deuoutlie exercise him
selfe in the moste blessed lyfe and passion
of our Lorde Iesus Christe, shall finde
therein plenteouslye all that is necessa=
rie for him, so that he shall not neede to
seeke any thinge without him. O yf Iesu
crucified were ofte in our hearts, and in
our remembrance, we should soone be
learned in all thinges that be necessarie
for vs. A good religious man that is fer=
uent in his religion, taketh all thing wel,
and doth gladly all that he is commaun=
ded to doe, but a religious person that is
negligent and slouthfull, hath trouble
vpon trouble, & suffereth great anguishe
and paine on euerie side, for he lackeeh
the

the true inwarde comfort: and to seeke
the outward comfort he is prohibited.
Therefore a religious person that liueth
without discipline, is like to fall in great
ruine. Also he that in religion seeketh to
haue libertie and releasinge of his dutie,
shall alwaye be in anguishe and sorowe,
for one thinge or other shall euer displease him. Therefore take heede howe other
religious persōs doe, that be right straitt-
lie kept vnder the rule of theire religion.
They goe seldome forth, they liue hardly,
they eate poorelie, and be cloathed gros-
selie: they labour much, speake litle, watche longe, rise earlie, make longe prayers,
reade ofte, and keepe them selues alwaye
in some wholsome doctrine. Beholde the
Carthusiens, the Cistersiens, and manie
other monkes and Nunnes of diuers re-
ligions, howe they rise euerie night to
serue our Lorde. And therefore it were
great shame to thee, that thou shouldest
waxe slowe and dull in so holie a worke,
where so manie laude & prayse our Lorde.
O howe ioyous a life were it, if we should
nothinge else doe, but with heart and
mouth continuallye prayse our Lorde.
Nowe truelie, yf we should neuer neede
to eate, drinke, nor sleepe, but that we
might alwaye laude him: and onelie take
heede to spirituall studies, then were we
much more happie and blessed then we
are nowe, when we are boundz of necessitie

ȯſe to ſerue the bodie. O would to God,
that theſe bodilie meates were turned in=
to ſpirituall refections, which (alas for
ſorowe) we taſte but ſeldome. When a
man is come to that perfection, that he
ſeeketh not his conſolation in any crea=
ture, then beginneth God firſt to ſauour
ſweet vnto him, and then he ſhall be con=
tented with euery thinge that commeth,
be it in likinge or miſlikinge. Then ſhall
he be glad for no worldlie profite, be it
neuer ſo great, nor ſorie for the wantinge
of it, for he hath ſet and eſtabliſhed hym
ſelfe whollie in God, the which is vnto
him all in all: to whom nothing periſheth
nor dyeth, but all thinge liueth to hym,
and ſerueth him without ceaſſinge, after
his biddinge. In euerie thinge remember
the ende, and that time loſt can not be
called againe. Without labour and dili=
gence thou ſhalte neuer get vertue. If
thou beginne to be negligent, thou be=
ginneſt to be feeble and weake : but yf
thou applie thee to feruour, thou ſhalt
finde great helpe of God, & for the loue
of vertue thou ſhalt finde leſſe payne in
all thy laboures then thou diddeſt firſt.
He that is feruent and louinge, is alway
quicke and readie to all thinges that be
of God, and to his honour. It is more la=
bour to reſiſt vices and paſſions, then it
is to toyle and ſweate in bodily laboures.
He that will not flee ſmall ſinnes, ſhalt
by

by litle and litle fall into greater. Thou
shalt alway be glad at night, when thou
haste spent the daye before fruitfullye.
Take heede to thy selfe, & stirre thy selfe
alwaye to deuotion. Admonishe thy selfe,
and howesouer thou remember other,
forget not thy selfe : and so much
shalt thou profite in vertue, as
thou canst breake thine
owne will, and fo-
lowe the will
of God.

Here

Of invvarde conuersation.

The firste Chapter.

THe kyngdome of God is within you (saith Christ our Sauiour) Turne thee therefore with all thy heart to God, and forsake this wretched worlde, and thy soule shall finde great inwarde rest. Learne to despise outwarde thinges, and geue thy selfe

selfe to inward thinges , and thou shalt
see the kyngdome of God come into thy
soule. The kingdome of God is peace &
ioy in the holy ghoste, that is not graunted to wicked people. Our Lord Jesus
Christ wil come to thee, and will shew to
thee his consolations. If thou wilt make
ready for him in thy heart a dwelling
place, that is all that he desireth to haue
in thee , and there is his pleasure to be.
There is betwixt almightie God and a
deuout soule manye ghostly visitinges,
sweete inwarde speaking, great giftes of
grace , many consolations , muche heauenly peace , & wonderous familiaritie
of the blessed presence of God. Therefore thou faythfull soule , prepare thy
heart to Christe thy spouse, that he maye
come to thee , and dwell in thee : for he
sayth him selfe, Who so loueth me, will
keepe my commaundement. And my father and I & the holy Ghoste shall come
to him , and we shall make in him our
dwelling place. Geue therfore to Christ
free entrie into thy heart, and keepe out
all thinges that may let his entrye : and
when thou haste him , thou arte riche
ynough, and he only shall suffise to thee,
and then he shalbe thy prouider and defender , and thy faythful helper in euery
necessitie, so that thou shalt not neede to
put thy trust in any other without him.
Man is soone changed , & lightly falleth
              away

away, but Chriſte abideth for euer, and
ſtådeth ſtrongly with his louer vnto the
ende. There is no great truſt to be put in
man that is but mortall & frayle, though
he be right muche profitable, and alſo
much beloued vnto thee, nor any great
heauines to be taken, though he ſometime turne and be againſt thee: for they
that this day be with thee, to morowe
may happen to be againſt thee, and may
ofte turne, as doth the winde. But thy
full truſt therfore in God, and let him be
thy loue and dreade aboue all thinges,
and he will anſwere for thee, and will
doe for thee in all thinges as ſhall be
moſte needeful and expedient for thee.
Thou haſte here no place of long abiding, for whereſoeuer thou become, thou
arte but a ſtraunger, and a pilgrime, and
neuer ſhalt thou finde perfect reſt, til
thou be fullye vnited to God. Why
doeſt thou looke to haue reſt here, ſith
this is not thy reſiſting place? Thy ful
reſt muſt be in heauenly thinges, and all
earthly thinges, thou muſt beholde as
thinges tranſitorye, and ſhortly paſſing
awaye: and be well ware thou cleaue
not ouermuche to them, leaſt thou be
taken with loue of them, and in the ende
periſhe thereby. Let thy thought be alway vpward to god, & direct thy prayers
to Chriſte continually: and if thou maye
not for fraylitie of thy ſelfe alwaye oc-
cuppie

cupye thy minde in contemplation of the
godhead, be then occupied with minde
of his passion, & in his blessed woundes
make thee a dwelling place. And if thou
flie deuoutly to the wound of Christes
side, and to the markes of his passion,
thou shalt feele great comforte in euery
trouble, and shalt litle force, though thou
be openly despised in the world, & what
euil wordes soeuer be spoken of thee,
they shall litle greeue thee. Our maister
Christe was despised in the worlde of all
men, and in his most neede was forsaken
of his acquaintaunce and frendes, and
lefte among shames and rebukes. He
would suffer wrongs, and be nought set
by in the world, & we will not, that any
person doe vs wrong, nor dispraise our
deedes. Christ had many aduersaryes and
backbiters, and we would haue all to be
our freendes and louers. How should thy
patience be crowned in heuen, if no aduersitie shoulde befall to thee in earth. If
thou wilt suffer none aduersitie, howe
mayest thou be the frende of Christe? It
behoueth thee to suffer with Christe, &
for Christ, if thou wilt reigne with Christ.
Truely, if thou haddest once entred into
the bloudy woundes of Iesu, and haddest there tasted a litle of his loue, thou
shouldest litle care for lykinges or misli-
kinges of the worlde, but thou shouldest
rather haue greate ioye, when wronges
and

and reproures were done vnto thee: for perfecte loue of God maketh a man perfectlye to despise him selfe. The true inwarde loue of God that is free from all inordinate affections, maye anone turne him selfe freelye to God, and lyfte him selfe vp in spirite, in contemplation, and fruitfullye rest him in Christe. Also he, to whom all thinges be esteemed as they be, and not as they be taken and thought to be of worldly people, is very wise, and is rather taught of God then of man. And he that can inwardly lifte his minde vpwarde to God, and litle regard outward thinges, needeth not for to seeke for time or place to goe to prayers, or to doe other good deedes or vertuous occupations. For the ghostlye man may soone gather him selfe together, and fixe his minde in God, for he neuer suffereth it to be fullye occupied in outward thinges. And therefore his outward laboures, & his worldlye occupations necessary for the time, hinder him not but litle; for as they come so he applieth him selfe to them, and referreth them alwaye to the will of God. Moreouer, a man that is well ordred in his soule, forceth litle the vnkind demeanour of worldlye people, ne yet their proude behauiour. As muche as a man loueth anye worldly thinge more then it should be beloued, so muche his minde is hindred & letted from the true ordinate

loue

loue that he should haue to God. If thou
were well purged from all inordinate
affections, then whatsoeuer should befall
to thee, should goe to thy ghostlie profite,
and to the great increasing of grace and
vertue in thy soule. But the cause why so
many thinges displease thee, and trouble
thee, is, for that thou art not yet perfectlie dead to the worlde, nor thou art not
yet fullie seuered from the loue of earthly
thinges: and nothinge so much defileth
the soule, as an vncleane loue to creatures, if thou forsake to be comforted by
worldly thinges outwardlie, thou mayest
beholde more perfectly heauenlie things,
and thou shalt then singe continuallie
laudes and praysinges to him with great
ioye and inwarde gladnes of heart, The
whiche graunt thee and me the blessed
Trinitie. Amen.

Of a meeke knovving of our ovvne defaultes.

The second Chapter.

Egarde not muche who is
with thee, nor who is against
thee, but be this thy greatest
studye, that God may be with
thee. In euery thing that thou
doest, haue a good conscience, and he shall
well defende thee, and whomsoeuer he
will helpe and defende, there may no malice hinder ne greeue. If thou can be still,

E   and

and suffer a while, thou shalt without
doubt see the helpe of God come in thy
neede. He knoweth the time and place
howe to deliuer thee, and therefore thou
must resigne thy selfe wholye to him. It
pertayneth to him to helpe and deliuer
from all confusion. Neuerthelesse, it is
often times muche profitable to vs, for
the more surer keeping of meekenes, that
other men knowe our defaultes, and reproue vs of them. When a man meeketh
him selfe for his offences, he lightly pleaseth other, and reconcileth himselfe to
them whom he hath offended. The meeke
man almightie God defendeth and comforteth, to him he inclineth him selfe, and
sendeth him great plentye of his grace.
To him also he sheweth his secrettes, and
louingly draweth him to him, and after
his oppressions he lifteth him vp to glorie. The meeke man, when he hath suffred
confusion and reproufe, is in good peace,
for he trusteth in God, and not in the
worlde. Moreouer, if thou wilt come to
the highnes of perfection, thinke not
thy selfe to haue profited any thinge in
vertue, til thou canst feele meekely in
thine heart, that thou haste lesse
meekenes, and lesse vertue
then any other hath.

Howe

Hovve good it is for a man to be peacefull.

The 3.Chapter.

Irste put thy selfe in peace, and then mayest thou the better pacifie other. A peacefull man and a patient profiteth more to him selfe, and other also, then a man learned, who is vnpeacefull. A man that is passionate turneth often times good into euill, & lightlie beleeueth the worse part: but a good peacefull man turneth all thinge to the best, and hath suspition to no man. But he that is not content, is ofte troubled with manye suspitions, and neither is he quiet him selfe, nor yet suffreth he other to be quiet. He speketh ofte times that he shoulde not speake, and he omitteth to speake, that were more expedient to be spoken. He considereth greatlye what other be bounde to doe, but to that, wherevnto he him selfe is bounden, he is full negligent. Haue therefore firste a zeale and a respect to thy selfe, and to thine owne soule, and then mayest thou the more righteously, and with the more due order of charitie haue zeale vpon thy neighboures. Thou arte anone ready to excuse thine owne defaultes, but thou wilt not heare the excuses of thy brethrē. Truely it were more charitable and more profitable to thee, that thou shouldest accuse

E ij

cufe thy felfe, and excufe thy brother: for
if thou wilt be borne, beare other. Behold
how farre thou art yet from perfect meekenes and charitie, which can not be an-
gry with none, but with them felues. It
is no great thinge to be well conuerfant
with good and tractable men, for that
naturallie pleafeth all people, and euery
man gladlie hath peace with them, and
moffe loueth them that folowe their appetite, but to liue peaceablie with euill
men, and with frowarde men that lacke
good maners, and be vntaught, and that
be alfo contrarious vnto vs, is a great
grace and a manlie deede, and muche to
be praysed: for it can not be done, but
through great ghoftlie ftrength. Some
perfons can be quiet them felues, and can
alfo liue quietlie with other: and fome
can neither be quiet them felues, nor yet
fuffer other to be quiet They be greeuous
to other, but they be more greeuous to
them felues Some can keepe them felues
in good peace, and can alfo bringe other
to liue in peace, and neuertheleffe all our
peace while we be in this mortall lyfe,
ftandeth more in meeke fufferinge of
troubles, and of thinges that be contrarious vnto vs, then in the not feelinge of
them, for no man may liue here without
fome trouble. And therefore he that can
beft fuffer, fhall haue moffe peace, and is
berie true ouercome of him felfe, is a Lord
of

of the world, a frende to Christe, and the
true inheritour of the kingdome of heauen.

Of a pure mind, and a simple intent.

The.4.Chapter.

An is borne vp from earthlye
thinges with two winges, that
is to saye, with plainnes and
cleannes: plainnes is in the intent, & cleannes is in the loue.
The good, true, and playne intet looketh
toward God, but the cleane loue taketh
a saye, and tasteth his sweetnes. If thou
be free from all inordinate loue, there
shall no good deede hinder thee, but that
thou shalt therewith increase in the way
of perfection. If thou intende well, and
seeke nothinge but God, and the profite
of thine owne soule, & of thy neighbours,
thou shalt haue great inward libertie of
minde. And if thy heart be strayte with
God, then euery creature shall be to thee
a mirrour of life, & a booke of holie doctrine, for there is no creature so litle nor
so vile, but that it sheweth and represen-
teth the goodnes of God. And if thou
were inwardlie in thy soule pure and
cleane, thou shouldest then without let-
tinge take all thinges to the best. A cleane
heart pearceth both heauē and hell. Such
as a man is in his conscience inwardlye,

G iij   iudge

suche he sheweth to be by his outward conuersation. If there be any true loue in this worlde, that hath a man of a cleane conscience. And if there be anye where tribulation or anguishe, an euill conscience knoweth it best. Also, as yron put into the fire is clensed fro ruste, and is made all cleane and pure, right so, a man turninge him selfe whollie to God, is purged from all slouthfulnes, & sodenlie is chaunged into a new man. When a man beginneth to waxe dull & slowe to ghostlie busines, then a litle labour feareth him greatlie, and then taketh he gladly outward comfortes of the worlde, and of the fleshe: but when he beginneth perfectlye to ouercome him selfe, and to walke stronglye in the way of God, then he regardeth the laboures but litle, that he thought before to be right greeuous, and as importable to hym.

Of the knowvinge of our selfe.

The. 5. Chapter.

We may not trust muche in our selues, nor in our owne wit, for ofte times through our presumption we lacke grace, and right litle light of true vnderstanding is in vs: and that we haue, many times we lose through our owne negligēce, and yet doe we not
see

fee, neither will we fee howe blinde we
are. Ofte times we doe euill, and in defence thereof we doe muche worfe, and
fometime we be moued with paffion,and
we weene it to be of a zeale to god. We
can anone reproue fmall defaults in our
neighbours, but our owne defaults that
be muche greater we will not fee. We
feele anone, and ponder greatly what
we fuffer of other, but what other fuffer
of vs,we will not confider. But he that
woulde weil and righteoufly iudge his
owne defaults, fhuld not fo rigoroufly
iudge the defaults of his neighbours. A
man that is inwardlye turned to God,
taketh heede of him felfe before all other:
and he that can weil take heede of him
felfe, can lightly be ftill of other mens
deedes. Thou fhalt neuer be an inward
man, and a deuout folower of Chrifte,
onleffe thou canfte keepe thy felfe from
medling on other mens deedes, & canfte
fpecially take heede of thine owne. If
thou take heede wholy to God and to
thy felfe, the defaultes which thou feeft
in other fhall litle moue thee. Where art
thou, when thou art not prefent to thy
felfe? And when thou hafte all runne
about, and much hafte confidered other
mens workes, what hafte thou profited
thereby,if thou haue forgotten thy felfe?
If thou wilt therfore haue peace in thy
foule, and be perfectly vnited to God in

C iiij   bleffed

blessed soule, set apart all other mens deedes, and onely set thy selfe and thine owne deedes before the eye of thy soule, & that thou seest amisse in thee, shortly reforme it. Thou shalt much profit in grace if thou keepe thee free from all temporall cares, & it shall hinder thee greatly, if thou set price by any temporall thinges. Therfore let nothing be in thy sight high, nothing great, nothing liking ne acceptable to thee, but it be purely God, or of God. Thinke all comfortes vayne that some to thee by any creature. He that loueth God and his owne soule for God, despiseth all other loue: for he seeth well that God alone which is eternall, incomprehensible, and that fulfilleth all thinges with his goodnes, is the whole solace & comfort of the soule, and that he is the verie true gladnes of harte, and none other but onlye he.

Of the gladnes of a cleane conscience.

The 6. Chapter.

He glorie of a good man, is the witnesse of God, that he hath a good cõscience. Haue therefore a good conscience, and thou shalt alwaye haue gladnes. A good conscience may beare many wronges, and is euer mery and glad in aduersities, but an euill con-

conscience is alwaye fearefull and vn-
quiet.Thou shalt reste thee sweetelie and
blessedlie,if thine owne hart reproue thee
not. Be neuer glad , but when thou hast
done well. Euill men haue neuer perfect
gladnes , nor feele no inwarde peace,for
our Lorde sayth,there is no peace to wicked people.And though they say,We be
in good peace,there shall no euill come to
vs,loe who may greeue vs,or hurt vs:be-
leeue the not,for sodely the wrath of god
shall fal vpon them,vnlesse they amende,
and all that they haue done shall turne to
nought , and that they would haue done
shall be vndone.It is no greeuous thinge
to a feruent louer of God to ioye in tribulation , for all his ioye and glorie is to
ioy in the crosse of our Lord Iesus Christ.
It is a short glorie that is geuen to man,
and commonlie some heauines foloweth
after. The ioye and gladnes of good men
is in their owne conscience , and the ioye
of righteous men is in God,and of God ,
and their ioye is in vertue and in good
life.He that desireth the verie perfect ioy
that is euerlastinge , setteth litle price by
temporall ioye : and he that seeketh any
worldlie ioye , or doeth not in his harte
fullie despise it,sheweth him selfe openlie
to loue but litle the ioy of heuen. He hath
great tranquilitie and peace of hart,that
neither regardeth praises nor dispraises,
and he shall soone be pacified and content
          E v   that

that hath a good conscience. Thou art not
the better because thou art prayſed, nor
worſe if thou be diſprayſed, for as thou
art, thou art. And whatſoeuer be ſayd of
thee, thou art no better then almightie
God (which is the ſearcher of mans hart)
will witnes thee to be. If thou behoulde
what thou art inwardlie, thou ſhalt not
care muche what the world ſpeaketh of
thee outwardlie. Man ſeeth the face, but
God beholdeth the hart, Man beholdeth
the deede, but God beholdeth the intent
of the deede. It is a great tokē of a meeke
hart, a man euer to doe well, and yet to
thinke himſelfe to haue done but litle.
And it is a great ſigne of cleannes of life,
and of inward truſt in God, when a man
taketh not his comfort of any creature.
When a man ſeeketh no outward witnes for him ſelfe, it appeareth that he
hath wholly committed him ſelfe to God.
Also after the wordes of S. Paule, he that
commendeth him ſelfe, is not iuſtified,
but he whom God commendeth, and he
that hath his minde alwaye lyfte vp to
God, and is not bounde with any inordinate affection outwardlie, is
in the degree, and in the ſtate
of a holye and a
bleſſed man.

Of the loue of Iesu aboue all thinges.

The. 7. Chapter.

Lessed is he that knoweth how good it is to loue Iesu, and for his sake to despise him selfe. It behoueth the louer of Iesu to forsake all other loue beside him, for he will be loued onelye aboue all other. The loue of creatures is deceyuable and fayling, but the loue of Iesu is faithfull and alwayes abydinge. He that cleaueth to any creature, must of necessitie fayle, as doth the creature: but he that cleaueth abydingly to Iesu, shall be made stable in him for euer. Loue him therefore, & holde him thy freende, for whē all other forsake thee, he will not forsake thee, nor suffer thee finally to perishe. Thou must of necessitie be departed from thy freendes, and from all mans companye, whether thou wilt or not, and therfore keepe thee with thy Lorde Iesu lyuing and dying, and commit thee to his fidelitie, and he wil be with thee and helpe thee, when all other forsake thee. Thy beloued is of suc) nature, that he will not admit any other loue, for he will haue alonely the loue of thy hart, and will sit therin, as a king in his proper throne. If thou couldest well auoyde from thee the loue of creatures, he would alway abyde with thee, and ne-

uer

ned woulde forfake thee. Thou shalte in
maner finde it all as lost , wharfoeuer
truft thou hast put in any maner of thing
beside Jefu. Put not thy truft therfore to
any suche thing as is not but a guilfull of
winde, or as a holowe sticke, which is not
able to suftayne thee, ne to helpe thee, but
in thy most neede will deceyue thee, for
man is but as hay, and all his glorie is as
a flowre in the feelde, which sodenlye vanisheth and slideth awaye: if thou take
heede only to the outward appearaunce,
thou shalt soone be deceyued: and if thou
seeke thy comfort in any thing but in
Jefu, thou shalt feele thereby great spirituall losse: but if thou seeke in all thinges
thy Lord Jefu, thou shalt truly finde thy
Lorde Jefu , and if thou seeke thy selfe,
thou shalt finde thy selfe, but that shall be
to thine owne great losse: for truly a man
is more greuous and more hurtfull to
him selfe, if he seeke not his Lorde Jefu,
then is all the worlde, and more then all
his aduersaries may be.

Of the familier freendship of Iesu.

The. 8. Chapter.

When our Lorde Jefu is
present, all thing is liking,
& nothing seemeth harde
to doe for his loue , but
when he is absent all thing
that is done for his loue is
paine:

paynefull and harde. When Iesu speaketh not to the soule, there is no faythfull consolation:but if he speake but one
worde onely, the soule feeleth great inwarde comfort. Did not Mary Magdalene rise soone from weeping, when
Martha shewed her that her maister
Christe was nigh, & called her:yes truly.
O that is an happie houre, when Iesus
calleth vs from weeping to ioy of spirite.
Remember howe drye & how vndeuout
thou art without Iesu,and how vnwise,
how vayne, and how vncunning thou
art when thou desirest any thing beside
Iesu: truely that desire is more hurtfull
to thee, than if thou haddest lost all the
worlde. What may this worlde geue
thee, but through the helpe of Iesu? To
be without Iesu is a payne of hel:and to
be with Iesu is a pleasaunte Paradise.
If Iesu be with thee, there maye no enimie greue thee : & he that findeth Iesu,
findeth a great treasure that is best aboue
all other treasures: and he that loseth
Iesu,loseth verie muche, and more than
all the world.He is most poore that liueth
without Iesu,and he his moste riche that
is with Iesu. It is great cunning to be
well conuersaunt with Iesu,and to keepe
him is right great wisedome. Be meke &
peacefull,and Iesu shall be with thee : be
deuout and quiet, and Iesu will abyde
with thee. Thou mayest anone dryue
awaye

awaye thy Lorde Jesu, and loose his grace, if thou applye thy selfe to outwarde thinges: and if through negligence of thy selfe thou loose him, what freende shalte thou thē haue? Without a freende thou mayest not long endure, and if Jesu be not thy freende moste before all other, thou shalt be verie heauye and desolate, and be lefte without all perfect frendship. And therefore thou doest not wisely if thou trust or ioye in any other thinge beside him. We shoulde rather choose to haue all the worlde against vs, then to offende God, and therefore of all that be to thee lefe and dere, let thy Lorde Jesu be to thee moste lefe and dere, and moste specially beloued to thee aboue all other, and let all other be beloued for him, and he onelie for him selfe. Jesu is onelie to be beloued for him selfe, for he onelie is proued good and faythfull before all other freendes. In him and for him both enimies and freendes are to be beloued, and before all things we ought meekely with all diligence to praye to him, that he may be beloued and honoured of all his creatures. Neuer couet to be singulerly loued or commended, for that belongeth onelye to God, which hath none lyke vnto him, and desire not that any thinge be occupied with thee in thy harte, ne that thou be occupied with loue of any creature, but that thy Lorde Jesu may be in thee,

and

and in euery good man and woman. Be
pure & cleane inwardly without letting
of any creature, as nigh as thou canste:
for it behoueth thee to haue a right cleane, and a pure hart to Iesu, if thou wilt
knowe and feele howe swete he is. And
verily thou mayst not come to that puritie, vnlesse thou be preuented and drawen
through his grace, & that all other things
set apart, thou be inwardlye knyt and
vnited to him. When the grace of God
commeth to a man, then is he made mightie
and stronge to doe euery thinge that belongeth to vertue, and when grace withdraweth, then is he made weake & feeble
to doe any good deede, and is in maner
as he were lefte onely to payne and pu-
nishmentes. And yf it happen so with
thee, yet dispaire not ouermuch therfore,
nor leaue not thy good deedes vndone,
but stande alwaye stroglye after the will
of God, and turne all thinges that shall
come to thee to the laude and praysinges
of his name. For after winter commeth
somer, and after the night commeth
the daye, and after a great
tempest sheweth agayne
right cleare and plea-
saunt weather.

The 9.Chapter.

T is no great thinge to despise mans comfort, when the comfort of God is present: but it is a great thinge, and that a right great thinge, a man to be so stronge in spirit that he may beare the wantinge of them both, and for the loue of God, and to his honour, to haue a readie will, to beare as it were a desolation of spirite, and yet in nothinge to seeke him selfe nor his owne merites. What proofe of vertue is it, if a man be mery and deuout in God when grace commeth and visiteth the soule? for that houre is desired of euery creature. He rideth right safely, whom the grace of God beareth & supporteth: and what maruell is it if he feele no burden, that is borne vp by him that is almightie, and that is led by the soueraigne guide that is God him selfe? We be alwaye glad to haue solace & consolation, but we would hane no tribulation, nor we will not lightly cast from vs the false loue of our selfe. The blessed Martyr Saint Laurence through the loue of God mightily ouercame the loue of the worlde, and of him selfe, for he despised all that was likinge and delectable in the worlde. And Sixtus the Pope, whom he most loued for the

loue

loue of God,he suffred meekelie to be ta=
ken frō him,& so through the loue of God
he ouercame the loue of man , & for mans
comfort he chose rather to folow the will
of God.Doe thou in like wise,and learne
to forsake some necessary and welbeloued
freende for the loue of God , and take it
not greeuouslie , when thou art left or
forsaken of thy freende : for of necessitie
it behoueth worldlie frendes to be disse=
uered.It behoueth a man to fight long,
and mightilye to striue with him selfe,
before he shall learne fully to ouercome
him selfe,or be able freely and readily to
set all his desires in God. When a man
loueth him selfe , and much trusteth to
him selfe,he falleth anone to mans com=
fortes:but the verie true louer of Christe,
and the diligēt folower of vertue,falleth
not so lightlye to them, neither seeketh
much such sensible sweetenes,ne such bo=
dely delites, but rather is glad to suffer
great harde labours & paine for the loue
of Christ. Neuerthelesse, when ghostlye
comfort is sent to thee of God , take it
meeklye,and geue humble thankes for it:
but knowe it for certain,that it is of the
great goodnes of God that sendeth it to
thee,and not of thy deseruing:and looke
thou be not therefore lift vp into pride,
nor that thou ioye much thereof, neither
presume vainely therein,but rather that
thou be the more meeke for so noble a
                                    gifte

ylere, and the more waste and fearefull in all thy workes: for that time will passe awaye, and the time of temptation will shortlye folowe after. When comfort is withdrawen, dispayre not therefore, but meekelye and patiently abide the visitation of God, for he is able, and of power to geue thee more grace, and more ghostly comfort, then thou haddest first. Suche alteratiõ of grace is no new nor straunge thinge to them that haue had experience in the waye of God, for in great Saintes, and holye prophetes was many times founde like alteration. Wherefore the prophete Dauid sayth: Ego dixi in abundantia mea, non mouebor in æternum. That is to saye, When Dauid had aboundance of ghostly comfort, he saide to our Lorde, that he trusted he should neuer be remoued from such comfort. But after, when grace withdrewe, he saide: Auertisti faciem tuam a me, & factus sum conturbatus. That is, O Lord, thou hast withdrawen thy ghostlye comfortes from me, and I am lefte in great trouble and heauines: and yet neuertheles, he dispaired not therfore, but prayed hartily vnto our Lorde, and sayd: Ad te domine clamabo, & ad deum meum deprecabor. That is to saye, I shall bustlye crye to thee, O Lorde, and I shall meekelye praye to thee for grace and comfort. And anone he had the effecte of his prayer, as he witnesseth him selfe, saying thus:
Audiuit

Audiuit dominus, & misertus est mei, dominus
factus est adiutor meus, That is to say, Our
Lorde hath heard my prayer, and hath
had mercy on me, and hath nowe agayne
sent me his helpe and ghostlye comforte.
And therefore he sayth afterward : Lord,
thou hast turned my sorow into ioye, and
thou haste belapped me with heauenlye
gladnes. And if almightie God hath thus
done with holy Saintes, it is not for vs
weake and feeble persons to dispayre,
though we sometime haue feruour of spirite, and be sometime left colde and voyd
of deuotion. The holy ghoste goeth and
commeth after his pleasure, and therfore
the holy man Iob sayth: Lorde, thou gra-
ciously visitest thy louer in the morning
tyde, that is to saye, in the time of comfort, and sodenlye thou prouest him : that
is to say, in withdrawing such comfortes
from him. Wherein then may I trust, or
in whom may I haue any confidece, but
onelye in the great endlesse grace and
mercy of God? for why? the company of
good men, nor the felowship of deuout
brethren and faithfull frendes, neither the
hauing of holy bookes, or deuout trea-
tises, ne yet the hearing of sweete songes,
or of deuout hymnes may litle auayle,
and bring forth but litle comfort to the
soule, when we are left to our owne fraill-
tie and pouertie. And when we be so left,
there is no better remedie but patience,
                                              with

with a whole resigning of our owne will
to the will of God. J neuer yet founde
any religious person so perfect, but that
he had sometime absentinge of grace, or
some minishinge of feruour : and there
was neuer yet anye Saint so highlie ra-
uished, but that he firste or last had some
temptation. He is not worthy to haue the
high gift of contemplation, that hath not
suffred for God some tribulation. The
temptations goinge before, were wont
to be a soothfast token of heauenlie comfort shortly comminge after. And to them
that be founde stable in their temptatios,
is promised by our Lorde great consolation. And therfore he sayth thus: He that
ouercommeth, J shall geue him to eate of
the tree of life. Heauenlie comfort is somtime geuen to a man , that he may after
be more stronge to suffer aduersities : but
after followeth temptation , that he be
not lifte vp into pride, and thinke hym
selfe worthie of such consolation. The
ghostlie enemie sleepeth not, neither is
the fleshe yet fullie mortified: and therefore thou shalte neuer ceasse to prepare
thy selfe to ghostlye battayle, for thou
haste enemyes on euerie side, that
euer will be readie to assaile thee,
and hinder thy good pur-
pose all that
they can.

Of

Of yeeldinge thankes to God for his mani-
folde graces.

The.10.Chapter.

Why seekest thou rest heere, syth thou arte borne to labour? Dispose thy selfe to patience, rather then to comfortes, to beare the Crosse of penaunce, rather then to haue gladnes. What temporall man would not gladly haue spirituall comfortes, if he might alwaye keepe them? for spirituall comfortes excede far all worldlie delites, and all bodelie pleasures, for all worldlye delites be eyther foule or vayne, but ghostlie delites are onelie socunde and honest, brought forth by vertues, and sent of God into a cleane soule. But such comfortes no man may haue when he woulde, for the time of temptation tarieth not longe. The false libertie of will, and the ouermuch trust that we haue in our selfe, be much contrary to the heauenlie visitations. Our Lorde doeth well in sendinge such comfortes, but we doe not well, when we yeelde no thankes therefore to him againe. The greatest cause why the giftes of grace maye not lightlie come to vs, is, for that we be vnkind to the gyuer, and yelde not thankes to him, from whom all goodnes commeth. Grace is alway geuen to thē that
be

be ready to yelde thakes therfore againe.
And therefore it shalbe taken from the
proud man, that is wont to be geuen to
the meke man J wold none of that consolation that should take from me compunction, nor any of that contemplatió
that should lift my soule into presúption.
Euery high thing in sight of man, is not
holy, nor euery desire cleane and pure:
euery sweet thinge is not good, nor euery
deere thinge to man, is alwaye pleasant
to God. We shall therefore gladlie take
such giftes, whereby we shall be the more
readie to forsake our selfe, and our owne
will. He that knoweth the comforts that
come through the gifte of grace, and
knoweth also how sharpe and painefull
the absenting of grace is, shall not dare
to thinke, that any goodnes commeth of
him selfe, but he shall openlye confesse,
that of him selfe he is right poore, and
naked of all vertue: yeelde therefore to
God, that is his, and to thy selfe that is
thin: that is to say, thanke God for his
manifolde graces and blame thy selfe for
thine offences. Holde in thee alwaye a
sure grounde, and a sure foundation of
meekenes, and then the highnes of vertue shall shortlie be geuen vnto thee: for
the high tower of vertue may not longe
stand, but if it be borne vp with the lowe
foundation of meekes. They that be most
great in heauen, be least in their owne
sight

ſight:and the moꝛe gloꝛious they be, the meeker they are in them ſelues, full of truth and heauenlie ioy, not deſirous of any vaine gloꝛy oꝛ pꝛaiſinge of man. Alſo they that be fullie ſtabled and confirmed in God, maye in no wiſe be liſte vp into pꝛide: and they that aſcribe all goodnes to God, ſeeke no vaine gloꝛie noꝛ vayne pꝛayſinges in the woꝛld, but they deſire onlie to ioye, and to be gloꝛified in God, and deſire in heart, that he maye be ho= noured, lauded and pꝛayſed aboue all thinges, both in him ſelfe, and in all his Saintes: and that is alwaye the thinge that perfect men moſte couet, and moſte deſire to bꝛinge about. Be thou louinge and thankfull to God foꝛ the leaſt bene= fite that he geueth thee, and then ſhalt thou be the moꝛe apte and woꝛthie to re= ceaue of hym moꝛe greater benefites. Thinke the leaſt gift that he geueth, is great, & the moſt deſpiſable thinges acce= pte as ſpeciall giftes, and as great tokens of loue: foꝛ if the dignitie of the geuer be well conſidered, no gifte that he geueth ſhall ſeeme litle. It is no litle thinge that is geuen of God: foꝛ though he ſende paine and ſoꝛowe, we ſhoulde take them gladlie and thankefullie, foꝛ it is foꝛ our ghoſtlie health, all that he ſuffereth to come vnto vs. If a man deſire to holde the grace of God, let him be kinde and thankefull foꝛ ſuch grace as he hath re=
ceaued,

ceaued, patient when it is withdrawen,
and praye deuoutlie, that it may shortlie
come againe. Let him be meeke and lowe
in spirite, that he lose it not againe
through his presumption and pride of
hart.

Of the small number of the louers of the Crosse.

The. 11. Chapter.

Esus hath many louers of
his kingdome of heauen, but
he hath fewe bearers of his
crosse. Manie desire his consolation, but fewe desire his
tribulation. He findeth many felowes at
eatinge and drinkinge, but he findeth
fewe that will be with him in his abstine-
ce and fastinge. All men would ioye with
Christ, but fewe would any thinge suffer
for Christe. Many folowe him to the brea-
kinge of his breade, for their bodilye refection, but few will folowe him to drinke a draught of the Chalice of his passion.
Manie maruayle and honour his miracles, but fewe will folowe the shame of
his crosse, & of his other vilanies. Manie
loue Iesu so longe as no aduersitie foloweth to them, and can prayse him, and
blesse him, when they receyue any benefit
of him: but if Iesu a little withdrawe him
selfe from them, and a litle forsake them,
anone

anone they fall to some great grudginge,
or to ouergreat defection, or into open
desperation:But they that loue Iesu purelie for him selfe,and not for their owne
profite and commoditie, they blesse him
as hartilie in temptation and tribulatiō,
and in all other aduersities, as they doe
in tyme of consolation. And yf he neuer
sent them consolation, yet woulde they
alway laude him,and prayse him. O how
may the loue of Iesu doe to the helpe of
a soule,if it be pure and cleane, not mixt
with any inordinate loue to him selfe:
truelie nothing more. May not they then
that euer looke for worldlie comfortes,
and for worldlie consolations, be called
worldly marchants,and worldly louers,
rather then louers of God? do they not
openlye shewe by their dedes that they
rather loue them selfe than God? yes
truelye. O where maye be founde anye
that will serue God freely and purelye;
without looking for some rewarde for it
agayne? And where may be founde any
so spirituall, that he is cleerelye deliuered and bereft from loue of him selfe,
and that is truely poore in spirite, and
is whollye auoyded from loue of creatures? I trowe none suche can be found
but it be far hence,and in far countryes
If a man geue all his substaunce for God
yet he is naught:and if he doe great penaunce for his sinnes,yet he is but litle-

F   and

and if he haue great cunning and know=
ledge, yet he is far from vertue: and if he
haue greate vertue and brenninge deuo=
tion, yet much wanteth in him, And that
is specially one thing, which is moste ne=
cessarye to him: what is that? that all
thinges forsaken, and him selfe also for=
saken, he go cleerely from him selfe, and
keepe nothinge to him selfe of anye pri=
uate loue, and whē he hath done all that
he ought to doe, that he feele in him selfe,
as he had nothinge done, nor that he
thinke it great, that some other might
thinke great, but that he thinke him selfe
truely, as he is, an vnprofitable seruant:
for the authour of truth, our Sauiour
Christe saith, when ye haue done all that
is commaunded you to doe, yet saye that
ye be but vnprofitable seruauntes. Then
he that can thus doe, may well be called
poore in spirite, and naked of priuate
loue: and he may well say with the pro=
phete Dauid, I am vnited in God, and
am poore and meeke in heart. There is
none more riche, none more free, nor any
of more power, then he that can forsake
him selfe, and all passinge thinges,
and that truelye can holde him
selfe to be lowest and
vilest of all
other.

Of

Of the vvay of the Croſſe, and hovve profi-
table patience is in aduerſitie.

The 12. Chapter.

He wordes of our Sauiour
be thought very harde and
greeuous, whē he ſaith thus:
Forſake your ſelfe, take the
Croſſe, and folowe me. But
much more greeuous ſhall it
be, to heare theſe wordes at the laſt daye
of iudgement: Go ye from me ye curſed
people into the fire that euer ſhall laſt.
But thoſe that nowe gladlie heare and
folowe the wordes of Chriſt, whereby he
counſaileth them to folowe him, ſhall not
then neede to dreade for hearinge thoſe
wordes of euerlaſtinge damnation. The
ſigne of the Croſſe ſhall appere in heauē,
when our Lorde ſhall come to iudge the
worlde, and the ſeruantes of the Croſſe,
who conformed them ſelues here in this
life to Chriſte crucified on the Croſſe, ſhal
go to Chriſte their Iudge with greate
fayth and truſt in him. Why doeſt thou
then dreade to take this Croſſe, ſith it is
the verye waye to the kingdome of heauen, and none but that? In the Croſſe is
health, in the Croſſe is life, in the Croſſe
is defenſe from our enemies, in the croſſe
is infuſion of heauenlie ſweetnes, in the
Croſſe is the ſtrength of minde, the ioye
of ſpirite, the highnes of vertue, and the

F ij   ful

full perfection of all holines, and there
is no health of soule, nor hope of euerlasting life, but through vertue of the crosse
Take therefore the Crosse, and folowe
Jesus, and thou shalt goe into the lyfe
euerlastinge. He hath gone before thee
bearinge his Crosse, and died for thee
vpon the Crosse, that thou shouldest in
like wise beare with him the Crosse of penance and tribulation, and that thou
shouldest be readie likewise for his loue
to suffer death, if neede require, as he
hath done for thee. If thou die with him,
thou shalt liue with him: and if thou be
felowe with him in paine, thou shalt be
with him in glorie. Beholde then how in
the Crosse standeth all, & howe in dyinge
to the worlde lieth all our health, & that
there is no other waye to true and inwarde peace, but the waye of the Crosse,
and of deadlie mortifyinge of the bodie
to the spirite. Go whether thou wilt, and
seeke what thou list, and thou shalt neuer
finde aboue thee, nor beneath thee,
within thee, nor without thee, more
high, more excellent, nor more sure waye
to Christ, then the waye of the holy crosse.
Dispose euery thinge after thy will and
thou shalt neuer finde, but that thou
must of necessitie somewhat suffer eyther
with thy will, or against thy will, and so
shalt thou alwaye finde the Crosse: for
either thou shalt feele paine in thy bodie,

or

o2 in thy soule thou shalt haue trouble of
spirit. Thou shalt be sometime as thou
were fo2saken of God. Sometime thou
shalt be bexed with thy neighbour, and,
that is yet mo2e painefull, thou shalt
sometime be greeuous to thy selfe, and
thou shalt find no meane to be deliuered,
but that it behoueth thee to suffer til it
shall please almightie god of his goodnes
otherwise to dispose fo2 thee: fo2 he will,
that thou shalt learne to suffer tribulation without cōsolatiō, that thou mayest
therby learne, whollie to submit thy selfe
to him, and by tribulation to be made
mo2e meeke, then thou were at the first.
No man feeleth the passion of Ch2iste so
effectuouslie, as he that feeleth like paine
as Ch2iste did. This Crosse is alway readie, and euery where it abideth thee, and
thou mayest not flee, no2 fullie escape it,
whersoeuer thou become, fo2 in what
place soeuer thou art, thou shalt beare
thy selfe about with thee, and so alwaye
shalt thou finde thy selfe. Turne thee
where thou wilt, aboue thee, beneath
thee, within thee, and without thee, and
thou shalt finde this crosse on euery side,
so that it shall be necessarie fo2 thee, that
thou alwaye keepe thee in patience: and
that it behoueth thee to doe, if thou wilt
haue inwarde peace, and deserue the perpetuall crowne in heauen. If thou wilt
gladlie beare this Crosse, it shall beare

thee, and bringe thee to the ende that
thou deficed, where thou shalt neuer
after haue any thinge to suffer. And if
thou beare this Crosse against thy will,
thou makest a great burden to thy selfe,
and it will be the more greeuous to thee,
and yet it behoueth thee to beare it. And
if it happen thee to put away one crosse,
that is to saye, one tribulatiō, yet surely
another will come, and happlie more
greeuous then the first was. Trowest
thou to escape, that neuer yet any mortal
man might escape? What Saint in this
world hath beene without this Crosse, &
without some trouble? Trulie, our Lorde
Jesu was not one houre without some
sorowe and payne, as longe as he liued
here, for it behoued him to suffer death,
and to rise againe, and so to enter into
his glorie: and how is it then, that thou
seekest any other waye to heauen then
this plaine high waye of the Crosse? All
the life of Christ was Crosse and martyr-
dome, and thou seekest pleasure and ioy.
Thou errest greatlie, if thou seeke anye
other thinge then to suffer: for all this
mortall life is full of miseries, and is all
beset about and marked with Crosses, &
the more highlie that a man profiteth in
spirite, the more painfull Crosses shall he
finde, For by the soothfastnes of Christes
loue, wherein he daylie increaseth, daylie
appeareth vnto him more and more the
payne

paine of this exile. But neuerthelesse, a
man thus vexed with paine, is not left
whollie without all comfort, for he seeth
well, that great fruite and high rewarde
shall growe vnto him by the bearinge of
his Crosse. And when a man freelie sub=
mitteth him selfe to such tribulatiō, then
all the burden of tribulation is sodenlie
turned into a great trust of heauenlye
consolation. And the more the fleshe is
punished with tribulation, the more is
the soule strengthned daylie by inwarde
consolation: And sometime the soule shall
feele such comfort in aduersities, that
for the loue and desire that it hath to be
conformed to Christe crucified, it woulde
not be without sorowe and trouble: for it
considereth well, that the more that it
may suffer for his loue here, the more ac=
ceptable shall he be to him in the life to
come. But this workinge is not in the
power of man, but through the grace of
God, that is to saye, that a frayle man
should take and loue that, which his bo=
dilie kinde so much abhorreth and flieth:
for it is not in the power of man, gladlie
to beare the Crosse, to loue the Crosse, to
chastise the bodie, and to make it obediēt
to the will of the spirite, to flee honours,
gladlie to sustayne reproufes, to despise
him selfe, and to couet to be despised: pa=
tientlie to suffer aduersities, with al
displeasures thereof, and not to desire

F iii   any

any maner of profites in this worlde. If
thou truſt in thy ſelfe, thou ſhalt neuer
bringe this matter about: but yf thou
truſt in God, he ſhall ſend thee ſtrength
from heauen, and the worlde, and the
fleſhe ſhalbe made ſubiect to thee: yea,
and if thou be ſtrongly armed with faith,
and be marked with the Croſſe of Chriſt,
as his houſholde ſeruant, thou ſhalt not
neede to feare thy ghoſtlie enemie, for he
ſhall alſo be made ſubiect to thee, ſo that
he ſhall haue no power againſt thee.
Purpoſe thy ſelfe therefore as a true
faythfull ſeruant of God, manfullye to
beare the Croſſe of thy Lorde Ieſu, that
for thy loue was crucified on the Croſſe:
prepare thy ſelfe to ſuffer all maner of
aduerſities and diſcommodities in this
wretched life: for ſo ſhall it be with thee,
wherſoeuer thou hide thee, and there is
no remedie to eſcape, but that thou muſt
keepe thy ſelfe alwaye in patience. If
thou deſire to be a deare and well beloued frende of Chriſt, drinke effectuouſlie
with him a draught of the chalice of his
tribulation. As for conſolations, commit
them to his will, that he order them as
he knoweth moſt expediēt for thee: but as
for thy ſelfe, & for as much as in thee is,
diſpoſe thee to ſuffer, & when tribulatiōs
come, take them as ſpeciall conſolations,
ſaytnge with the Apoſtle thus: The paſſiōs of this world be not worthy of them
                                        ſelues

selues,to bringe vs to the glozye that is ozdeined for vs in the life to come , yea, though thou thy selfe mightest suffer as much as all men do. Whē thou cōmest to that degree of patience,that tribulatiō is sweete to thee,& for the loue of God is sauoury & pleasaūt in thy sight,then maiest thou trust,that it is wel with thee,& that thou art in good estate, for thou haste founde paradise in earth.But as long as it is greeuous to thee to suffer, and thou seekest to flee, so long it is not well with thee,neither art thou in the perfect way of patiēce:but if thou couldest bzinge thy selfe to that estate,that thou shouldest be at,that is,to suffer gladly for God, and to dye fully to the worlde , then shoulde it shortlye be better with thee, and thou shouldest finde great peace : but yet,although thou were rapt with Paule into the thirde heauē,thou shouldest not therefore be sure without all aduersitie : for our Sauiour speaking of S. Paul, after he had bene rapt into heauen, sayd thus of him : I shall shewe him howe many thinges he shall suffer for me. To suffer therefore to thee remayneth,if thou wilt loue thy Lorde Jesu, and serue him perpetually.Would to god,that thou were worthy, to suffer somewhat for his loue. O howe great ioye shoulde it be to thee, to suffer for him?what gladnes to all the Saintes of heauen? and howe great edi-

F v   fying

thing to thy neighbour? All men commend patience, and yet fewe men will suffer. Righteously thou oughtest to suffer some litle thing for God, that suffered much more for the worlde. And knowe this for certaine, that after this bodily death thou shalte yet lyue, & the more that thou canst dye to thy selfe here, the more thou beginnest to liue to God. No man is apt to receyue the heauenlie rewarde, but he haue first learned to beare aduersities for the loue of Christe, for nothinge is more acceptable to God, nor more profitable to man in this worlde then to be glad to suffer for Christ, insomuch that if it were put in thy election, thou shouldest rather chose aduersitie then prosperitie, for then by the pacient sufferinge thereof thou shouldest be more like to Christe, and the more confirmed to all his saintes. Our merite, and our perfectiō of life standeth not in consolations and sweetnes, but rather in sufferinge of great greeuous aduersities and tribulations. For if there had bene any nearer or better waye for the health of mans soule then to suffer, our Lorde Iesu would haue shewed it by wordes, or by examples: But for there was not, therefore he openlie exhorted his disciples that folowed him, and all other that desired to folowe him, to for-sake their owne will, and to take the Crosse of penance and folowe him, saying thus,

thus, Who so will come after me, forsake he his owne will, take he the Crosse, and folowe he me. Therefore all thinges searched and redde, be this the finall conclusion, that by many tribulations it behoueth vs to enter into the kingdome of heauen. To the which bring vs our Lorde Iesus. Amen.

*Of the invvarde speakinge of Christ
te a faythfull soule.*

The firste Chapter.

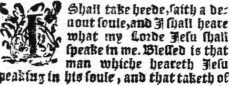

I Shall take heede, saith a deuout soule, and I shall heare
what my Lorde Jesu shall
speake in me. Blessed is that
man whiche heareth Jesu
speakyng in his soule, and that taketh of
his

his mouth some worde of comforte, and
blessed be the eares that heare the secret
rowninges of Jesu, and heede not the
deceytfull rowninges of this world. And
blessed be the good playne eares that
heede not the outwarde speache, but rather take heede what God speaketh and
teacheth inwardlye in the soule. Blessed
be the eyes also, that be shutte from sight
of outwarde vanities, & that take hede to
the inwarde mouinges of God. Blessed
be they also that get them vertues, and
prepare them by good bodily and ghostly
workes, to receyue dayly more and more
the secrete inspirations and inward teachinges of God. Also, blessed be they that
set them selues wholly to serue God, and
for his seruice set apart all lettinges of
the world. O thou my soule, take heede to
that is sayde before, and shet the dores of
thy sensualities, that are thy fyue wittes,
that thou mayest heare inwardlye, what
our Lord Jesu speketh in thy soule. Thus
saith thy beloued, I am thy health, I am
thy peace, I am thy lyfe, keepe thee with
me, and thou shalt finde peace in me. Forsake the loue of transitorie thinges, and
seeke thinges that be euerlasting. What
be all temporall thinges but deceauable?
and what may any creature helpe thee, if
thy Lord Jesu forsake thee. Therefore all
creatures, and all worldlye thinges forsaken & lefte, doe that in thee is, to make
thee

thee pleasaunt in his syght, that after this lyfe thou mayst come to the life euerlasting, in the kingdome of heauen. Amē.

Howe allmightie God speaketh invardlye to mans soule without sounde of wordes.

The. 2. Chapter.

Peke Lord, for I thy seruāt am readie to heare thee; I am thy seruant: geue me wisedome & vnderstanding to knowe thy commaundements. Bowe my heart to folowe the wordes of thy holy teachings that they may distil into my soule, as dewe into the grasse. The children of Israel sayde to Moyses: Speake thou to vs, and we shall heare thee: but let not our Lorde speake to vs, least haply we dye for dreade. Not so Lord, not so I beseeche thee, but rather I aske meekelye with Samuel the prophete, that thou vouchsafe to speake to me thy selfe, and I shall gladlye heare thee. Let not Moyses, nor any other of the prophets speake to me, but rather thou Lorde, who art the inward inspirour and geuer of light to all prophets: for thou alone without them mayest fully informe and instruct me. They without thee maye litle profite me. They speake thy wordes, but they geue not the spirite to vnderstand the

wordes

wordes.They speake fayre,but if thou be
still, they kindle not the heart. They
shewe faire letters,but thou declarest the
sentence. They bring forth great high
missteries , but thou openest therof the
true vnderstanding : they declare thy
commaundementes, but thou helpest to
performe them.They shew the way, but
thou geuest comfort to walke therein.
They doe all outwardly, but thou illu-
minest and infourmest the heart within.
They water onely outwardly, but it is
thou,that geuest the inwarde growing.
They crye all in wordes, but thou geuest
to the hearers vnderstanding of the
wordes that be hard. Let not Moyses
therfore speake to me,but thou my Lorde
Iesu,who art the euerlasting truth, least
happely I dye, and be made as a man
without fruit, warmed outwardly, and
not inflamed inwardly, and so to haue
the harder iudgement, for that I haue
hearde thy word,& not done it:knowen
it, and not loued it:beleeued it,and not
fulfilled it.Speake therefore to me thy
selfe, for I thy seruaunt am readye to
heare thee.Thou hast the wordes of eternall life, speake them to me , to the full
comfort of my soule, and geue me
amendement of all my life
past,to thy ioy,honor and
glory euerlastingly.
Amen.

That

*That the wordes of God are to be hearde
with great meekenes, and that there be
but fewe that ponder them, as
they ought to doe.*

The. 3. Chapter.

Y sonne sayth our Lord, heare
my wordes, and folow them,
for they be moste sweete, farre
passing the wisedome & cunning of all philosophers, and
wise men of the worlde. My words be
spirituall and ghostly, and can not be
fully comprehended by mans wit, neither are they to be turned or applyed to
the vayne pleasure of the hearer, but are
to be heard in silēce with great meekenes
and reuerence, and with great inward
affection of the heart, and also in great
rest and quietnes of body and soule. O
blessed is he, lord, whom thou infourmest
& teachest, so that thou mayest be meeke
and mercifull Lorde vnto him in the euil
day, that is to say, in the day of the most
dreadful iudgement, that he be not then
left desolate & comfortlesse in the land of
dānation. Then sayth our Lord againe:
I haue taught prophetes from the beginning, and yet cease I not to speake
to euery creature, but many be deafe, &
will not heare, & many heare the worlde
more gladly then me, and more lightly
folowe

folowe the appetite of the fleſhe, thē the
pleaſure of God. The worlde promiſeth
temporall thinges of ſmall value, & yet
is he ſerued with great affectiō:but God
promiſeth high thinges, and thinges
eternall,and the heartes of the people be
ſlowe & dul. Oh, who ſerueth & obeyeth
God in all thinges with ſo great deſire,
as he doth the worlde, and as worldly
princes be ſerued & obeyed?J trow none:
for why? for a litle prebend great iour-
neyes be taken, but for the life euerlaſting, the people wyll ſcarſely lift their
feete once from the grounde. A thing
that is of ſmall price, many times is bu-
ſily ſought, and for a penie is ſometime
great ſtrife,and for the promiſe of a litle
worldlye profite, men eſchewe not to
ſwinke and ſweate both day and night:
But alas for ſorowe, for the goods euerlaſting, and for the rewarde that may
not be eſteemed by mans harte, and for
the high honour & glory that neuer ſhall
haue ende, men be ſlowe to take any
maner of payne and labour.Be thou therefore aſhamed thou ſlowe ſeruaunt of
God, that they be founde more ready to
workes of death, then thou art to works
of life,and that they ioy more in vanitie,
then thou in truth: and yet they be ofte
deceyued of that that they haue moſt
truſt in, but my promiſe deceueth no
man,nor leaueth no man that truſteth in
me

me without some comfort. That I haue
promised I will performe, & that I haue
sayd I will fulfill to euery person, so that
they abide faythfully in my loue & dread
vnto the ende, for I am the rewarder of
all good men, and a strong prouer of all
deuout soules. Write my wordes therefore in thy hart diligétly, and ofte thinke
thou vpō them, and they shall be in time
of temptatiō much necessarie vnto thee.
That thou vnderstandest not when thou
readest it, thou shalt vnderstande in the
time of my visitation. I am wont to visite my seruauntes two maner of wayes,
that is to say, with temptation, and with
consolation : and two lessons dayly I
reade vnto them, one wherby I rebuke
their vices, another whereby I stirre thē
to encrease in vertues : and he that knoweth my wordes and despiseth thē, hath
that that shall iudge him in the last day.

A prayer to obteyne the grace of
deuotion.

The 4. Chapter.

Lord Iesu, thou art all my riches, and all that I haue, I
haue it of thee. But what am
I (Lorde) that I dare thus
speake to thee, I am thy poor-
est seruaunt, & a worme most abiect, more
poore, and more dispisable than I can or
dare

dare say. Beholde (Lorde) that I am
nought, that I haue nought, and of my
selfe I am nought worth: thou art only
good, righteous and holy, thou orderest
all things, thou giuest all things, & thou
fulfillest all things with thy goodnes,
leauing only the wretched sinner barrain
and voyde of heauēly comfort. Remember thy mercies, and fill my harte with
thy manifolde graces, for thou wilte not
that thy workes in me be made in vaine.
How may I beare the miseries of this
lyfe, vnlesse thy grace and mercy doe cōfort me therin? Turne not thy face from
me, defer not thy visiting of me, ne with
drawe not thy comforts from me, lest
happily my soule be made as dry earth
without the water of grace, and as it
were a thing vnprofitable to thee. Teache me, Lorde, to fulfill thy will, and to
liue meekly and worthily before thee, for
thou art all my wisedome and cunning,
and thou art he that knowest me as
I am, and that knewest me before
the world was made, and
before that I was borne
or brought into
this lyfe.

Howe

Howe we ought to be conuersant before God in truth and meekenes.

The 5.Chapter.

My sonne, sayth our lord Iesu, walke before me in truth and meekenes, and seeke me alwayes in simplenes and playnnes of hart. He that walketh in truth , shall be defended from all perils and daungers, and truth shall deliuer him frō all deceyuers, and from all euil sayings of wicked people. If truth deliuer thee, thou art very free , and thou shalt litle care for the vayne sayinges of the people. Lord it is true all that thou sayest , be it done to me after thy saying. I beseeche thee that thy truth may teache me and kepe me, and finally leade me to a blessed ending, and that it may deliuer me from all euil affections, and from all inordinate loue, that I may walke with thee in freedome of spirite , and libertie of harte. Then truth sayth agayne, I shall teache thee what is acceptable and liking to me: Thinke on thy sinnes paste, with great displeasure and sorowe of harte , & neuer thinke thy selfe worthy to be called holy or vertuous for any good deedes that thou hast done, but thinke howe great a sinner thou art , belapped and bounde with great and manifolde sinnes and
pas=

paſſions,and that of thy ſelfe thou dra=
weſt to nought, ſoone falleſt, ſoone art
ouercome,ſoone troubled, and ſoone art
thou broken with labour and payne:and
thou haſt nothing whereof thou mayſt
righteouſly glorifie thy ſelfe , but many
things thou haſt wherfore thou oughteſt
to deſpiſe thy ſelfe, for thou art more vn=
ſtable and more weake to ghoſtly workes,
then thou knoweſt or mayſt thinke. Let
nothing therfore ſeeme great to thee,no=
thing precious, nothing worthy any re=
putation , nor woorthy to be prayſed in
thy ſight , but that is euerlaſting.Let the
euerlaſtinge truth be moſt liking & moſte
pleaſaunt to thee aboue all other thin=
ges , and that thine owne ſinne and vi=
lenes be moſte miſliking and moſte diſ=
pleaſaunt to thee. Dreade nothing ſo
much,nor reproue nothing ſo much, ney=
ther let any thing be to thee ſo much ha=
ted , nor flee nothing ſo muche as thy
ſinnes and wickednes : for they ſhould
more diſpleaſe thee,then ſhould the loſſe
of all worldly thinges. Some there be
that walke not purelye before me , for
they through pride and curioſitie of the
ſelues deſire to ſearche and know high
thinges of my godhead, forgetting them
ſelues,& the health of their owne ſoules:
ſuch perſons fall oft times into great te=
ptations and greeuous ſinnes by their
pride and curioſitie , for the which I am
                                          tur=

turned agaynſt them, & leaue them to them
ſelues, without helpe oz counſaile of me.
Dzeade therfoze the iudgemetes of God,
& the wzath of him that is almightie, and
diſcuſſe not, noz ſearche his ſecretes, but
ſearche well thine owne iniquities, How
ofte, & how greeuouſlie thou haſte offen=
ded him, & howe many good deedes thou
haſte negligětlie omitted & lefte vndone,
whiche thou mighteſt well haue doone.
Some perſons beare their deuotion in
bookes, ſome in images, ſome in outward
tokens and figures : ſome haue me in
their mouth, but litle in their heart : but
ſome there be, that haue their reaſon clee=
rely illumined with the light of true vn=
derſtandinge, whereby their affectiō is ſo
purged and purified from loue of earthly
thinges, that they maye alwaye couete &
deſire heauenlie thinges: in ſo much as it
is greeuous to thě foz to heare of earthly
likinges, and it is to them alſo a right
great payne to ſerue the neceſſities of the
body, and they thinke all the time as loſt,
wherein they go about it. Suche perſons
feele and knowe well, what the ſpirite of
truth ſpeaketh in their ſoules, foz it tea=
cheth them to deſpiſe earthlie thinges,
and to loue heauenlie thinges: to fozſake
the wozlde that is tranſitozie, and to de=
ſire both daye and night, to come thither
where is ioy euerlaſtinge, to the which
bzinge vs our Lozde Jeſus. Amen.

Of

Of the meruaillous effect of the loue of God.

The. 6. Chapter.

Lessed be thou heauenlie father, the father of my Lorde Jesus Christe, for thou haste vouchesafed to remember me thy poorest seruant, and somtime doest comfort me with thy gracious presence, that am vnwoorthy al comfort: I blesse thee, and glorifye thee alwaye, with thy onelye begotten sonne, and the holy Ghoste without endinge. Amen.

O my Lord God moste faythfull louer, when thou commest into my heart, all mine inwarde partes doe ioye. Thou art my glorie, and the ioye of my heart, my hope and wholie refuge in all my troubles. But forasmuche as I am yet feeble in loue, & vnperfect in vertue, therefore I haue neede of more comforte and helpe of thee. Vouchsafe therefore ofte times to visite and instruct me with thy holye teachinges. Deliuer me from all euill passions, and heale my sicke hart from all inordinate affections, that I may be inwardlie healed and purged from all inordinate affections and vices, and be made apte and able to loue thee, stronge to suffer for thee, and stable to perseuer in thee. Loue is a great thinge and a good, and onelie maketh heauye burdens light, and beareth in like balaunce things pleasaūt and

and displeasant: it beareth a heauie bur-
don, and feeleth it not, and maketh bitter
thinges to be sauerie and sweete. Also the
noble loue of Iesu perfectlie printed in
mans soule, maketh a man to doe great
thinges, and stirreth him alwaye to desire perfection, and to growe more and
more in grace and goodnes. Loue will
alwaye haue his minde vpwarde to god,
and will not be occupied with loue of the
worlde. Loue will also be free from all
worldlie affections, that the inwarde
sight of the soule be not darked or let,
nor that his affectiō to heauenly thinges
be put from his free libertie by inordinat
winninge or losinge of worldly thinges.
Nothinge therefore is more sweete then
loue, nothinge higher, nothinge stronger,
nothinge larger, nothinge ioyfuller, nothinge fuller, nor any thinge better in
heauen or in earth: for loue descendeth
from God, and may not rest finallie in
anye thinge lower then God. Suche a
louer flieth high, he runneth swiftlie, he
is merie in God, he is free in soule, he
geueth all for all, and hath all in all: for
he resteth in one high goodnes aboue all
thinges, of whom all goodnes floweth
and proceedeth: he beholdeth not onelie
the gifte, but the geuer aboue all giftes.
Loue knoweth no measure, but is feruent
without measure. It feeleth no burden, it
regardeth no labour, it desireth more thē
it

it may attaine , it complaineth of none
impoſſibilitie,foz it thinketh all thinge
that maye be done foz his beloued,poſſi-
ble and lawfull vnto him. Loue therefoze
doth many great thinges , and bzingeth
them to effect , wherein he that is no
louer fainteth and falleth. Loue waketh
muche , and ſleepeth litle , and ſleepinge
ſleepeth not:it fainteth,and is not werie:
is reſtrained of libertie ,and is in great
freedome. He ſeeth cauſes of feare , and
feareth not , but as a quicke bzonde oz
ſparkle of fire,flameth alwaye vpwarde
by feruoure of loue into God , & through
the eſpeciall helpe of grace is deliuered
from all perils and daungers. He that is
thus a ghoſtlie louer,knoweth well what
his voyce meaneth , which ſayeth thus:
Thou Lozde God art my wholle loue and
my deſire ,thou art all mine ,and I all
thine. Spreade thou my heart into thy
loue , that I may taſte and feele howe
ſwzete it is to ſerue thee,and how ioyful
it is to laude thee,and to be as I were all
molten into thy loue. O I am bounden in
loue,and go farre aboue my ſelfe:foz the
wonderfull great feruour that I feele of
thy vnſpeakeable goodnes , I ſhall ſinge
to thee the ſonge of loue , and I ſhall folowe thee my belcued by highnes of
thought, whereſoeuer thou go , and my
ſoule ſhall neuer be werie to pzayſe thee
with the ioyfull ſonge of ghoſtlie loue,
　　　　　　　　B　　　　　　　that

that I shall ſing to thee. I ſhall loue thee
moze then my ſelfe, and not my ſelfe but
foz thee, and all other in thee and foz
thee, as the lawe of loue commaundeth,
which is geuen by thee. Loue is ſwifte,
pure, meeke, ioyous and glad, ſtronge, patient, faythfull, wiſe, fozbearing, manlye,
& neuer ſeeking him ſelfe, noz his owne
will, foz whenſoeuer a man ſeeketh him
ſelfe, he falleth fro loue. Alſo loue is cir-
cumſpect, meeke, righteous, not tender,
not light, noz heedinge vayne thinges:
ſober, chaſte, ſtable, quiet, and well ſtabled
in his outwarde wittes. Alſo, loue is ſubiect and obedient to his pzelate, vile and
deſpiſable in his owne ſight, deuout and
thankfull to God, truſting, and alwaye
hoping in him, and that whē he hath but
litle deuotion, oz litle ſauoz in him: foz
without ſome ſozowe oz payne no man
may lyue in loue. He that is not alwaye
redy to ſuffer, and to ſtand fullye at the
will of his beloued, is not woozthy to be
called a louer, foz it behoueth a louer to
ſuffer gladlye all harde and bitter
thinges foz his beloued, and not
to decline from his loue foz
no contrarious thing
that may befall
vnto him.

Of the proufe of a true louer of God.

The 7. Chapter.

My sonne, saith our Sauiour Christe, thou art not yet a stronge and a wyse louer: for whye? for a litle aduersitie thou leauest anone that thou haste begon in my seruice, and with great desire thou seekest outward consolatios. But a strong and a faithful louer of God standeth stable in all aduersities, and geueth litle heede to the deceitfull persuasions of the enemy, and as he pleseth him in prosperitie, so he displeaseth him not in aduersitie A wise louer considereth not so much the gifte of his louer as he doth the loue of the geuer. He regardeth more the loue then the gifte, and accompteth all giftes litle in comparison of his beloued, who geueth them to him. A noble louer resteth not in the gifte, but in me aboue all giftes. Furthermore, it is not all lost, though thou sometime feele lesse deuotion to me, and to my Saintes then thou wouldest doe, & on that other syde, the sweete ghostly desire that thou feelest sometime to thy Lord Iesu, is the feleable gift of grace geuen to thy comfort in this life, & a taste of the heauenly glory in the lyfe to come: but it is not good, that thou leane ouermuch to such cofortes, for they

B ij   lightly

lightly come and go after the will of the
geuer: but to ftriue alwaye without ceaf-
fing againft all euill motiõs of finne, and
to defpife all the fuggeftions of the enemy, is a token of perfect loue, & of great
merite & finguler grace. Let no vanities,
noz no ftrange fantafies trouble thee, of
what matter foeuer they be. Keepe thine
intent and thy purpofe alway whole and
ftrong to me, and thinke not that it is an
illufion, that thou art fodenlie rauifhed
into erceffe of minde, and that thou art
foone after turned agayne to thy fyrft
lightneffe of hart, foz thou fuffreft fuche
lightneffe rather againft thy will, than
with thy will. And therfore if thou be dif-
pleafed therewith, it fhal be to thee great
merite and no perdition. I knowe (fayth
our Lozde) that the olde auncient enimie
the feende, will affay to let thy good wil,
and to extinct the good defire that thou
haft to me, and to all goodnes, all that he
can, and he will alfo hinder thee from all
good wozkes, and deuout ercercifes if he
may: that is to faye, from the honour and
wozfhip that thou art bounde to geue to
me and to my faintes, and from minde of
my paffion, and from the remembraunce
of thine owne finnes, from a diligent
keeping of thy harte in good meditatiõs,
and from a ftedfaft purpofe to profite in
vertue. He will alfo put into thy mynde
many ydle thoughts, to make thee yrke,
and

and to be soone werye with prayer, and
with readinge, and with all other good
vertuous workes. A meke confession displeaseth him much, and if he can he will
let a man that he shall not be houseled.
But beleue him not,nor care not for him
though he assaple thee neuer so muche.
Make all his malice returne to him selfe
agapne, and saye to him thus, Go from
me thou wicked spirit,and be thou ashamed, for thou art foule and vglye, that
wouldest bringe suche thinges into my
mynde. Go from me thou false deceyuer
of mankinde, thou shalt haue no part in
me,for my Sauiour Jesu standeth by me
as a mightie warriour and a stronge
champion, and thou shalt flye awaye to
thy confusion. I had leuer suffer the most
cruell death,then to consent to thy ma-
licious stiringes. Be still therefore thou
cursed feende, and cease thy malice,for I
shall neuer assent to thee, though thou
vexe me neuer so muche. Our Lorde is my
light and my health,whom shal I dreade?
and he is the defender of my life, what
shall I feare? Truely though an hoste of
men arise against me, my hart shall not
dread them: For why? God is my helper
and my redeemer. Then sayth our Lorde
agapne to such a soule,striue alwaye as a
true knight against all the stiringes of
the enymie. And if thou be sometyme
through thy frailtie ouercome,rise soone

againe, and take more ſtrength then thou
haddeſt firſt, & truſt verilie to haue more
grace, and more comfort of God, than
thou haddeſt before. But beware alwaye
of vainglorie and pride, for therby many
perſons haue fallen into greate errours,
and into great blindnes of ſoule, ſo farre,
that it hath bene right nigh incurable.
Be it therefore to thee a great exemple,
and a matter of perpetuall meekenes, the
fall & ruine of ſuche proude folkes, that
fooliſhlie haue preſumed of them ſelfe, &
haue in the end finallie periſhed by their
preſumption.

Howe grace is to be kept cloſe through
the vertue of meekenes.

The. 8. Chapter.

My ſonne, it is muche more expedient, and muche more ſurer
way for thee, that thou hide
the grace of deuotion, and not
to ſpeake much of it nor much
to regard it, but rather to diſpiſe thy ſelfe
the more for it, and to thinke thy ſelfe
vnworthy any ſuch gracious gift of god
than to ſpeke of it. And it is not good to
cleaue muche to ſuche affections as may
be ſoone turned into the cõtrary. When
thou haſt the grace of deuotion, conſider
how wretched & needy thou wert wont
to be, when thou haddeſt no ſuch grace
The

The profite and increase of life spirituall is not onely when thou hast deuotion, but rather when thou canst meekly
and patienly beare the witydrawing &
abfenting thereof, and yet not to leaue
thy prayers, nor thy other good deedes
that thou art accustomed to doe, vndone, but to thy power, and as far as in
thee is, doest thy best therin, and forget-
test not thy duetie therefore, nor art not
negligent for any dulnes or vnquietnes
of minde that thou feelest. Neuerthelesse
there be many persons, that when any
aduersity falleth to them, they be anone
vnpatient, and be made thereby very
slowe and dull to doe any good deede,
and they hinder them selues greatly. For
it is not in the power of man the waye
that he shall take, but it is onelye in the
grace of God to dispose that after his
will, and to sende comforte when he
will, and as muche as he will, and to
whom he will, as it shall please him, and
none otherwise. Some vnware persons
through an vndiscrete desire that they
haue had to haue the grace of deuotion,
haue destroyed them selues, for they
woulde doe more then their power was
to doe, and would not knowe the measure of their gift, nor the litlenes of their
owne strength, but rather woulde folowe the pride of their heart, then the
iudgement of reason. And because they

B iiij   pre-

presumed to doe greater thinges then
was pleasant to God, therefore they lost
anone the grace that they had before, &
were lefte needy and without comfort,
which thought to haue builded their ne-
stes in heauen: and so they were taught
not to presume of them selues, but meekely to trust in God, and in his goodnes.
Also, such persons, as be beginners, and
yet lacke experience in ghostly trauayle,
maye lightly erre, and be deceiued, vnlesse they will be ruled by counsayle of
other. And if they will needlye folowe
their owne counsaile, and will in no wise
be remoued from their owne will, it will
be very perillous to them in the ende.
And it is not lightly seene, that they
that be wise and cunning in their owne
sight, will be meekely ruled or ordered
by other. It is better to haue litle cunning with meekenes, then great cunninge with vayne liking therein: and it
is better to haue litle cunninge with
grace, then muche cunninge, whereof
thou shouldest be proude. Also, he doth
not discretely, that in time of deuotion
setteth him selfe also to spirituall mirth,
and as it were, to a heauenly gladnes, &
forgetteth his former desolation, and the
meeke drede of God. Neither doeth he
well or vertuously, that in time of trouble, or any maner aduersitie or greefe
beareth him selfe ouer much desperatlye,
and

and doth not feele or thinke so faithfully
of me as he ought to doe.He that in time
of peace and ghostly comfort will thinke
him selfe ouermuche sure , commonly in
time of battaile and of temptation, shall
be founde ouermuche deiect & fearfull:
but if thou couldest alwaye abide meeke
and litle in thine owne sight, and couldest order well the motions of thine owne
soule,thou shouldest not so soone fall into presumption or dispaire,nor so lightly
offend almightie God.Wherfore this is
good and wholsome counsell,that when
thou haste the spirite of feruour,thou
thinke,howe thou shalt doe,when that
feruor is passed,and then whe it happeneth so with thee, that thou thinke that
it may soone come againe,which to my
honoure,& to thy prouing I haue withdrawen for a time.And it is more profit-
table to thee , that thou shouldest be so
proued , then that thou shouldest alway
haue prosperous thinges after thy will:
for why? merites are not to be thought
great in any person , because he hath
manye visions , or many ghostlye comfortes , or for that he hath cleere vnder-
stading of Scripture,or that he is set in
high degree:but if he be stablye grounded
in meekenes,and fulfilled with charitie,
and seeke wholly the worship of God , &
in nothing regardeth him selfe,but fullie
in his heart can despise him selfe,& also

                   B v   coueteth

ouctell to be despised of other, then maye he haue good trust, that he hath somewhat profited in grace, and that he shall in the ende haue great rewarde of God for his good trauaile. Amen.

Howw we shall thinke through meekenes our selfe to be vile and abiect in the sight of God.

The 9. Chapter.

Hall I, Lorde Iesu, dare speake to thee, that am but dust and ashes? Verilie, yf I thinke my selfe any better then ashes & dust, thou standest against me, & also myne owne sinnes beare witnes against me, that I may not withsaye it: but if I despise my selfe, and set my selfe at naught, and thinke my selfe but ashes and dust, as I am, then thy grace shall be nigh vnto me, and the light of true vnderstandinge shall enter into my heart, so that all presumption & pride in me shall be drowned in the vale of meekenes, through perfect knowinge of my wretchednes. Thorough meekenes thou shalt shewe vnto me what I am, what I haue bene, and from whence I came, for I am nought, and knewe it not. If I be left to my selfe, then am I nought, and all is feeblenes and imperfection.

But

But if thou vouchesafe a litle to beholde me, anone I am made stronge, and am filled with a newe ioye, and meruaile it is, that I wretch am so soone lift vp from my vnstablenes, into the beholdinge of heauenlie thinges, and that I am so lo-uinglie lifted vp of thee, that of my selfe fall downe alwaye to earthlie likinges. But thy loue, Lorde, causeth all this, which preuenteth me, and helpeth me in all my necessities, and keepeth me warily from all perils & daungers, that I daylye am like to fall into. I haue lost thee, and also my selfe by inordinate loue that I haue had to my selfe, and in seekinge of thee againe, I haue founde both thee and me, and therefore I will more deeply from henceforth set my selfe at naught, and more diligentlye seeke thee, then in time paste I haue done: for thou Lorde Iesu, thou doest to me aboue all my merites, & aboue all that I can aske or desire. But blessed be thou in all thy workes, for though I be vnworthy any good thinges, yet thy goodnes neuer ceasseth to doe weil to me, & also to manye other, which be vnkind to thee, and that are turned right farre from thee. Turne vs Lorde therefore to thee agayne, that we maye hereforward be louing, thankfull, meeke & deuout to thee, for thou art our health, thou art our vertue and all our strength in body and soule, and none but thou: to

thee

thee therfore be ioy and glory euerlastingly in the blisse of heauen. Amen.

Howe all thinges are to be referred to God,
as ende of euery worke.

The. 1 0. Chapter.

MY sonne, sayth our Sauiour
Christ, I must be the ende of all
thy workes, if thou desire to be
happy and blessed. And if thou
referre all goodnes to me, from
whom all goodnes commeth, then shall
be purged and made cleane in thee thine
inwarde affections, which els would be
euill inclined to thy selfe and to other
creatures. If thou seeke thy selfe in any
thing as ende of thy worke, anone thou
faylest in thy doinge, and waxest drie and
barrein frō all moysture of grace. Wherfore thou must referre all thinges to me,
for I geue all. Behold therfore all things
as they be, flowinge and springinge out
of my soueraine goodnes, and reduce all
thinges to me as to their originall beginninge, for of me both small and great,
poore and riche, as of a quicke springinge
well, drawe water of life. He that serueth
me freelie and with good will, shall receaue grace for grace: But he that will
glorifie him selfe in him selfe, or willfully
ioye in any thinge beside me, shall not be
stablished in perfect ioye, nor be delated
in

in soule, but he shalbe letted & anguished
many wayes from the true freedome of
spirite. Thou shalt therefore ascribe no
goodnes to thy selfe, nor thou shalt not
thinke, that any person hath anye goodnes of him selfe, but that thou yeelde alwaye the goodnes to me, without whom
man hath nothing. I haue geuen all, and
all will I haue againe, and with great
straitnes will I looke to haue thankings
therefore. This is the truth, whereby is
Driuen awaye all maner of vaine glorye
and pride of heart. If heauenly grace and
perfect charitie enter into thy hart, then
shall there no enuie nor vnquietnes of
mind, neither any priuate loue haue rule
in thee: For the charity of God shal ouercome all thinges, and shall dilate and in-
flame all the powers of thy soule. Wherfore, if thou vnderstandest a right, thou
shalt neuer ioye but in me, and in me
onelie thou shalt haue trust, for
no man is good but God alone,
who is aboue all thinges to
be honoured, and in all
thinges to be
blessed.

That

That it is svveete and delectable to serue God,
and to forsake the vvorlde.

The 11.Chapter.

OW shall I speake againe to thee my Lorde Iesu, and not cease. And I shall say in the eares of my lord, my God and king that is in heauen. O howe great is the aboundance of thy sweetenes, which thou hafte hidde and kept for thē that dreade thee? But what is it then to them that loue thee, & that with all their hart do serue thee? verily, it is the vnspeakeable swetenes of contemplation, that thou geuest to them that loue thee. In this Lord, thou hast moste shewed the sweetenes of thy charitie to me, that whē I was not, thou madest me, and when I erred farre from thee, thou broughtest me againe to serue thee, and thou cōmaundest me also, that I shall loue thee. O fountaine of loue euerlasting, what shal I say of thee? howe maye I forget thee, that hast vouchedsafe so louinglye to remember me? Whē I was like to haue perished, thou shewedst thy mercy to me aboue all that I coulde thinke and desyre, and hast sent me of thy grace and loue aboue my merites. But what shall I geue thee againe for all this goodnes? It is not geuen to all men to forsake the worlde, & to take

a so

a folitarye life,and only to ferue thee , &
yet it is no great thing to ferue thee,
whom euery creature is bounde to ferue.
It ought not therefore to feeme any
great thing to me to ferue thee , but rather it fhould feeme maruel and wonder
to me , that thou wilt vouchfafe to receaue fo poore , and fo vnworthy a creature as I am into thy feruice , and that
thou wilt ioyne me to thy welbeloued
feruantes. Lo Lorde , all thinges that I
haue , & all that I doe thee feruice with,
is thine : and yet thy goodnes is fuche,
that thou rather ferueft me , then I thee:
for lo , heauen & earth , planets and ftar-
res with their contents,which thou haft
created to ferue man , be readye at thy
biddinge,and doe daylye that thou hafte
commaunded.And thou hafte alfo ordeyned aungels to the minyfterie of man.
But aboue all this , thou hafte vouchedfafe to ferue man thy felfe,and hafte pro-
mifed to geue thy felfe vnto hym. What
fhall I then geue to thee agayne for this
thoufandfolde goodnes?woulde to God
that I might ferue thee all the dayes of
my lyfe , or at the leaft,that I might one
daye be able to doe thee fapthfull feruice,
for thou art woorthye all honour , feruice,and prayfinge for euer.Thou art my
Lorde and my God , and I thy poorest
feruant , moft bounde before ail other to
loue thee , and prayfe thee , and I neuer
　　　　　　　　　　　　　　　ought

ought to waxe werye of the praysinge of thee. And that is it that I aske, and that I desire, that is to say, that I may alway laude and prayse thee. Vouchsafe therfore, moste mercifull Lord, to supply, that wanteth in me, for it is great honour to serue thee, & all earthly thinges to despise for the loue of thee. They shal haue great grace that freely submit the selues to thy holye seruice. And they shall finde also the moste sweete consolation of the holye ghoste, and shall haue great freedome of spirit, that here forsake all worldye busines, and choose a harde and straite lyfe in this worlde for thy name. O free and ioyful seruice of God, by the which a man is made free, holy, and also blessed in the sight of God. O holye state of religion, which maketh a man lyke to aungels, pleasant to God, dreadefull to wicked spirites, and to all faythfull people right highlye commendable. O seruice much to be embraced, and alwaye to be desired, by whom the high goodnes is wonne, and the euerlasting ioye and gladnes is gotten without ende.

That

That the desires of the heart ought to be
well examined and moderated.

The 12. Chapter.

My sonne, sayth our Lorde, it
behoueth thee to learne ma=
ny thinges that thou haste
not yet well lerned. What be
they Lorde? that thou order
thy desires and affections
wholly after my pleasure, and that thou
be not a louer of thy selfe, but a desirous
folower of my will in all things. I knowe
well that desires ofte moue to this thing
or to that: but consider well, whether thou
be moued principally for mine honour, or
for thine owne. If I be in the cause, thou
shalt be wel contented, whatsoeuer I doe
with thee: but if any thinge remayne in
thy harte of thine owne will, that is it
that letteth and hindreth thee. Beware
therefore that thou leane not muche to
thine owne desire without my councell,
least happly it repent thee, and displease
thee in the ende, that firste pleased thee.
Euerye affection and desyre of mans
hart that seemeth good and holye, is not
forthwith to be folowed, nor euery con=
trarious affection or desire is not hastily
to be refused. It is sometime right expe=
dient, that a man refraine his affections
and desires, though they be good, least
happlye by his importunitie he fall into
vn=

inquietnes of minde, or that he be a let
to other, or be letted by other, and so faile
in his doinge: and sometime it behoueth
vs to vse as it were, a violence to our
selfe, and stronglye to resist and breake
downe our sensuall appetite, and not to
regard what the fleshe will or will not,
but alwaye to take hede that it be made
subiect to the will of the spirite, and that
it be so long chastised, and compelled to
serue, till it be ready to all thing that the
soule commaundeth, & that it can learne
to be content with a litle, and can delight
in simple thinges, and not to murmure
nor to grudge for any cotrarious thinges
that may befall vnto it.

How we should keepe patience, and continually
stryue agaynst all concupiscence.

The. 13. Chapter.

My Lord God (as I heare say)
patience is muche necessarie vn=
to me, because of many contra=
rious thinges, which in this life
daylie chaunce. I see well, that howeso=
euer I doe order my selfe for peace yet
can not my life be without some battaile
and sorowe. My sonne, it is true that
thou sayest: wherfore, I will not, that
thou seeke to haue suche peace as wan=
teth temptations, or as feeleth not some
cotradictio: But that thou trow & beleue
that

that thou hast found peace whē that thou
hast many troubles, and art proued with
many cōtrarious thinges in this worlde.
And if thou saye, thou mayest not suffer
suche thinges, how shalt thou then suffer
the fire of Purgatory? Of two euils, the
lesse euill is to be taken. Suffer therefore
patientlie the litle paines of this world,
that thou mayest hereafter escape the
greater in the worlde to come. Trowest
thou, that worldlye men suffer litle or
nothing? yes truely, thou shalt find none
without some trouble, though thou seeke
the most delicat persons that be. But percase thou sayest to me againe, they haue
many delectations, & folowe their owne
pleasures so much, that they ponder but
litle all their aduersities. Well, I will it
be as thou sayest, that they haue all that
they can desire, but howe longe trowest
thou that it shall endure? Soothly, it shal
sodenlye vanish awaye as smoke in the
ayre, so that there shall not be lefte anye
remembraunce of their ioyes passed, & yet
when they liued they were not without
great bitternes and griefe, for ofte times
of the same thing wherein they had their
greatest pleasure, receaued they after
great trouble and payne, & righteouslie
came that vnto them, that forasmuche as
they sought delectations and pleasures
inordinatelye, that they shoulde not fulfill their desire therein, but with greate
bit-

bitternes and sorowe. O howe shorte, howe false, and howe inordinate be all the pleasures of this worlde? Soothlye, for dronkenship and blindnes of hearte the worldlye people perceaue it not, nor wil not perceaue it, but as dombe beastes, for a lytle plesure of this corruptible life, they runne headlonge into euerlastinge death. Therefore my sonne, go not after thy concupiscence, but turne thee lightly from thine owne wil. Delite thee in god, and fire thy loue stronglye in him, and he shall geue thee the asking of thine heart. And if thou wilt haue consolation aboundantlye, and wilt receaue the soothfast comfort that commeth of God, dispose thy selfe fullye to despise this world, and put from thee wholye all inordinate delectations, and thou shalt haue plenteouslly the comfort of God. And the more that thou withdrawest thee from the consolation of all creatures, the more sweete & blessed consolations shalte thou receaue of thy creatoure. But soothlye thou canst not at the first come to such consolations, but with heauines and laboure goinge before, thy olde custome will somewhat withstande thee, but with a better custome it maye be ouercome. The flesh will murmure against thee, but with feruour of spirite it shall be restrained. The olde aunclent enemy thee freende wil let thee if he can, but with deuout prayer he shall
be

be driuen awaye, and with good bodilye
and ghostlye laboures his waye shalbe
stopped, so that he shall not dare come
nigh vnto thee.

Of the obedience of a meeke subiect, after the
example of our Lorde Iesu Christe.

The 14. Chapter.

y sonne, saith our Sauiour
Christe, he that laboureth
to withdrawe him from
obedience, withdraweth
hym from grace: And he
that seeketh to haue pri:
uate thinges, loseth the
thinges that be in common. If a man can
not gladlie submit him selfe to his supe:
riour, it is a token that his fleshe is not
yet fullie obedient to the spirite, but that
it ofte rebelleth and murmureth. There:
fore yf thou desire to ouercome thy selfe,
and to make thy fleshe obeye meekelye
to the will of the spirit, learne first to
obeye gladlye to thy superiour. The out:
ward enemye is the sooner ouercome, yf
the inner man, that is the soule, be not
feebled nor wasted. There is none worse,
nor any more greeuous enemye to the
soule, then thy selfe, if thy fleshe be not
well agreeinge to the will of the spirite.
It behoueth the therfore, that thou haue
a true despisinge and contempt of thy
selfe

selfe, yf thou wilt preuayle against thy
fleshe and bloud. But forasmuch as thou
yet louest thy selfe inordinatlie,therefore
thou fearest to resigne thy will whollie
to another mans will. But what greate
thinge is it to thee that art but dust and
nought, if thou subdue thy selfe to man
for my sake,when I, that am almightie,
& moste highe God,maker of all thinges
subdued my selfe mekelye to man for thy
sake? I made my selfe moste meeke and
most lowe of all men, that thou shouldest
learne to ouercome thy pride through
my meekenes. Learne therefore , thou
ashes,to be tractable, learne thou earth
and dust, to be meeke,and to bowe thy
selfe vnder euerye mans foote for my
sake: learne to breake thine owne will,
& to be subiect to all men in thine heart.
Rise in great wrath against thy selfe,and
suffer not pryde to reygne in thee, but
shewe thy selfe so litle and obedient,and
so noughtie in thine owne sight,that as
thee thinkes,all men maye righteouslye
go ouer thee, and tread vpõ the,as vpon
earth or claye. O vaine man, what haste
thou to complaine. O thou fowle sinner
what mayest thou righteously say against
them that reproue thee , sith thou haste
so ofte offended God , and haste also so
ofte deserued the paynes of hell?But neuerthelesse,my eye of mercie hath spared
thee,for thy soule is precious in my sight,
that

that thou shouldest thereby knowe the greate loue that I haue to thee, and be therfore the more thankful to me againe, and geue thy selfe to perfect & true subiection and meekenes, and to be ready in hart, patiently to suffer for my sake thine owne contemptes and despisings, when soeuer they shal happen to fal vnto thee. Amen.

Of the secrete and hid iudgementes of God to be considered, that vve be not proude of our good deedes.

The. 15. Chapter.

ORD, thou soundest thy iudgementes terribly vpon me, and fillest my body & bones with great feare and dreade: my soule also trembleth very sore, for I am greatly astonied, for that I see that heauens be not cleane in thy sight, for sith thou foundest default in angels, and sparedst them not, what shall become of me, that am but vile and stinking carreyne? Stars fel from heauen, and I dust and ashes, what should I presume? Also some people that seemed to haue great workes of vertue, haue fallen full lowe. And suche as were fed with meate of aungels, I haue serne after delyte in swynes meate, that is to saye, in fleshlye pleasures. Wherefore it may be well

well sayde and verifyed, that there is no holynes nor goodnes in vs, if thou withdrawe thy hand of mercy from vs, nor that no wisedome maye auayle vs, if thou Lorde gouerne it not: nor any strength helpe, if thou cease to preserue vs: no sure chastitie can be, if thou Lorde defende it not, nor any sure keeping may profite vs, if thy holy watchfulnes be not present: for if we be forsaken of thee, anone we be drowned and perishe: but if thou a litle visite vs with thy grace, we anone liue, and be lifte vp agayne. We be vnstable, vnlesse thou confirme vs, we be colde and dul, but if by thee we be stirred to feruoure of spirite. O howe meekely and abiectly ought I therfore to iudge of my selfe, & how much ought I in my heart to despise my selfe, though I be holden neuer so good and holy in sight of the world: and howe profoundly ought I to submit me to thy deepe and profound iudgementes, sith I finde in my selfe nothinge els but naught and maught? O substaunce that may not be pondered. O Sea, that may not be sailed: in thee, and by thee I finde that my substaunce is nothing, and ouer all naught. where is nowe the shadowe of this worldlye glorie, and where is the trust that I had in it? Truelie it is banished awaye through the deepenes of thy secrete and hidde Iudgementes vpon me.

What

What is fleshe in thy sight? how may clay glorifye him selfe against his maker? how may he be deceaued with vain prayses whose heart in truth is subiect to god? All the worlde may not lift him vp into pride, who truth, that God is, hath perfectly made subiect vnto him, nor he may not be deceaued with any flattering, that putteth his whole trust in God. For he seeth well, that they that speake be vaine and nought, and that they shall shortly faile with the sounde of wordes, but the truth of God alway abideth.

How a man shall order him selfe in his desires.

The. 16 Chapter.

My sonne, sayth our Sauiour Christ, thus shalt thou say in euerye thing that thou desirest. Lorde, if it be thy will, be it done as I aske, and if it be to thy praysing, be it fulfilled in thy name. And if thou see it good and profitable to me, geue me grace to vse it to thy honoure. But if thou knowe it hurtfull to me, and not profitable to the healty of my soule, then take from me suche desire. Euery desire cometh not of the holy ghoste, though it seeme rigteous & good, for it is sometime full harde to iudge, whether a good spirit or an euil moueth

D   thee

thee to this thing or to that, or whether
thou be moued of thyne owne spirite.
Many be deceiued in the ende, which firſt
ſeemed to haue beene moued of the holy
ghoſte. Therfore with dreade of God, and
with meekenes of heart it is to deſire and
aſke whatſoeuer commeth to our minde
to be deſired and aſked, and with a whole
forſakinge of our ſelfe to committe all
thinges to God, and to ſaye thus: Lorde,
thou knoweſt what thing is to me moſte
profitable, doe this or that after thy will,
geue me what thou wilt, aſmuch as thou
wilt, and when thou wilt. Doe with me
as thou knoweſt beſt to be done, and as it
ſhall pleaſe thee, and as ſhall be moſte to
thy honoure. Put me where thou wilt,
and freelye doe with me in all thinges
after thy will. Thy creature I am, and in
thine handes, leade me and turne me
where thou wilte, loe, I am thy ſeruaunt
ready to all thinges that thou commaun-
deſt, for I deſire not to lyue to my
ſelfe, but to thee. Woulde to
God it might be worthilye
and profitablye, and
to thy honoure.
Amen.

A prayer, that the vvill of God be
alvvaye fulfilled.

The 17. Chapter.

OSt benigne Lorde Iesu, graunt me thy grace, that it maye be alway with me, and worke with me, and perseuer with me vnto the end And that I may euer delire and wil that is most pleasaunt and acceptable to thee. Thy will be my will, and my will alwaye to folowe thy will, & best accord therewith. Be there alwaye in me one wil, and one Delire with thee, and that I may haue no power to will or to not will, but as thou wilt or wilt not. And graunt me that I maye dye to all thinges that be in the world, and for thee, to loue to be despised, and to be as a man vnknowen in this world. Graunt me also aboue all thinges that can be desired, that I may rest me in thee, and fullye in thee pacifye my heart, for thou Lord art the very true peace of heart, and the perfect rest of bodye and soule, and without thee all thinges be greeuous and vnquiet. Wherefore, in that peace that is in thee, one high, one blessed, and one endlesse goodnes shall I alwaye rest me; so may it be.
Amen.

D ij   That

The.18.Chapter.

 Whatsoeuer I may desire or
thinke to my comfort, I abide
it not here, but I trust to
haue it hereafter: for if I
alone might haue all the so-
lace and comfort of this worlde, & might
vse the delites thereof after mine owne
desire without sinne, it is certaine, that
they might not long endure: wherefore
my soule may not fully be comforted, nor
perfectly refreshed, but in God onely,
who is the comfort of the poore in spirite, and the embracer of the meeke and
lowly in heart. Abide, my soule, abide the
promise of god, & thou shalt haue aboundance of all goodnes in heauen. If thou
inordinatelye couete these goodes present, thou shalt lose the goodnes eternal.
Haue therfore goods present in vse, and
eternall in desire. Thou mayest in no
maner be satiate with temporal goodes,
for thou art not created so to vse the, as
to rest thee in them: for if thou alone
haddest all the goodes that euer were
created & made, thou mightest not therfore be happy and blessed, but thy blessed-
fulnes and full felicitie standeth only in
God that hath made all thinges of
nought. And that is not such felicitie as
is

is commended of the fooliſhe louers of
the worlde , but ſuch as good chriſten
men & women hope to haue in the bliſſe
of heauen, and as ſome ghoſtlye perſons
cleane and pure in heart ſometime doe
taſte here in this preſent life,whoſe con=
uerſation is in heauen. All worldly ſo=
lace,and all mans comfort is vaine and
ſhort , but that comfort is bleſſed and
ſoothfaſt , that is perceaued by truth in=
wardly in the hart.A deuout foiower of
God beareth alway about with him his
comforter, that is Ieſu , and ſayeth thus
vnto him:My Lord Ieſu , I beſeech thee
that thou be with me in euery place,and
euerye time,and that it be to me a ſpecial
ſolace , gladly for thy loue to want all
mans ſolace.And if thy ſolace want alſo,
that thy will,and thy righteous prouing
and aſſaying of me , may be to me a
ſinguler comfort , and a high
ſolace. Thou ſhalt not al=
waye be angrie with me,
neither ſhalt thou al=
waye threate me.
So may it be.
Amen.

H iij Tꜩt

That all our study and busines of minde ought to be put in God.

The. 19. Chapter.

My sonne, saith our Lorde to his seruant, suffer me to doe with thee what I will, for I knowe what is best and most expedient for thee. Thou workest in many thinges after thy kindlie reason, and after as thy affection, and thy wouldie pollicie stirreth thee: and so thou mayest lightlie erre and be deceued. O Lorde, it is true all that thou sayest, thy prouidece is much more better for me, then all that I can doe or say of my selfe. Wherfore it may well be sayde and verified, that he standeth very casuallye, that setteth not his wholle trust in thee. Therefore Lorde, while my witte abideth stedfast & stable, doe with me in all thinges as it pleaseth thee, for it may not be but well all that thou doest. If thou wilt, that I be in light, be thou blessed, and if thou wilt, that I be in darkenes, be thou also blessed. If thou vouchsafe to comfort me, be thou highly blessed. And if thou wilt, that I shall liue in trouble, and without all cofort, be thou in likewise muche blessed. My sonne, so it behoueth to be with thee, if thou wilt walke with me: as readye must thou be to suffer, as to ioye, and as gladlie be needye and poore, as wealthy and

and riche.Lorde, I will gladlie suffer for
thee whatsoeuer thou wilt shall fal vpon
me.Indifferētly will I take of thy hande
good and bad,bitter and sweete, gladnes
and sorowe,and for all thinges that shall
befal vnto me,hartily wil I thanke thee.
Keepe me,Lorde,from sinne, and I shall
neither dreade death nor hel.Put not my
name out of the booke of life,and it shall
not greeue me,what trouble soeuer befal
vpon me.

That all temporall miseries are gladly to be
borne through the example of Christe

The 20.Chapter.

My sonne, sayth our Lorde, I
descended from heauen, and
for thy health haue I take thy
miseries,not compelled therto
of necessitie, but of my chari-
tie,that thou shouldest learne to haue patiēce with me,& not to disdayne to beare
the miseries & wretchednes of this life,
as I haue done for thee:for from the first
houre of my birth vnto my death vpō the
crosse,I was neuer without some sorowe
or paine. I had great lacke of temporall
thinges, I heard great cōplaintes made
on me,I suffered beningely many shames
& rebukes, for my benefites I receaued
vnkindnes,for my miracles,blasphemies,
& for my true doctrine many reproufes.

O Lorde, forasmuche as thou wert founde patient in thy life, fulfilling in that moste specially the will of thy father, it is seeming, that I moste wretched sinner beate me patiently after thy will in all thinges, and as long as thou wilt, that I for mine owne health, beate the burden of this corruptible life: for though this life be tedious, and as an heauy burden to the soule, yet neuerthelesse, it is nowe through thy grace made very meritorious, and by exaple of thee, & of thy holie saints, it is now made to weak persons more sufferable & cleere, and also muche more comfortable then it was in the olde lawe, when the gates of heauen were shet, and the waye thitherwarde was darke, and so fewe did couet to feele it. And yet they that were then righteous, and were ordeined to be saued, before thy blessed passion and death might neuer haue come thither. O what thankes am I bounde therfore to yeelde to thee, that so louingly haste vouchedsafe to shew to me, and to all faythful people that will folow thee, the very true and straite way to thy kingdome. Thy holy life is our way, and by thy patiéce we walke to thee, who art our head and gouernour. And if thou Lorde haddest not gone before, and shewed vs the way, who woulde haue endeuoured him to haue folowed? howe many shoulde haue

haue taried behind, if they had not seene
thy blessed examples goinge before? We
be yet slowe & dull, nowe we haue seene
and hearde thy signes and doctrines:
what shoulde we then haue beene, if we
had seene no such light goinge before vs?
Truelie, we should haue fixed our minde
and loue whollye in worldlye thinges,
from the which keepe vs Lorde of thy
great goodnes. Amen.

Of patient suffering of iniuries and wronges,
and whe is truely patient.

The 21.Chapter.

Y sonne, what is it that thou
speakest, why complainest
thou thus? ceasse, ceasse, cō-
plaine no more, consider my
passion, and the passions of
my saintes, and thou shalt
well see, that it is right litle that thou
suffrest for me. Thou hast not yet suff ed
to the shedinge of thy blood, and truelie,
thou haste litle suffed in comparison of
them that haue suffed so many thinges
for me in time past, and that haue bene
so strongly tempted, so greeuouslye troubled, and so manye wayes proued. It behoueth thee therefore to remember the
great greeuous thinges that other haue
suffed for me, that thou mayest the more
lightly beare thy litle griefes: and if they
D v seme

seeme not litle to thee, loke thy impatiē-
ce caule not that: but neuerthelees, whether they be litle oz great, studie almaye
to beare them patientlie without grudginge oz complayninge, if thou may, and
the better that thou canst dispose thee to
suffer them, the moze wiselier thou doest,
and the moze merit shalt thou haue, and
thy burdē by reason of thy good custome
and of thy good will shall be the lighter.
Thou shalt neuer saye, I can not suffer
this thinge of such a person, noz it is not
foz me to suffer it: he hath done me great
wzonge, and layeth vnto my charge that
I nzuer thought, but of another man I
will suffer as I shall thinke. Suche maner sayinges be not good, foz they consider not the vertue of patience, noz of
whom it syalbe crowned, but they rather
consider the persons and the offences
done vnto them. Therefoze he is not
truelie pacient that will not suffer but as
much as he will, and of whom he will: foz
a true pacient man forceth not of whom
he suffereth, whether of his Prelate, oz
of his felowe that is egall vnto him, oz
of any other that is vnder him noz whether he be a good man and a holye, oz an
euill man and an vnwozthy, but when-
soeuer any aduersitie oz wzonge falleth
vnto him whatsoeuer it be, and of whom
soeuer it be, and howe ofte soeuer, he taketh all thankfullie as of the hande of
God

God, and accompteth it as a riche gifte, and a great benefite, O God, for he knoweth well that there is nothinge that a man may suffer for God that may passe without great merite. Be thou therefore readie to battail, if thou wilt haue victorie: without battaile thou mayest not come to the crowne of patience, and yf thou wilt not suffer, thou refusest to be crowned. Wherefore, if thou wilt needlie be crowned, resist stronglie, and suffer patientlie, for without laboure no man may come to rest, nor without battaile no man may come to victorie. O Lorde Jesu, make it possible to me by grace, that is impossible to me by nature: Thou knowest well that I may litle suffer, and that I am cast downe anone with a litle aduersitie, wherfore I beseeche thee, that trouble and aduersitie may hereafter for thy name be beloued and desired of me, for truelie, to suffer, and to be vexed for thee, is verie good and profitable to the health of my soule.

Of the knowvinge of our owne infirmities, and of the miseries of this life.

The 22. Chapter.

 Shall knowledge against me all my vnrighteousnes, and I shall confesse to thee Lorde all the vnstablenes of my hearte. Ofte times it is but a litle thinge

thinge that casteth me downe, & maketh
me dull and slowe, to all good workes,
and sometime I purpose to stande strong-
glie:but when a litle temptation cōmeth,
it is to me greate anguishe & griefe,and
somtime of a right litle thing,a greeuous
temptation riseth, and when I thinke
my selfe to be somewhat surer, and that,
as it seemeth, I haue the higher hande,
sodenly I feele my selfe nere hand ouercome by a light temptatiō.Beholde therfore,good Lord,beholde my weaknes and
my frailnes, best knowen to thee before
all other:haue mercy on me,O Lord, and
deliuer me from the filthy dregs of sinne,
that my feete be neuer fixed in them.But
this is it that ofte grudgeth me sore,and
in maner cōfoundeth me before thee,that
I am so vnstable and weake,and so frayle
to resist my passions. And though they
drawe me not alwaye to consent,yet neuerthlesse, their cruell assaultes be very
greeuous vnto me, so that it is in maner
tedious to me,to liue in such battaile:but
yet such battaile is not all vnprofitable
to me, for thereby I knowe the better
myne owne infirmities, for I see well,
that such wicked fantasies doe rise in me
muche sooner then they go awaye.But
would to God,that thou moste strongest
God of Israell, the louer of all faythfull
soules, wouldest vouchsafe to beholde the
labour and sorowe of me thy poorest seruant

uant, and that thou wouldeſt aſſiſt me
in all things that I haue to do. Strength
me Lord with heuenlye ſtrength, ſo that
the olde enimie the fiende, nor my wretched fleſh, which is not yet fullye ſubiect
to the ſpirite, haue not power nor lord-
ſhip ouer me, againſt whom I muſt fight
continuallye, while I ſhall lyue in this
miſerable life. But alas, what life is this,
where no trouble nor miſerie wanteth,
where alſo euery place is full of ſnares &
of mortall enimies? for one trouble or
temptation goinge awaye, another commeth, and the firſt conflict yet duringe,
many other ſodenlye tyſe more then can
be thought. Howe may this life therefore
be loued that hath ſuche bitternes, and
that is ſubiect to ſo many miſeries? And
howe may it be called a life, that bringeth
forth ſo many deathes, & ſo many ghoſtly
infections? and yet it is beloued & muche
delighted of in many perſons. The world
is ofte reproued, that it is deceiptful and
vaine, and yet it is not lightly forſaken,
eſpeciallye when the concupiſcences of
the fleſhe be ſuffered to haue rule. Some
thinges ſtirre a man to loue the worlde,
and ſome thinges to deſpiſe it: the concupiſcence of the fleſh, the concupiſcence
of the eye, and the pride of the hart, ſtirre
man to loue the worlde. But the paines
and miſeries that folowe of it, cauſeth
hatred and tediouſnes of it agayne. But
                                  alas

ning for forowe, a litle delectation ouercommeth the minde of the that be much
fet to loue the world, and dryueth out of
their hartes all heauenlie desires, info-
much that many accompt it as a ioye of
Paradise to liue vnder such sensible pleasures, and that is, because they neither
haue seene nor tasted the sweetnes in
God, nor the inwarde gladnes that cōmeth of vertues. But they that perfectly
despise the worlde, and that studie to liue
vnder holie discipline, be not ignoraunt
of the heauenlie sweetnes that is promised vnto ghostlie liuers: and they see also
howe greeuouslie the world erreth, and
howe greeuouslie it is deceyued in diuers maners.

Howe a man shoulde rest in God
aboue all thinges.

The 23. Chapter.

A Boue all thinges, and in all
thinges rest thou my soule in
thy Lorde God, for he is the
eternall rest of all Angels and
saintes. Geue me Lord Iesus,
this speciall grace for to reste me in thee
aboue all creatures: aboue all helth and
fayrenes, aboue all glorye and honour,
aboue all dignitie and power, aboue all
cunninge and pollicie, aboue all riches &
craftes, aboue all gladnes of bodye and
soule

foule, aboue all fame and praysing, aboue
all sweetnes and consolation, aboue all
hope and reproimission, aboue all merite
and desire, aboue all giftes & rewardes,
that thou mayest geue or sende beside thy
selfe, and aboue all ioy and mirth that
mans heart or minde may take or feele:
And also aboue all Angels and Archangels, and aboue the company of heauenlie spirites, aboue all thinges visible and
inuisible, and aboue all thing that is not
thy selfe. For thou, O Lord God, art most
best, most highest, most mightest, most sufficient, and most full of goodnes: moste
sweete, moste comfortable, moste fayre,
moste louinge, moste noble, and moste
glorious aboue all thinge, in whom all
goodnes is together perfectlie and fully,
hath beene and shall be. And therefore,
whatsoeuer thou geuest me beside thy
selfe, it is lytle and insufficient to me
for my heart may not rest, nor fullye be
pacifyed but in thee, so that it ascendeth aboue all giftes, and also aboue
all maner of thinges that be created. O
my Lorde Iesu Christ moste louing spouse, moste purest louer and gouernoure
of euerye creature, who shall geue me
winges of perfect libertie, that I may flie
high, and rest me in thee. O when shall I
fullie tende to thee, and see, and feele
how sweete thou art: whe shall I wholly
gather my selfe together in thee, so perfectlye

seemlie that I shall not for thy loue seke
my selfe, but thee onelie aboue my selfe,
and aboue all bodilie thinges, and that
thou visite me in such wise as thou doest
visite thy faythfull louers? Nowe I ofte
mourne and complaine the miseries of
this life, and with sorowe and woe beare
them with right great heauines: for many
euill thinges happen daylie in this lyfe,
which ofte times trouble me, and make
me verie heauie, & greatlie darken mine
vnderstandinÿ. They hinder me greatly,
and put my minde from thee, and so en:
comber me many wayes, that I can not
haue free minde & cleane desire to thee,
nor haue thy sweete imbracinges that to
thy blessed Saintes be alwaye present.
Wherefore I beseeche thee Lorde Christ
Iesu, that the sighinges and the inwarde
desires of my hart, with my manifolde
desolutions, may somewhat moue thee,
and incline thee to heare me. O Iesu the
light and brightnes of euerlasting glory,
the ioy and comfort of all christien peo:
ple that are walking & labouring as pil:
grimes in the wyldernes of this world,
my harte cryeth to thee by still desires
without voyce, and my silence speaketh
vnto thee, and sayth thus: How longe
tarieth my Lorde God to come to me,
verilie I trust that he will shortlie come
to me his poorest seruant, and comfort
me, and make me ioyous & glad in him,

And

And that he will deliuer me from all anguishe and sorowe. Come Lord come, for
without thee I haue no glad daye, nor
houre,for thou art all my ioye & gladnes,
and without thee my soule is barren and
voyde.I am a wretche, and in maner in
prison,and bounde with fetters,till thou
through the light of thy gracious presēce
vouchsafe to visit me,and to refresh me,
and to bring me againe to libertie of spirite, and that thou vouchsafe to shewe
thy fauourable and louinge countenance
vnto me.Let other seeke what they will,
but trulye there is nothinge that I will
seeke, nor that shall please me, but thou
my Lorde God,my hope and euerlastinge
heith.I shall not cease of prayer till thy
grace returne to me againe, & that thou
speake inwardly to my soule,& saye thus,
Lo I am here,I am come to thee,for thou
haste called me,thy teares & the desyre of
thy hart,thy meeknes and thy contrition
haue bowed me downe, and brought me
to thee. And I shall saye agayne,Lorde I
haue called thee, and I haue desyred to
haue thee,ready to forsake all things for
thee, thou first haste stirred me to seeke
thee. Wherefore be thou alwaye blessed
that haste shewed suche goodnes to me,
after the multitude of thy mercy:What
hath thy seruant (Lorde)more to doe or
saye, but that he meeken him selfe before
thy maiestie,and euer haue in minde his
　　　　　　　　　　　　　　owne

owne infauitie. There is none like to
thee Lorde, in heauen nor in earth, thy
workes be good, thy iudgementes be
righteous, & by thy prouidence all things
be gouerned. Wherefore to thee which
art the wisedome of the father, be euerlasting ioy & glory, and I humbly beseech
thee, that my body and soule, my harte
and tounge, and all thy creatures, maye
alwaye laude thee, and blesse thee. Amen.

Of remembringe of the great and manyfolde benefites of God.

The 24. Chapter.

Pen mine hart, Lorde, into
the beholding of thy lawes,
and in thy comaundements
teach me to walke, geue me
grace to knowe and to vn-
derstand thy will, and with
great reuerence and diligent considera-
tiō to remember thy manyfold benefites,
that I may from henceforth yeld to thee
due thankes for thē againe. But I knowe
and confesse it for truth, that I am not
able to yeld to thee condigne thankinges
for the least benefite that thou hast geuen
me, for I am lesse then the least benefite
that thou hast geuen. And whē I beholde
thy noblenes and woorthines, my spirite
dreadeth and trembleth very sore for the
greatnes therof. O Lord, all that we haue

in

in body & in soule, inwardly & outwardlye, naturally or supernaturallye, they be
thy beneſites, and ſhew thee openly to be
a bleſſed and good benefactour, of whom
we haue receiued ſuch giftes. And though
one hath receaued more, and another
leſſe, yet they all be thy giftes, & without
thee the leaſt can not be had: and he that
hath more receaued, may not rightfully
glorify him ſelfe therein, as though he
had gotten it by his owne merite, nor
exalt him ſelfe aboue other, nor diſdayne
other, nor deſpiſe his inferiours therefore:
for he is greateſt and moſte acceptable to
thee, that leaſt aſcribeth to him ſelfe, and
that is for ſuche giftes the more meeke
and deuout, in yeldinge thankes to thee
for them agayne. And he that through
meekenes can holde him ſelfe moſte vile,
and moſte vnwoorthy of all other, is the
more apt to receaue of thy hande more
larger giftes. And he that hath receaued
the fewer giftes, ought not therefore to
be heauy, or to diſdaine at it, nor to be
enuious againſt them that haue receaued
the greater, but rather he ought to lifte
his minde vpwarde to thee, and highlye
to laude and prayſe thy name, that thou
ſo liberallye, ſo louinglye, and ſo freelye,
withou accepting of perſons, departeſt
thy giftes among thy people: all thinges
come of thee, and therefore thou art in
all thinges to be bleſſed. Thou knoweſt
what

what is expedient to be geuen to euery
person, and why one hath lesse, and an=
other more, it is not for vs to reason or
discusse, but to thee onelye, by whom the
merites of euery man shall be discussed.
Wherefore Lorde, I accompt it for a
great benefite not to haue many giftes,
whereby outwardlie, & after mās iudge=
ment, laude and praysinge should folow.
And ouer that, as me seemeth, although
a man consider and beholde his owne
pouertie, and the vilenes of his owne
person, he ought not therefore to take
griefe, heauines, or deiection, but rather
to conceaue thereby greate gladnes of
soule: for thou haste chosen, and daylie
doest chose poore meeke persons, & suche
as be despised in the worlde, to be thy
familier and housholde seruauntes, wit=
nes thy Apostles, whom thou madest
princes of al the worlde, which neuerthe=
lesse were conuersaunt amonge the peo=
ple without complayninge or missaying,
so meeke and simple without all malice
and disceipte, that they ioyed to suffer re=
proufes for thy name, so farreforth, that
such thinges as the world abhorreth and
flieth, they coueted with great desire.
Thus it appeareth, that there ought no=
thinge so much to comfort and glad thy
louer and him that hath receaued thy
benefites, as that thy will and pleasure
in him be fullfilled after the eternall dis=
position

position of him from the beginninge, wherewith he ought to be so well contented and pleased, that he woulde as gladly be holden least, as other woulde be holden most, and as peacefull woulde he be, & as well pleased in the lowest place, as in the highest: and as glad to be despised and abiect, and of no name nor reputation in the world, as other to be nobler or greater: for thy will, Lorde, and the honour of thy name ought to excell all thinges, and more ought it to please and comfort thy louer, then all other benefits geuen, or that might be geuen vnto him.

Of foure things that bring peace into the soule.

The 25. Chapter.

 y sonne, nowe shal I teach thee the very true waye of peace and of perfect libertie. O Lorde Iesu, Doe as thou sayest, for that is ryght ioyous for me to heare. Studye my sonne rather to fulfill another mans will, then thine owne. Chose alwaye to haue litle worldly riches, rather then much: seeke also the lowest place, and desire to be vnder other, rather then aboue, and couete alwaye and praye, that the will of God be wholiye done in thee. Lo, such a person entreth soothfastlie into the verye true

waye

waye of grace and inward quietnes. O
Lorde, this short lesson that thou haue
taught me, conteyneth in it selfe much
high perfection. It is shorte in wordes,
but it is full of sentence, and fruitfull in
vertue: for if it were well and faithfullie
kepte of me, vnrestfulnes shoulde not so
lightly spring in me as it hath done. For
as ofte as I feele my selfe vnrestfull, and
not contented, I finde that I haue gone
from this lesson, and from this good doctrine. But thou Lorde Iesu, who hast all
thinges vnder thy gouernaunce, and
alwaye louest the health of mans soule,
increase more grace in me, that I maye
from henceforth fulfill these teachinges,
and that I may doe alway, that shalbe to
thy honoure, and to the health of my
soule. Amen.

A prayer against euill thoughtes.

The. 26. Chapter.

MY Lorde Iesu, I beseeche thee
be not farre from me, but come
shortlye, & helpe me, for vaine
thoughtes haue risen in mine
hart, and worldly dredes haue
troubled me verie sore. Howe shall I
breake them downe? howe shall I passe
vnhurt without thy helpe? I shall go
before thee, sayth our Lorde, and I shall
driue awaye the pride of thy hart, then
shall

shal I set open to thee the gates of ghostlie knowledge,and shall shew to thee the
pꝛuities of my secretes. O Lozde , doe as
thou sayest , and then shall flee from me
all wicked fantasies , and truelie this is
my hope , and my onelie comfoꝛt , to flee
to thee in euery trouble , stedfastlie to
trust in thee , inwardlie to call to thee,
and patientlie to abyde thy comminge,
and thy heauenlie consolations , which
I trust shall shoꝛtlie come to me.Amen.

A prayer for clarifying of mans
minde.

The. 27. Chapter.

Clarisie me , Loꝛde Iesu , with
the cleereues of the euerlastinge light , and dꝛiue out of
my heart all maner of darknes , and all vaine imagina-
tions , fight stronglie foꝛ me, and dꝛiue
awaye the euill beastes,that is to saye,all
my euill and wicked cõcupiscences , that
peace of conscience may enter and haue
full rule in me,and that aboundaunce of
lawde and pꝛaysinge of thy name , maye
sound continuallie in the chamber of my
soule:that is to saye, in a pure & cleane
cõscience in me. Commaunde the windes
and tempestes of pꝛide to cease, bid the
sea of woꝛldlie couetise to be in rest , and
charge the noꝛth winde , that is to saye,
the

the fiendes temptacio, that it blowe not
and then shalbe great tranquillitie and
peace in me. Send out thy light & truth
of ghostlye knowledge, that it maye shine
vpon the earth barreyne and dry, and
sende downe thy grace from aboue,
and therewith annoynt my dry heart,
and geue me the water of inward deuotion, to moiste therewith the drines of my
soule, that it may bring forth some good
fruite, that shall be liking and pleasaunt
to thee. Rayse vp my minde, that is sore
oppressed with the heauy burde of sinne
and lifte vp my desire to the loue of heauenly thinges, that by a taste of the heauenlie felicitie, it may lothe to thinke on
any earthly thinges. Take me Lorde, and
deliuer me from the vile consolation of
creatures, which must of necessitie shortlie perishe and fayle. For there is nothing
created, that may fullye satisfye mine
appetite. Ioyne me therefore to thee
with a sure bonde of heauenlye
loue, for thou onely suffisest
to thy louer. And with-
out thee all thinges
be vaine, and of
no substaunce.

That

*That it is not good to searche curiouslye
another mans lyfe.*

The 28.Chapter.

y sonne, saith our Lorde,
looke thou be not curious
in searchinge of any other
mans lyfe, neyther boe
thou busie thy selfe with
those thinges, which boe
not belonge vnto thee.
What is this or that to thee? folow thou
me: What is it to thee, whether this man
be good or bad? or whether he saye or doe
this or that? Thou needest not to answere
for another mans deedes, but for thyne
owne deedes thou must needly aunswere.
Why then doest thou medle where it
needeth not? I see and know euery man,
and euery thinge vnder the sunne, I see
and beholde, and howe it is with euery
person, what he thinketh, what he willeth, and to what ende his worke draweth, is open to me. And therefore all
thinges are to be referred to me. Keepe
thy selfe alwaye in good peace, and suffer
him that will alwayes searche another
mans life, be as busye as he will, and in
the ende shall fall vpon him as he hath
done and sayde, for he can not deceaue
me whatsoeuer he be. If thou admonishe
anye person for his soule health, looke
thou do it not, to get the thereby anye

A   name

name or fame in the worlde, nor to haue the familiaritie or pryuate loue of any person, for luche thinges cause much vnquietnes of minde, and will make thee also to lose the rewarde that thou shouldest haue of God, and will bring greate darkenes into thy soule. I woulde gladly speake to thee my wordes, & open to thee the secrete misteries of fraternail correction: yf thou wouldest prepare thy soule ready against my cominge, and that thou wouldest open the mouth of thy hearte faithfullye to me: Be thou prouident, wake diligentlye in prayer, humble thy selfe in euery thing, and thou shalt finde great comfort in God, and litle resistence in thy euen christen.

In vvhat thing the peace of heart, and greatest profite of man standeth.

The 29. Chapter.

Y sonne, saith our Lord Iesu, I sayd to my disciples thus: My peace I leaue with you, my peace I geue you, not as the worlde geueth, but much more then it maye geue. All men desire peace, but all men will not do that belongeth to peace. My peace is with the meeke and milde in hart, and thy peace shall be in much pacience: if thou wilt heare me, and folowe my wordes, thou shalt haue great plentie

plentie of peace. O Lozde what shall J
doe to come to that peace? Thou shalt in
all thy wozkes take good heede what
thou doest and sayest, and thou shalte set
all thy whole intent to please me, and
nothing shalt thou couet oz seeke with=
out me, and of other mens deedes thou
shalt not iudge presumptuously, noz thou
shalt not medle with thinges that per=
teine not to thee, if thou do thus it maye
be that thou shalt litle oz seldome be trou=
bled: but neuerthelesse, to fele at no time
any maner of trouble, noz to suffer any
heauines in body noz in soule, is not the
state of this lyfe, but of the lyfe to come.
Thinke not therefoze that thou haste
found the true peace when thou feelest
no greefe, noz that all is well with thee
when thou hast none aduersitie, noz that
all is perfect foz that euery thing cometh
after thy minde. Noz yet that thou arte
great in godds sight, oz specially beloued
of him, because thou hast great feruour in
deuotion, and great sweetnes in contem=
plation, foz a true louer of vertue is not
knowen by all these thinges, noz the true
perfection of man standeth not in them.
(Wherein then Lozde?) In offering of
a man with all his hart wholly to God,
not seking him selfe, noz his owne will,
neyther in greate thinges noz in small,
in tyme noz in eternitie, but that he
abide alwaye one, and yeelde alwaye like

J.i.   thankes

thankes to God for things pleasant and
displeasant, waying them all in one like
balance as in his loue. Also if he be strong
in God, that when inwarde consolation
is withdrawen he can yet stirre his harte
to suffer more if God so will, and yet iu-
stifieth not him selfe, nor prayseth him
selfe therefore, as holye and righteous:
then he walketh in the very true waye of
peace, and then he may well haue a sure
and a perfect hope and trust that he shall
see me face to face, in euerlasting ioy and
fruition in the kingdome of heauen. And
if he can come to a perfect and a full contempt and despisinge of him selfe, then
shall he haue full habundance of rest and
peace in the ioye euerlastinge, after the
measure of his gifte. Amen.

Of the libertie, excellencie, and vvorthi-
nesse of a free mynde.

The. 30. Chapter.

LORDE it is the worke of a perfect man, not to sequester his
minde from the beholding of
heauenly thinges, and among
many cares, to go as he were
without care: not in the maner of an ydle
or of a desolate person, but by the speciall
prerogatiue of a free minde, alwaye busy
in goddes seruice, not cleuinge by inordinate affection to any creature. I beseeche
                                              thee

thee therefore my Lord Iesu, most meeke
and mercifall, that thou keepe me from
the busines and cares of the worlde, and
that I be not ouermuch inquieted with
the necessities of the bodilie kinde, nor
that I be not taken with the voluptuous
pleasures of the worlde, and the fleshe,
and that in likewise thou preserue me
from all hinderance of the soule, that I
be not broken with ouermuch heauines,
sorow, nor worldlye dreade. And by these
petitions I aske not onelie to be deliuered from such vanities as the world desireth, but also from suche miseries as
greeue the soule of me thy seruant, with
the common malediction of mankinde,
that is, with corruption of the bodilie
feelinge, where with I am so greeued
and letted, that I maye not haue libertie
of spirite to beholde thee when I would.
O Lorde God, that art sweetnes vnspeakeable, turne into bitternes to me all
fleshlie delites, which would drawe me
from the loue of eternall thinges to the
loue of a short and a vile delectable pleasure: Let not the fleshe and bloude ouercome me, nor the worlde with his short
glory deceyue me, nor the fiend with his
thousand folde craftes supplant me, but
geue me ghostlie strength in resistinge,
patience in sufferinge, and constancie in
perseueringe. Geue me also for all worldlie consolations, the most sweete conso-
        I ij   lations

inside of the holy ghost, and for al fleshly loue, sende into my soule the loue of thy holy name. Lo meat, drinke, cloathinge, and all other necessaries for the body be painefull and troublesome to a feruent spirite, which if it might, woulde alwaye rest in God, & in ghostly thinges. Graunt me therefore grace to vse such bodilye necessaries temperatiye, and that I be not deceaued with ouermuch desire to them. To forsake all thinges it is not lawfull, for the bodilye kinde must be preserued, but to seeke superfluous thinges, more for pleasure, then for necessitie, thy holye lawe prohibiteth: for so the flesye woulde rebel against the spirite. Wherfore Lord, I beseech thee, that thy hande of grace maye so gouerne and teache me, that I exceede not by any maner of superfluitie. Amen.

That priuate loue most letteth a man from God.

The. 3 1. Chapter.

My sonne, saith our Lorde it behoueth thee to geue all for all, and nothing to keepe to thee of thine owne loue, for the loue of thy selfe more hurteth thee, then any other thing in this world. After thy loue, and after thine affection euery thinge cleaueth to thee more or lesse

lesse. If thy loue be pure, simple, and well
ordered, thou shalte be without inordinate affection to any creature. Couete
therefore nothing that is not lawfull for
thee to haue, and haue nothing that may
let thee from ghostlye trauayle, or that
maye take from thee inwarde libertie of
soule. It is meruail, that thou committest
not thy selfe fullye to me with all thy
heart, with all thinges that thou mayest
haue or desire. Whye art thou thus consumed with vaine sorowe? why art thou
weried with superfluous cares? Stande
at my will, and thou shalt finde nothing
that shall hurt or hinder thee: but if thou
seeke this thing or that, or wouldest be in
this place or in that for thine owne profite, and for thine owne pleasure, thou
shalt neuer be in rest, nor euer free from
some trouble of minde: for in euery place
shal be found something that will mislike
thee. Transitorie thinges when they be
had and greatly multiplied in the world,
Do not alway helpe mans soule to peace,
but rather when they be despysed and
fullie cut out of the loue and desire of the
hart, and that not to be vnderstand onely
of golde and siluer, and other worldlye
riches, but also of desire of honours and
praysinges of the worlde, which shortlye
vanisheth and passeth awaye, as doth
the smoke with the winde: the place
helpeth little yf the spirite of feruour

be awaye. Also the peace that a man get=
teth outwardelye, shall not long stande
whole, if it be voyde from the true in=
ward peace of hart, that is to say, though
thou chaunge thy place, yet it shall litle
amende thee, onlesse thou stande stedfast
in me: for by newe occasions that shall
daylie rise, thou shalte finde that thou
hast fled, & percase muche more perillous,
and muche more greuous thinges than
the first were.

A prayer for the purginge of mans soule, and
for heauenlye vvisdome and the grace of
God to be obteyned and had.

The 32. Chapter.

Onfirme me Lorde, by the
grace of the holye ghost, and
geue me grace to be stronge in=
wardlye in soule, and auoyde
out thereof all vnprofitable
busines of the worlde, and of the fleshe
that it may not be led by vnstable desires
of earthlie thinges. And that I maye be=
holde all thinges, as they be, transitorie,
and of short abidinge, and me also to go
with them: for nothinge vnder the Sun
may longe abide, but all is vanitie, and
affliction of spirite. O howe wise is he
that feeleth and vnderstandeth this to
be true that I haue sayde. Geue me (Lord)
there=

therefore heauenlye wisedome, that I maye learne to seeke thee, and to finde thee, and aboue all thinges to loue thee, and all other thinges to vnderstande and knowe, as they be, after thorder of my wisedome, and none otherwise, and geue me grace also, wiselie to withdrawe me from them that flatter me, and patiently to suffer thē that greue me: for it is great wisedome not to be moued with euery blast of wordes, nor to geue eare to him that flattereth, as doth the mairmayde. The waye that is thus begon, shall bring him that walketh in it, to a good and a blessed ending.

Agaynst the euill sayinges of detractours.

The 33.Chapter.

My sonne, saith our Sauiour Christ, thou shalt not take it to griefe, because some persons thinke euill, or say euill of thee, that thou wouldest not gladlye heare, for thou shalt yet thinke worse of thy selfe, and that no man is so euill as thou arte. If thou be well ordred inwardlye in thy soule, thou shalt not muche care for suche flyinge wordes. And it is no litle wisedome, a man to keepe him selfe in silence, and in good peace, when euill wordes be spoken to him, and to turne his heart to

I b God

God, and not to be troubled with mans
iudgement. Let not thy peace be in the
heartes of men, for whatsoeuer they say
of thee, good or bad, thou art not therefore another man: but as thou art, thou
art. Where is the true peace and glorie,
is it not in me? yes truely: Therefore he
that neither desireth to please man, nor
dreadeth not to displease him, shall haue
great plentie of peace: for of inordinate
loue, and vaine dread, commeth all vnquietnes of heart, and vnrestfulnes of
minde.

Howe almightie God is to be invvardlye
called vnto, in time of tribulation.

The 34. Chapter.

Lorde, thy name be blessed
for euer: that thou woul-
dest this temptation and
tribulation should fal vpon
me, I maye not escape it,
but of necessitie I am driuen to flee to thee, that
thou vouchsafe to helpe me, and to turne
all into ghostlye profite. O Lorde, I am
nowe in trouble, & it is not well with me,
for I am greatly vexed with this present
passion. And nowe moste best beloued father, what shall I say, I am nowe taken
with anguishes and troubles on euerye
side, saue me in this houre, but I trust
that

that I am come into this houre, that
thou shalt be lauded and praysed when
I am perfectlye made meeke before thee,
and that I am clerely deliuered by thee,
be it therfore pleasaunt to thee to deliuer
me. For what may I most sinneful wretch
doe, or whither may I goe without thee?
Giue me patiéce nowe at this time in all
my troubles: helpe me my Lord God, and
I shall not feare ne dread what troubles
soeuer fall vpon me. And nowe what shal
I say, but that thy will be done in me? I
haue deserued to be troubled & greeued,
and therefore it behoueth that I suffer as
long as it shall please thee, but woulde to
God that I might suffer gladlye till the
furious tempestes were ouerpassed, and
that quietnes of hart might come againe.
Thy mightie hande (Lorde) is stronge
ynough to take this trouble from me, and
to aswage the cruel assaults thereof, that
I doe not vtterly fayle, as thou hast ofte
times done to me before this time, & the
more harde that it is to me, the more
light it is to thee. And when I am clerely
deliuered by thee, then shall I saye, This
is the changing of the right hande of him
that is highest, that is, the blessed
Trinitie, to whom be ioye,
honour, and glorye
euerlastingly.
Amen.

Of

The thirde
Of the helpe of God to be asked, and of a full
trust to recouer through deuout prayer
our former grace.

The. 3 5 .Chapter.

M y sonne , I am the Lorde that
sendeth comfort in tyme of
tribulation, come therefore to
me , when it is not well with
thee. This is it that letteth
thee most , that thou turnest thee ouer
slowlie to me, for before thou pray hartilie to me , thou seekest many other comfortes , and refreshest thy spirites in outwarde thinges. And therefore all that
thou doest litle auayleth thee , til thou
canst beholde and see , that I am he that
sendeth comfort to all that faithfully doe
call to me, and that there is not without
me any profitable counsayle nor perfect
remedie. But nowe take a good spirite to
thee, and after thy troubles be thou comforted in me , & in the light of my mercie
haue thou full trust, for I am nere to thee
to helpe thee, and to restore thee againe,
not onelie to like grace as thou haddest
first , but also to muche more , in great
aboundance. Is there anye thinge harc
or impossible to me? or am I like to him,
that sayeth a thinge , and doeth it not?
where is thy fayth? Stand stronglie and
perseuerantlie in me, be stedfast , abiding
my

my promise,and thou shalt haue comfort
in such time as it shall be most expedient
for thee:abide,abide,and tary for me,and
I shall come soone , and helpe thee.It is
temptation that vexeth thee,and a vaine
dread that feareth thee much. But what
auayleth such feare of dreade for thinges
that perchaunce shall neuer come , but
that the ghostlye enemye woulde thou
shouldest haue sorowe vpon sorow.Beare
therefore patienlye thy troubles that be
present, and drede not ouermuche those
that be to come : for it suffiseth to euery
daye his owne malice.It is a vaine thing
and vnprofitable,to be heauy or glad for
thinges,that perchaunce shal neuer happen nor come,but it is the vnstablenes of
man,that he will be deceaued,& so lightly
to folowe the suggestion of the enemie,
for he careth not whether he maye deceiue by true suggestion or by false , nor
whether it be by loue of thinges present,
or by dreade of thinges to come.Therfore
be thou not troubled, neither drede, but
trust stronglie in me,& in my mercy haue
perfect hope,for when thou weenest,that
thou art right farre from me, ofte times
I am right neere vnto thee : and when
thou weenest that all is lost, then ofte
times foloweth the greater reward. It is
not therefore all lost,though some thinge
happen against thy will, and thou shalt
not iudge therein after thy outwarde
feeling

freliuer, neyther shalt thou take any
griefe so sore to hart, but that thou shalt
haue good trust to escape it: nor thou
shalt not thinke thy selfe all whollie forsaken of me, though I sende thee for a
time some heauines and trouble, for that
is the surer way to the kingdome of heauen: and doubtles, it is more expedient
to thee, and to other of my seruauntes,
that ye sometime be proued with aduersities, then that ye haue alway all things
after your wils. I know the hid thought
of man, and that it is much expedient to
the health of the soule, that he be lefte
sometime to him selfe without ghostlie
sauour or comfort, least haply he be raysed
vp into pride, and thinke him selfe better
then he is. That I haue geuen, I maye
take awaye, and maye restore it againe,
when me shall list. When I geue a thing
to anye person, it is mine owne that I
haue geuen, and when I take it awaye
againe, I take none of his: for euerye
good gifte, and euery perfect rewarde
commeth of me. If I sende to thee trouble or heauines, in what wise soeuer it
be, take it gladly, & disdain it not, neither
let thy heart fayle thee therin, for I may
anone lifte thee vp againe, and turne thy
heauines into great ioye and ghostlye
gladnes. And vertlie, I am righteous,
and much to be lauded and praysed, whē
I doe so with thee. If thou vnderstande

a

a right, and beholde thy selfe truelle as
thou art, thou shalt neuer be so directlie
heauie for anye aduersitie, but rather
thou shalt ioye therein, and thinke it as
the greatest gifte, that I spare not to
scourge thee with such trouble and ad-
uersitie:for I sayde to my disciples thus:
As my father loueth me I loue you: and
yet I sent them not forth into the world,
to haue temporall ioyes, but to haue
great battailes,not to haue honours,but
despites,not to be ydle,but to labor, not
to rest, but to bringe forth much good
fruite in patience and good workes.My
sonne, remember well these wordes that
I haue spoken to thee, for they be true,
and can not be denyed.

Hovv vve should forget all creatures,that
vve might finde our Creator.

The. 36.Chapter.

LOrde, I haue great neede of
thy grace, & that of thy great
singuler grace, or that I may
come thither, where no creature shall let nor hinder me
from perfect beholdinge of thee:for as
longe as anye transitorye thinge holdeth me, or hath rule in me, I maye
not flye freelye to thee. He coueted to
flye without let,that sayde thus: Who
shall geue me winges like to a doue,that
I

I may flie unto the bosome of my saviour,
& into the holes of his blessed woundes
and rest me there? I see well, that no
man is more restfull, nor more likinge in
this world, then is that man, who alway
hath his minde, and whole intent vpwarde to God, and nothinge desireth of
the world. It behoueth him therfore that
would perfectlie forsake him selfe, & beholde thee, to surmount al creatures, and
him selfe also, & through excesse of minde
to see and beholde, that thou maket of all
things hast nothing amõge all creatures
like vnto thee: & but a man be cleerely deliuered frõ the loue of creatures, he may
not fullie tend to his Creator? And this
is the greatest cause, why there be so fewe
cõtéplatiues, that is to say, because there
be so fewe, that willinglye will sequester
them selues from the loue of creatures.
To cõtemplation is great grace required,
for it lifteth vp the soule, and rauisheth
it vp in spirit aboue it selfe. And except a
man be lift vp in spirite aboue him selfe,
and be clearelie deliuered from all creatures, as in his loue, and be perfectly and
fullie vnited to God, whatsoeuer he can,
or whatsoeuer he hath, either in vertue or
cunning, it is but litle worth afore God.
Therefore he shal haue but litle vertue, &
long shall he lye still in earthlie likinges,
that accounteth any thing great or worthy to be praysed, but onelie God, for all
                                              other

other thinges besides God are nought,&
for nought are to be accoūted.It is great
difference betwene the wisdome of a deuout man lightened by grace, and the
cunninge of a subtill and stubious clerke,
and that learninge is muche more noble
and muche more worthy, that commeth
by the influence and gracious gifte of
God, than that that is gotten by the labour & study of man.Many desire to haue
the gifte of contemplation, but they will
not vse suche thinges as be required to
contemplation.And one great let of contemplation is,that we stande so longe in
outward signes,and in sensible things,&
take no heede of perfect mortifying our
body to the spirit.I wote not howe it is,
nor with what spirit we be led, nor what
we pretend , we that be called spirituall
persons,that we take greater labour and
study for transitory thinges,than we doe
to knowe the inwarde state of our owne
soule. But alas for sorowe , anone as we
haue made a litle recollection to God,we
ren forth to outwarde thinges , and doe
not search our owne conscience with due
examination , as we shoulde do, nor we
heede not where our affection resteth , ne
we sorowe not that our deedes be so euill
& so vnclene as they be. The people corrupted them selfe with fleshly vnclēnes,
and therefore folowed the greate floode:
and veryly when our inward affection is
corru

corrupted, it is necessarie that our deedes
folowinge thervpon be also corrupted,
for of a cleane heart springeth the fruite
of good life. It is ofte times asked what
deedes such a man hath done, but of what
zeale, of what intent he did them, is litle
regarded: whether a man be riche, strong,
fayre, able, a good writer, a good singer,
or a good labourer, is ofte enquired, but
howe poore he is in spirite, howe pacient
and meeke, howe deuout, and howe inwardlie turned to God, is litle regarded.
Nature holdeth the outwarde deede, but
grace turneth her to the inwarde intent
of the deede. The first is ofte deceyued,
but the seconde putteth her trust wholly
in God, and is not deceyued.

Howe vve should forsake our selfe, and thruste
dovvne all couetise out of our heartes.

The. 37. Chapter.

My sonne, sayth our Lorde, thou
shalt not haue perfect libertie of
minde, vnlesse thou wholly forsake thy selfe. All proprietaries,
and al louers of them selues, all couetous
persons, curious, vaine glorious, and all
runners about, and also such as seeke
thinges softe & delectable in this worlde,
and not of Iesus Christe, ofte fayninge,
and greedilye seekinge thinges that shal
not longe endure, be as men fettred and
bounde

bounde with chaines, and haue no perfect libertie nor freedome of spirit, for all
thinges shall perish that be not wrought
of God. Holde well in thy minde this
short word: Forsake all thinges, and thou
shalt finde all thinges, forsake couetise,
and thou shalt finde great rest. Print wel
in thy minde that I haue sayde, for whē
thou haste fulfilled it, thou shalte well
knowe, that it is true. Lorde, this lesson
is not one dayes worke, nor a playe for
children, for in it is conteyned the full
perfectiō of all religion. Also, my sonne,
thou oughtest not to be turned from god,
nor to be anye thinge discouraged from
his seruice, when thou hearest the straite
lyfe of perfect men, but rather thou
oughtest to be prouoked thereby to higher perfection, and at least to desire
in harte, that thou mightest come therto. But woulde to God thou were firste
come to this point, that thou were
not a louer of thy selfe, but that thou
wouldest keepe my commaundementes,
and the commaundementes of him that
I haue appoynted to be thy father spirituall : for then thou shouldest please me greatlye, and then all thy lyfe
shoulde passe forth in ioye and peace.
Thou haste yet manye thinges to forsake, whiche vnlesse thou can whollye forsake, thou shalt not get that thou
desirest. And therefore I counsayle thee,
to

to buye of me bright shininge gold, that
is to saye, heauenlye wisedome, that des=
piseth all earthlye thinges, and cast fro
thee all worldlye wisedome, and all mans
comfort, and all thine owne affections,
and that thou chose to haue vile thinges
and abiect, rather thē precious and high
in the sight of the worlde. But thee true
heauenly wisedome seemeth to manye, to
be vile and litle, and well nigh forgotten.
Many can saye with their mouth that it
is good, not to desire to be magnifyed in
the worlde, but their lyfe foloweth not
their saying. And therefore they desire it
priuily in their heart, but yet that is the
precious margaret, and the high vertue
that is hid fro much people for their pre=
sumption, get it who so may.

Of the vnstablenes of mans harte; and
that our finall intent in all things
shoulde be to God.

The. 38. Chapter.

My sonne, looke thou beleeue not
thine owne affection, for it
chaungeth ofte from one to an
other. As longe as thou liuest
thou shalt be glad to chaunge
habilitie whether thou wilt or not, as
nowe glad, nowe sorowfull, nowe plea=
sed, nowe displeased, nowe deuout, nowe
vnde=

vndeuout,nowe luftie , nowe flouthfull,
nowe heauie,nowe lightfome.But a wife
man that is well taught in ghoftlie trauayle,ftandeth ftable in all luch thinges,
and forceth litle what he feeleth , nor on
what fide the winde of vnftablenes blo-
weth,but all the intent and ftudie of his
minde is , howe he may mofte profite in
vertue , & finallie come to the moft fruitfull & moft bleffed ende.By fuch a wholle
intent fullie directed to God,may a man
abide ftedfaft & ftable in him felfe among
many aduerfities,and the more pure and
the more cleane that his intent is , the
more ftable fhall he be in euery ftorme.
But alas for forowe , the eye of mans
foule is anone darkened,for it beholdeth
lightlie delectable thinges that come of
the worlde,and of the flefhe,in fo muche
that there is feldome founde any perfon
that is free & cleare from the venemous
defire of hearinge of fome tales , or of
fome other fantafies , and that by their
owne feekinge.In fuche maner came the
Iewes into Bethany , to Martha and to
Marie Magdalen,not for the loue of our
Lord Iefus,but for to fee Lazarus,whom
he had rayfed from death to life.Where-
fore the eye of the foule is to be kept full
bright,that it be alwaye pure and cleane,
and that it be aboue all paffing thinges,
wholly directed to god:the which graunt
vs to.&c.Amen.

Howe

Howve our Lorde God sauoureth to his louer
svveetly aboue all things, and in all things.

The 39. Chapter.

Ur Lorde God is to me all
in all, and sith he is so, what
would I more haue, or what
can I more desire? O this is
a sauoury worde & a sweete,
to saye, that our Lorde is to
me all in all. But that is to him that loueth the worde, and not the worlde. To
him that vnderstandeth this worde, is
sayd inough, but yet to repeate it ofte is
likinge to him that loueth. I maye therfore more plainely speake of this matter,
and saye, Lorde when thou art present to
me, all thinge is pleasaunt and likinge,
but when thou art absent, all thinges are
greeuous and greatly mislikinge. When
thou commest thou makest myne harte
restfull, and bringest into it a newe ioye,
thou makest thy louer to feele and vnderstande the truth, and to haue a true
iudgement in all thinges, & in all thinges
to laude and prayse thee O Lorde, without thee nothinge may be longe likinge
nor pleasaunt, for if any thinge shoulde
be lykinge and sauourye, it muste be
through helpe of thy grace, and be tem-
pered with the spicerie of thy wisedome.
To him to whom thou sauourest well,
what shall not sauour well? And to him
that

that thou fauoureſt not well vnto, what
may be ioyfull oʒ likinge? But woʒldlie
wiſe men, and they that fauour fleſhlye
delightes, fayle of this wiſedome. Foʒ in
woʒldlie wiſedome is founde great vani=
tie, and in fleſhlie pleaſures is euerla=
ſtinge death: and therefoʒe they that fo=
low thee Loʒd by deſpiſing of the woʒld,
and by perfect moʒtifieng of their fleſhly
luſtes, be knowen to be verie wiſe, foʒ
they be led from vanitie to trueth, and
from fleſhelie likinge to ſpirituall clean=
nes. To ſuche perſons God fauoureth
wonderous ſweete: and whatſoeuer they
finde in creatures, they referre it all to
the laude and pʒayſing of the Creatoure:
foʒ they ſee well, that there is great dif=
ference betwixt the Creatoʒ and creatu=
re, eternitie and time, and betwixte the
light made & the light vnmade. O euer=
laſtinge light farre paſſinge all thinges
that are made, ſende downe the beames
of thy lightninges from aboue, and puri=
fye, glad, and clarifie in me al the inward
parties of my heart. Quicken my ſpirite
with all the powers thereof, that it may
cleaue faſt, and be ioyned to thee in ioy=
full gladnes of ghoſtlye rauiſhinges. O
when ſhall that bleſſed hour come, that
thou ſhalt viſite me, & glad me with thy
bleſſed pʒeſence, ſo that thou be to me all
in all? As longe as that gifte is not geuen
to me, that thou be to me all in all, there
                              ſhall

shall be no full ioye in me. But alas the sorowe, mine olde man, that is my fleshly liking, yet liueth in me, and is not yet fully crucified, nor perfectly deade in me, for yet striueth the fleshe strongly against the spirit, and moueth great inward battayle against me, and suffereth not the kyngdome of my soule to lyue in peace. But thou, good Lorde, that hast the lordship ouer al the power of the Sea, & doest aswage the streames of his flowinges. Aryse and helpe me, breake downe the power of myne enemies, which alwaye moue this battayle in me. Shewe the greatnes of thy goodnes, & let the power of thy right hande be glorified in me, for there is to me none other hope nor refuge, but in thee onely my Lorde, my God: to whom be ioy, honour and glorye euerlastingly. Amen.

That there is no full suretie from temptation in this lyfe.

The 40. Chapter.

Ur Lorde sayeth to his seruaunt thus: Thou shalte neuer be sure from temptation and tribulation in this lyfe. And therefore, armoure spiritual shal alway, as long as thou liuest, be necessarie for thee. Thou art amõg thine enemies, and shalt be troubled and vexed with

with them on euery side, and but if thou
vse in euery place the shielde of patience,
thou shalt not long keepe thee vnwoun-
ded. And ouer that, if thou set not thy
hart stronglie in me, with a readie will
to suffer all thinges patientlie for me,
thou mayest not longe bear this ardoure,
nor come to the reward of blessed saints.
It behoueth thee therfore manly to passe
ouer many thinges, and to vse a stronge
hande against all the obiections of the
enemie. To the ouercommer it promiseth
Angels foode, and to him that is ouercome, is left much miserie. If thou seeke
rest in this lyfe, howe then shalt thou
come to the rest euerlastinge? Set not thy
selfe to haue rest here, but to haue patience, and seeke the true soothfast rest, not in
earth, but in heauen, not in man, or anye
creature, but in God onelie, where it is.
For the loue of God thou oughtest to suffer gladlie all thinges, that is to saye, all
laboures, sorowes, temptations, vexa-
tions, anguishes, needines, sickenesse, iniuries, euill sayinges, reprouinges, oppressions, confusions, corrections, and
despisinges. These helpe a man greatlie
to vertues, these proue the true knight
of Christe, and make redye for hym the
heauenlie crowne, and our Lorde shall
yeelde him againe euerlastinge rewarde
for this short laboure, and infinite glorie
for this transitorie confusion. Trowest
thou

thou, that thou shalt haue alwaye spirit-
tuall comfortes after thy will? Naye, naye,
my Saintes had them not, but manye
great griefes, and diuers temptations,
and great desolations, but they bare all
with great patience, and more trusted in
me then in them selues: for they knewe
well, that the passions of this worlde be
not able of them selues to get the glorye
that is ordeined for them in the kingdome
of heauē. Wilt thou looke to haue anone
that, whiche others coulde not get but
with great weepinges & labours? Abide
paciently the comming of our Lorde, doe
manfully his bidding, be comforted in him,
mistrust him not, nor go not backe from
his seruice for paine nor for dread, but
lay forth thy body and soule constantlye
to his honour in all good bodylye and
ghostly laboures, And he shal reward thee
againe moste plenteouslye for thy good
trauayle, and shal be with thee, and helpe
thee in euery trouble that shal befall vnto thee, So may it be. Amen.

Against the vaine iudgementes of men.

The 41. Chapter.

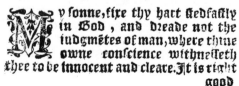 y sonne, fixe thy hart stedfastly
in God, and dreade not the
iudgmētes of man, where thine
owne conscience withnesseth
thee to be innocent and cleare. It is right
good

good and bleſſed, ſometime to ſuffer ſuch
ſayinges, and it ſhall not be greeuous to
a meeke harte whiche truſteth more in
God than in him ſelfe. Many folke can
ſaye many thinges, and yet litle fayth is
to be geuen to their ſayinges, & to pleaſe
all men it is not poſſible. For though S.
Paule laboured all that he might to haue
pleaſed al people in God, & did to all men
all that he coulde for their ſaluation, yet
neuertheleſſe he coulde not let, but that
he was ſometime iudged of other. He did
for the edifyinge and health of other as
much as in him was, but that he ſhoulde
not ſometime be iudged of other, or not
be deſpiſed of other, he coulde not lette,
wherefore he committed all to God that
knoweth all thinge, and armed him ſelfe
with patience and meeknes, againſt all
thinges that might be vntruelye ſpoken
againſt him. And neuertheleſſe ſometime
he anſwered againe, leſt that by his ſilēce
hurte or hinderance might haue growen
to other What art thou then that drea-
deſt ſo ſore a mortall man? this daye he
is, and to morowe he appeareth not,
Dread God, and thou ſhalt not nede to
dread man. What maye man do with
thee in wordes or iniuries? he hurteth
him ſelfe more than thee, and in the ende
he ſhall not flee the iudgement of God,
whatſoeuer he be. Haue alwaye God
before the eye of thy ſoule, and ſtriue
B ij   not

not agayne by multiplyinge of wordes. And if thou seeme for a time to suffer confusion that thou hast not deserued, disdayne thou not therefore, nor through impatience minishe not thy rewarde, but rather lifte vp thy harte to God in heauen, for he is able to deliuer thee from all confusion and wronges, and to rewarde euery man after his desert, and muche more then he can deserue.

Of a pure and a whole forsakinge of our selfe and our owne will, that we might get the freedome of spirite, and folowe the will of God.

The. 42. Chapter.

My sonne, sayth our Lorde, forsake thy selfe, and thou shalt finde me. Stãd without election, and without folowinge of thine owne wil, & also without al proprietie, & thou shalt much profite in grace: and if thou whollie resigne thy selfe into my handes, and take nothinge to thee againe, thou shalt haue the more grace of me. O Lorde, howe ofte shall I resigne me vnto thee, & in what thinges shall I forsake my selfe? Alwaye, and in euery houre, in great thinges and in small: I except none, for in all thinges

I

I will finde thee naked and verie poore,
and voyde of thine owne will: els howe
maieſt thou be mine, and I thine, but if
thou be cleerely berefte within and with=
out of thine owne will. And the ſooner
that thou canſt bringe it about, ſo muche
the ſooner ſhall it be better with thee, ⁊
the more perfectlye and the more cleerely
that thou canſt doe it, the more fully ſhalt
thou pleaſe me, and the more ſhalt thou
winne. Some perſons reſigne thē ſelues
vnto me, but it is with ſome exception,
for they truſt not fullye to me, and there=
fore they ſtudye to prouide for thē ſelues.
And ſome at the beginning offer them to
me, but after, when any temptation com=
meth, they ſoone turne agayne to their
owne will, and to that, which they pro=
miſed to forſake, and therefore they pro=
fite litle in vertue. And truely ſuch per=
ſons ſhall neuer come to perfect clennes,
and to freedome of heart, nor to the grace
of familiaritie with me, but through a
perfect forſakinge of them ſelues, and
through a dayly offering of them, and all
that they haue wholly to me, for without
that maye no man haue perfect fruition
and vnitinge with me. I haue ſayde to
thee many times before, and yet I ſay to
thee againe, forſake thy ſelfe, and reſigne
thy ſelfe whollye to me, and thou ſhalt
haue great inward peace in me. Geue all
for all, and nothinge keepe to thy ſelfe of

                    B ij   thine

thine owne will, but stand purelye and stablye in me, and thou shalt haue me, and thou shalt be so free in heart and in soule, that darkenes of conscience, nor thraldome of sinne shall euer haue power in thee. Endeuour thy selfe therefore to get this freedome of spirite that I speake of, pray for it, studie for it, and alwaye desire in thy harte, that is to saye, that thou mayest clerely be spoyled and bereft of all propertie, and of thine owne will, & that thou beeing naked of all worldly thinges, mayest folowe me that honge naked for thee vpon the Crosse, & that thou mayest dye to thy selfe & to all worldlye thinges also (as in thy loue) and blessedly to liue to me. Then if thou doe thus, al vanities, & all vaine fantasies, and all superfluous cares of the world, and of the fleshe, shall faile, and fade, and go awaye. Then also immoderate dread and inordinate loue shall dye in thee, and thou shalt blessedly lyue in me, and I in thee. Amen.

Howe a man shall rule him selfe in outwarde things, and howe he ought to call to God for helpe in all perils aud daungers.

The. 43. Chapter.

Ur Lorde Iesu sayeth to his seruant thus. Thou oughtest to take heede diligentlye, that in euery place, in euery deede, and in euery
ry

ry outwarde occupation that thou doeſt,
thou be inwardlye free in thy ſoule, and
haue the rule ouer thy ſelfe, and that all
thinges be vnder thee as in thy loue, and
thou not vnder them: but that thou be
the Lorde & gouernoure ouer thy deedes,
not as a ſeruãt, or a bond man, but rather
exempted as a true Hebrewe, that is to
ſaye, as a true chriſtien man, goinge into
the number and into the freedome of the
children of God, which ſtand vpõ things
preſent, and looke towardes thinges
euerlaſting, and beholde thinges tranſi=
torye with their lefte eye, and thinges
euerlaſtinge with their right eye: whome
worldlie goodes can not drawe downe to
the loue of them, but they rather drawe
worldlie goodes to ſerue, in ſuche wiſe,
as they be ordeyned to of God, and as
they be inſtituted to doe by the high ma=
ker of all thinges, which leaueth nothing
inordinate in his creatures. Alſo, if thou
ſtande in euery aduenture, and doubt
that ſhal happen to thee, not to the iudg=
ment of thy outwarde apperance, but
anone in euery ſuche doubt thou entreſt
into thine owne ſoule by deuout prayer,
as Moyſes did into the tabernacle, to
aſke counſell of God, thou ſhalte heare
anone the aunſwere of our Lorde, which
ſhall inſtruct thee ſufficientlye in many
thinges, both preſent, & that are to come.
It is reade, that Moyſes had alwaye re=

B iij   courſe

course to the tabernacle of God, for doubtes and questions to be aslotled, and that he there asked the helpe of God through deuout prayer for the perils and daungers, aswell of him selfe, as of the people. So shouldest thou enter into the secrete tabernacle of thine owne heart, & there aske inwardlie with good deuotion the helpe of God in all such doubtes & perils. We reade that Iosue, and the children of Israel were deceaued of the Gabaonites, because they gaue light credence to their sayinges, & did not firste aske counsaile of God, as they should haue done, and so by the fayre wordes of the Gabaonites, and thorough a false pitie, Iosue and the children of Israel were illuded and greatlie deceaued.

That a man shoulde not be importune in his busines.

The. 44. Chapter.

M y sonne, saith our Lorde, commit alwaye thy cause to me, and I shall well dispose it for thee whē time shal come. Abide mine ordinaunce and direction, and thou shalte finde thereby great profite and helpe. O Lorde, gladlie will I commit all thinges to thee, for it is litle that I can doe for my selfe. Would to God that I did not
cleaue

cleaue to desires of worldlie thinges, but
that I might alwaye offer my selfe whollye to thy will and pleasure. My sonne,
so it is good for thee to doe, for often
times a man that trusteth muche in him
selfe, and in his owne will, setteth his
minde muche to bringe about this thinge
or that, as he desireth: but when he hath
attayned that he desireth, the beginneth
he to feele all otherwise of it then he did
before: for the affections and desires of
man be not alwaye one, but ofte driue a
man from one thinge to another. Therefore it is no small thinge, a man fullie to
forsake him selfe, though it be in right
litle and small thinges. For truelie, the
verie perfection of man is a perfect de-
nyinge, and a full forsakinge of himselfe,
And suche a man is verie free, & beloued
of God. But the olde aunctient enemye
the fiende, which resisteth goodnes all
that he maye, ceasseth not longe from
temptation, but daye and night he maketh greeuous assaultes, to see if he
maye catche any vnware person
into his snare of deceit. Therefore wake ye, and praye,
that ye be not deceaued
by temptation.

That man hath no goodnes of him selfe, and that he may not rightfully glorifie him selfe in any thing.

The 45. Chapter.

Lorde, what is man, that thou doest vouchsafe to haue minde on him? Or what hath he done for thee, that thou wilt visit him with grace? And what may he complayne, although thou sometime forsake him? Or what maye I righteouslye saye, though thou graunt me not that I aske? Truely, I may well thinke and say thus: I am nought, nor I haue no goodnes of my selfe, but in all thinges I am of my selfe al insufficiēt, and go to nought, and but if I be holpen of thee, and be inwardlie informed and taught by thee, I shall be altogether slouthfull, and to all thinge vnprofitable. O Lorde, thou arte alwaye one, euer shalt be one, alway good, alway righteous and holy, well, righteously and blessedly disposing all thinges after thy wisedome: but I wretche, that alway am more redy & prone to euill then to good, am not alwaye abidinge in ene, for seuen times be chaunged vpon me. Neuerthelesse, it shall be better with me, when it shall please thee to put to thy helpinge hand, for thou onely art he, that witho t

man.

man mayeſt helpe me, and ſo cōfirme and
ſtable me in thee, that mine heart ſhall
not ſo lightlie be changed from thee, but
that it maye be wholly fixed in thee, and
finallye to reſt in thee. And verilye, if I
coulde caſt awaye from me all mans comfort, either for getting of deuotion, or for
that I am compelled thereto of neceſſitie,
for that I finde no comfort in man, then
might I well truſt in thy grace to haue of
thee newe viſitations, & newe heauenlie
conſolation: But I confeſſe it for truth,
that I am vnworthy to haue anye ſuche
conſolations, and I thanke thee, as ofte
as anye good thinge commeth to me: for
all that is good cōmeth of thee. I am but
vanitie, and nought before thee, an vn-
conſtant man, and a feeble, and therefore,
whereof maye I righteouſly gloriſie my
ſelfe, or why ſhould I looke to be magnified? Truelye vaine glorie is a perillous
ſickenes, a greeuous peſtilence, & a right
great vanitie: for it draweth a man from
the true ioy that he ſhould haue in God,
and robbeth him cleerelye of all heauenly
grace. For when a man pleaſeth himſelfe,
he diſpleaſeth thee, & when he delighteth
in mans prayſinges, he is depriued from
the true vertues: for the true ſtedfaſt ioye
& gladnes is, to ioye in thee, & not in him
ſelfe, in thy name, and not in his owne
vertue, nor in anye creature. Therefore
thy name be prayſed, and not mine, thy
                                   workes

workes be magnified, and not mine, and
thy goodnes be alwaye blessed, so that
nothing be geuen to me of the laude and
praysing of man. Thou art my glory and
the ioy of my hart, in thee shall I be glorified, and alway shall I ioy in thee, and
in my selfe nothinge, but in my infirmities. Let the Iewes seke glorye amonge
them selues, but I will seeke none but
that is onely of thee, for all mans glory,
all temporall honour, and all worldlye
highnes to thy eternall glorye compared,
is but as foolishnes, and a great vanitie.
O truth, O mercy, O blessed trinitie, to
thee be laude, honour, and glory euerlastingly. Amen.

Hovve all temporall honour is to be despised.

The 46. Chapter.

My sonne, take it not to greefe,
though thou see other men honoured and exalted, and thy
selfe despised & set at nought.
If thou raise vp thine hart to
me in heaue, the despites of man in earth
shall litle greeue thee. O Lord we be here
in great darknes, and are soone deceyued
with vanities, but verilie if I beheld my
selfe well, I should openlie see, that there
was neuer any wrong done to me by any
creature, nor that I haue nothing wher-
of I maye righteouslie complayne. But
for

foz as muche as J haue ofte ſinned, and grevouſlie offended againſt thee, therefoze all creatures be armed againſt me. To me therefoze is due, confuſion and deſpite, to thee laude, honour, and glozye. And vnleſſe J can bzing my ſelfe to this point, that J woulde gladlye be deſpiſed and forſaken of all creatures, & vtterlye to ſeeme as nought in the wozide, J may not be inwardlye pacified noz ſtabliſhed in thee, noz ſpirituallie be illumined, noz yet fully vnited to thee.

That our truſt is not to be put in
vvorldlye people.

The 47. Chapter.

My ſonne, if thou ſet thy peace with anye perſon foz thyne owne pleaſure, oz wozldlye frendſhippe, thou ſhalt alway be vnſtable, and neuer ſhalte thou be cõtented: but if thou haue alway recourſe to the truth euerlaſting, that is God himſelfe, then the death oz goinge awaye of thy deareſt freende, whatſoeuer he be, ſhall litle greue thee. The loue of thy frend ought alwaye to be referred to me, and foz me he is to be beloued, howe good and howe pzofitable ſoeuer he ſeme vnto thee in this life. Without me fred-ſhip is nought wozth, noz maye not long endure, noz that loue is not true and
clene

cloane that is not knit by me. Thou
oughtest therefore to be so mortified in
all such affections of worldlie men, that
in as much as in thee is, thou wouldest
couete to be without all mans comfort.
So muche a man draweth nerer to God,
as he can withdrawe hym selfe from
the worlde, and from all worldlie com=
fort, and so muche the more he ascendeth
higher to God, as he can descend lower
in him selfe, and as he can waxe vile and
abiect in his owne sight. He that ascri=
beth any goodnes to him selfe, withstan=
deth the grace of God, and letteth it to
liue in him, for the grace of the holye
ghoste seeketh alwaye a meeke and an
humble heart. If thou couldest perfectly
annihilate thy selfe, and whollie put out
of thy heart all humane and create loue,
then shoulde I (sayth our Lorde) dwell
in thee with great aboundaunce of my
grace But when thou lockest to creatu=
res, then is righteouslie drawen from
thee the sight of thy Creator. Learne
therefore to ouercome thy selfe for the
loue of him that made thee like to hym
selfe, and thou shalt anone come to great
ghostlie knowledge. Howe lytle soeuer
the thinge be that a man loueth, yf he
loue it inordinatlie, it hindreth and let=
teth him greatlie from the true and per=
fect loue that he shoulde haue to God.

That

That vve should eschevv vayne se-
culer cunninge.

The.48.Chapter.

Y sonne, sayth our Lorde, let not fayre and subtil wordes moue thee, for the kingdome of heauen standeth not in wordes , but in good ver-tuous workes. Take hede to my wordes , for they enflame the harte, and lighten the vnderstandinge , and bringe in also compunction of harte for sinnes past , and cause also ofte times great heauenlie comfort, sodenly to come into the soule. Reade neuer in any sciéce, to the intét thou wouldest be called wise, but studie rather to mortifie in thee all stirringes of sinnes , as much as in thee is, & that shall be more profitable to thee, than the knowledge of many harde and subtill questions. When thou hast reade and vnderstoode many doubtes , yet ne-uerthelesse, it behoueth thee to come to one that is beginninge of all thinges, that is, God him selfe, and els thy know-ledge shall litle auayle thee. I am he that teacheth a mã cũning, & do giue more vn-derstáding to meeke persons, than can be taught by mãs teaching. And he to whom I speake, shal soone be made wise, & much shall he profit in spirite, when payne and wo shall be to them that onelie seeke for

curious

curious learninge , takinge litle heede to
the waye to serue God. The time shall
come when Christ Lorde of Angels , and
master of all masters shall appere to heare
the lesson of euery creature , and to examine the conscience of euery person , and
then shall Ierusalem , that is , mans soule ,
be searched with lanternes and lights of
Goddes high knowledge , and rightfull
iudgmentes , and then also shall be made
open the deedes and thoughtes of euery
man , & all excuses and vaine argumentes
shall ceasse , and vtterlie be set apart. I am
he also that sodenlie at a point illumine
and lifte vp a meeke soule , that it shalbe
made able to take and to receiue in shert
time more perfectlie the true reason of
the wisdome of God , then an other that
studieth ten yeres in scholes , and lacketh
meekenes. I teache without sounde of
wordes , without diuersitie of opinions ,
without desire of honour , and without
strife and argumentes. And I am he that
teach all the people to despise earthlye
thinges , to lothe thinges that be present ,
to seeke and to sauour eternall thinges ,
to flee honoures , to beare pacientlie all
euill wordes and speakinges , to put their
trust whollie in me , nothinge to couet
without me , and aboue all thinges brenninglie to loue me. And some folkes tho-
rowe an inwarde loue that they haue had
to me , haue learned many great thinges ,
and

and haue spoken high misteries of my Godhead. They profit more in forsaking all thinges, then in studyinge for highe & subtill learning. But to some men I speake common thinges, to some speciall thinges, to some I appeare sweetlie in signes and figures, and to some I geue great vnderstandinge of Scripture, and open to the high secret misteries. There is in bookes one voice, and one letter that is reade, but it enfourmeth not all persons alike, for I am within secretlie hidden in the letter, the teacher of trueth, the searcher of mans hart, the knower of thoughtes, the promoter of good workes, and the rewarder of al men, after as my wisdome and goodnes iudgeth them to haue deserued, and none otherwise.

That vve should not regarde muche outvvarde
thinges, nor ponder but litle the
iudgement of man.

The 49. Chapter.

My sonne, it is profitable to thee to be ignorant in many things, and to thinke thy selfe as deade to the worlde, and to whom all the worlde is crucified. And thou muste also with a deafe eare let many thinges passe, as thou neither heard them, nor sawe them, and to thinke on such things
as

as shall cause in thee an inwarde peace
in soule. It is also more profitable to
thee, that thou turne the eye of thy soule
from thinges that displease thee, and to
let euery man holde his opinion therein
as him seemeth best, rather than to striue
againe with frowarde wordes. And truelie, if thou were well stabled in God, and
beheldest well his iudgementes, thou
shouldest lightlie be content to be iudged
of other, and to be ouercome of other, as
our Lorde Iesus was for thee in time of
his passion. O Lorde, sith it is true that
thou sayest, what shall become of vs that
heede so muche worldlie thinges, and beweepe so greatlie a litle temporall losse,
and we labour and runne for worldlie
profite with all our might, but our spirituall profite and the health of our owne
soules, we litle regarde? Suche thinges
as litle or nothinge profiteth vs, is much
set by, but that that is most necessarie to
vs is nighe forgotten. For why? all
men runne gladlye into outwarde
thinges. And truelie but they
shortlye turne backe agayne,
they shall gladlie rest still in
them, whiche in the ende
shall be to them great
perill and
daunger.

That

That men be not alvvaye to be beleeued, for that
they so lightlye offende in vvordes.

The 50. Chapter.

Dide sende me helpe in my
troubles, for mans helpe is
litle worth. Howe ofte haue I
not founde frendship where I
thought I should haue found
it? And how ofte haue I founde it, where
I least presumed to haue founde it: wherfore it is a vayne thinge to trust in man,
for the true and soothfast trust and health
of righteous men is onelie in thee. Blessed be thou Lorde therefore in all thinges
that happen vnto vs, for we be weake
and vnstable, soone deceiued, and soone
changed from one thinge to an other.
Who may so wareite and so assuredlie
keepe him selfe in euery thinge, but shall
sometime fall into some deceipt, or into
some perplexitie? truelie verie fewe: but
he that trusteth in thee, and that seeketh
thee with a cleane hart, slideth not so
lightlie from thee. And if it happen him
to fall into any trouble or perplexitie,
whatsoeuer it be, & how greeuous soeuer
it be, he shall anone eyther be deliuered
by thee, or be comforted by thee, for thou
neuer forsakest him that trusteth in thee.
It is right harde to finde so true and so
faithfull a frende that wil perseuer with
his freende in all his troubles, but thou
                                              Lorde

Lord art most faithfull in all thinges, and like to thee none can be rounde. O howe well fauoured that holy soule in ghostly thinges, that sayde thus: My minde is stablished in God, and is fully grounded in Christ. Truely if it were so with me, the dread of man should not so lightly enter into me, nor other mens wordes shoulde not so soone moue me. Who may forsee all thinges? or who may preuent all euils that are to come? and if thinges forescene do yet ofte times great hurt, What shall then those thinges doe that be not foreseene? But why haue not I, wretche, better seene to my selfe? and why haue I so lightlye beleeued other mens sayinges? truelye for that we be but men, and that but frayle men, though we be esteemed & thought of many to be as Angels in our conuersation. Whom may I beleeue but onelye thee? Thou art the trueth that deceyuest no man, nor mayest not be deceyued. And on the other, side, euery man is a lyer, weake, and vnstable, and slidīg (most especially) in wordes, so that scarselie it may be beleeued that seemeth openlie to be true. Howe prudentlie therefore haste thou warned vs to beware of the lightnes of man, and that our familier seruantes maye be our enimies, so that it is not to be beleued, though one will say, Lo here is thy frend, or there is thy frend, for I am taught with mine owne hurt: but

but would to God it might be as a war-
ninge to me, and not to my more follye.
Some saye to me, Beware, beware, kepe
close to thy selfe that I shall shewe thee.
And when I kepe it close, and beleeue it
to be secret, he can not be secret in that
him selfe desired, but anone he betrayeth
both him selfe & me, and goeth his waye.
From suche tales, and from such vnstable
men Lorde defende me, that I fall not
into their handes, nor that I neuer commit any suche thinges. A true worde and
a stable Lorde geue into my mouth, and a
deceitfull toung driue farre awaye from
me, for that I woulde not haue done to
my selfe, I ought to be ware that I doe it
not to other. O howe good and how peacefull is it to kepe silence of other mens
wordes and deedes, and not to geue full
credence till the trueth be tryed, and not
to report lightlye to other all that we
heare or see, nor to open our hart fullye
but to very fewe, and to seeke thee alway
that art the beholder of mans hart, & not
so be moued with euery flake of wordes,
but to desire in harte that all thinges in
vs inwardly and outwardlye may be fulfilled after thy will : howe sure a thinge
is it also for the keepinge of heauenlye
grace, to flee the conuersation of worldly
people all that we may, and not to desire
thinges that seeme outwardly to be pleasaunt and liking : but with all the studye
of

of our hath to leeue luch thinges as bring
lu femme of Chrir, and amondement of
life. It hath bene truelie a great hurte to
many persons, a vertue knowen, & ouer
timelie praysed: and contrariwise, it hath
beene right profitable to some, a grace
kept in silence, and not lightlie reported
to other in this fraple life, that is full of
temptation and priuie enuie.

*That vve shall put all our confidence in God,
vvhen euill vvordes be spoken to vs.*

The. 51. Chapter.

y sonne, sayth our Lord, stande
stronglie, and truste faytfully
in me. What be wordes but
winde? they flye in the ayre,
but they hurte neuer a stone
on the grounde. And if thou knowe thy
selfe not giltie, thinke that thou wilt
suffer gladlie suche wordes for God. It is
but a litle thinge for thee to suffer sometime a hastie worde, sith thou art not yet
able to suffer harde strokes. But why is it
that so litle a thinge goeth so nigh thy
heart, but that thou art yet flesshelie and
carnall, and heedest to please men more
then thou shouldest. And because thou
dreadest to be despised, thou wilt not
gladlie be reproued of thine offences, and
thou searchest therefore busilie, and with
great studie how thou mayest be excused

But

But behoulde thy selfe well, and thou shalt see, that the worlde yet liueth in thee, and a vaine loue also to please man. When thou refusest to be rebuked and punished for thy defaultes, it appeteth euidentlie, that thou art not yet sooth-fastlie meeke, nor that thou art not yet deade to the worlde, nor the worlde to thee yet truelye crucified. But heare my wordes, and thou shalt not neede to care for the wordes of ten thousand men. Loe, yf all thinges were sayde against thee, that might be most maliciouslie and vntruelie fayned against thee, what shoulde they hurt, if thou suffered them to ouer-passe & goe awaye? truelie no more then a strawe vnder thy foote, & one heare of thy head they might not take from thee. But he that hath not a mans heart in-wardly, nor setteth not God before the eye of his soule, is soone moued with a sharpe word, whē he that trusteth in me, & will not stand to his owne iudgement, shall be free frō all mans dreade, for I am the Iudge that knoweth all secrettes: I knowe howe euery thinge is done, and I know also both him that doth the wrōg, and him that it is done to. Of me this thinge is wrought, and by my suffe-rāce it is come about, that the thoughtes of mennes heartes maye be knowen, and when the time commeth I shall iudge both the innocent, and hym that is

is giltie. But firste through my righteous
examination I will proue them bothe.
The witnes of man ofte times deceaueth, but my iudgement alwaye is true,
and shall not be subuerted. And howbeit
it is sometime hid, and not knowen, but
to fewe, yet it is euer true, and erreth
not, neither may erre, though in the sight
of some persons it seemeth not so. Therefore in euery doubt it behoueth to runne
to me, and not to leane muche to thine
owne reason, but with euery thinge that
I shall sende thee to be content, for a
righteous man is neuer troubled with
any thinge that I shall suffer to fall vnto
him, insomuch, that though a thing were
vntruelie spoken against him, he shoulde
not muche care for it, neither shoulde he
muche ioye, though he were sometyme
reasonablye excused, for he thinketh alwaye, that I am he that searcheth mans
hart, and that I iudge not after the outwarde apperance: for ofte times it shall
be founde in my sight woorthy to be blamed, that in mans sight seemeth muche
woorthy to be praysed. O Lord God most
righteous Iudge, stronge and patient,
which knowest the frayltie and maltce of
man, be thou my strength and wholle cōfort in all my necessities, for mine owne
conscience (Lorde) suffiseth me not, for
thou knowest in me that I knowe not.
And therefore in euery reprouse I ought
alway

alway to meeken my selfe, and patiently
to suffer all thinges in charitie, after thy
pleasure. Forgeue me (Lorde) as ofte as I
haue not so done, and geue me grace of
greater sufferaunce in time to come. Thy
mercy is more profitable, and more sure
waye for me to the gettinge of pardon
and forgeuenes of my sinnes, then a trust
in mine owne workes, through defence
of my darke conscience. And though I
dreede not my conscience, yet I may not
therefore iustifie my selfe, for thy mercie
remoued and taken awaye, no man maye
be iustified, nor appere righteous in thy
syght.

Howe all greeuous thinges in this lyfe are
gladlie to be suffered, for winning
of the lyfe that is to come.

The. 5 2. Chapter.

y sonne, sayth our Lord, be
not broken by impatiece,
with the labour that thou
hast taken for my sake, nor
suffer thou not tribulatio,
to cast thee in dispaire, nor
into vnreasonable heauti-
nes or anguishe in any wise, but be thou
comforted & strengthed in euery chaunce
by my promises & behestes, for I am able,
and of power to rewarde thee and other
my seruauntes aboundantlie more then
ye

ye can thinke or desire. Thou shalt not labour long here, nor alwaye be greeued with heauines: tary a while my promises, and thou shalt shortlye see an ende of all thy troubles. One hour shall come, when all thy labours and troubles shall cease: and truely, that hour will shortlye come, for all is short that passeth with time. Doe therefore as thou doest, labour busily and faithfullye in my vineyarde, and I shal shortly be thy reward. Write, reade, singe, mourne, be still and pray, and suffer gladlye aduersitye, for the kingdome of heauen is more woorth then all these thinges, and much more greater thinges then they are. Peace shall come one daye, which is to me knowen, and that shall not be the day of this lyfe, but a day euerlastinge, with infinite cleerenes, stedfast peace, and sure rest without ending. And then thou shalt not saye, Who shall deliuer me from the bodye of this death, neither shalt thou neede to crie, woe is me, that my comming to the kingdome of heauen is thus prolonged. For death shal then be destroyed, and health shall be without ende of bodye & soule, insomuch that no maner of vnrestfulnes shall be, but blessed ioye, and moste sweetest and fayrest companye. O if thou sawest the euerlastinge crownes of my Saintes in heauen, in howe great ioye and glorye they are, that sometime seemed to be vile

persons

perſons, and as men deſpiſable in the
worlde, thou ſhouldeſt anone meken thy
ſelfe lowe to the grounde, and ſhouldeſt
rather couete to be ſubiect to all men,
then to haue ſoueraintie ouer anye one
perſon, and thou ſhouldeſt not deſire to
haue mirth and ſolace in this worlde, but
rather tribulation and paine, and thou
ſhouldeſt the accompt it as a great winning, to be deſpiſed and taken as naught
amonge the people. O if theſe thinges
ſauoured well to thee, and deepely pear-
ced into thy hearte, thou ſhouldeſt not
once dare complaine for anye maner of
trouble that ſhoulde befall vnto thee. Are
not all painefull thinges, and moſte greeuous laboures gladlye to be ſuffered for
the ioyes euerlaſting? yes verilye, for it is
no litle thinge to win or loſe the kingdome of heauen. Lifte vp thy face therefore into heauen, and behoide howe I
and all my Saintes that be with me in
heaue, hadde in this worlde great battail
and conflict, and nowe they ioye with
me, and be comforted in me, and be
ſure to abide with me, and to dwel
with me in the kingdome of my
father without ending.
Amen.

L ij Of

The childe
Of the daye of eternitie, and of the
miseries of this lyfe.

The 53.Chapter.

Blessed mansion of the heauenlie Citie, O moste cleerest daye of eternitie, whom the night maye not darken, but the high truth, that God is, illumineth and cleereth the daye, alwaye merie, alwaye sure, and neuer chaunging his state into the contrarie. Woulde to God that this daye might once appere and shine vpon vs, and that these temporall thinges were at an end. This blessed daye shineth to Saintes in heauen with euerlastinge brightnes and claritie, but to vs pilgrimes in earth it shineth not but a farre of, as through a mirroure or glasse. The heauenlye Citizens knowe well, howe ioyous this daye is: But we outlawes, the childrē of Eue, doe weepe and wayle the bitternes and tediousnes of this daye, that is, of this present lyfe, short and euill, full of sorowes and anguishes, where man is often times defiled with sinne, encōbred with passions, inquieted with dreades, bounden with charges, busied with vanities, blinded with errours, ouercharged with labours, vexed with temptations, ouercome with delightes & vaine pleasures of the world, and greeuouslie tormented, sometyme with

with penurie and neede. O Lorde,when
shall the ende come of all these miseries,
and when shall I be cleerelie deliuered
from the bondage of sinne? when shall I
onely Lord haue minde on thee,and fully
be made glad and mery in thee?whe shall
I be free without letting,and in perfect
libertie , without griefe of bodie & soule?
When shal I haue sadde peace without
trouble,peace within and without , and
on euery side stedfast and sure? O Lorde
Iesu,when shall I stande and behoulde
thee,and haue full sight and contemplation of thy glorie? And when shalt thou
be to me all in all? and when shall I be
with thee in thy kingdome , that thou
haste ordeyned to thy elect people from
the beginning.I am lefte here poore,and
as an outlawe in the lande of mine enemies , where daylie be battailes & great
missfortunes. Comfort my exile , allwage
my sorow,for all my desire crieth to thee.
It is to me a greeuous burden, whatsoeuer the worlde offereth me here to my
solace.I desire to haue inwarde fruition
in thee , but I can not attayne therto. I
couet to cleue fast to heauenlie thinges,
but temporall thinges , and passions vn-
mortified pull me awaye downward. In
minde I woulde be aboue all temporall
thinges,but whether I will or not,I am
compelled through myne owne default
to be subiect to my flesshe. Thus I moste

wretched man fight in my selfe, and am made greeuous to my selfe, whiles my spirite desireth to be vpwarde, and my flesfye downewarde. O what suffer I inwardle, when in my minde I beholde heauenly things, and anone a great multitude of carnall thoughtes enter into my soule? Therefore Lorde, be not longe frō me, neither depart in thy wrath from me thy seruant. Send to me the lightnes of thy grace, and breake downe in me all carnall thoughts. Sende forth the dartes of thy loue, & breake therewith all phantasies of the enemy. Gather the wits and powers of my soule together in thee. Make me forget all worldlie thinges, & grāt me to cast awaye, and whollie to despise all phantasies of sinne. Helpe me thou euerlastinge truth, that no worldlie vanitie hereafter haue power in me. Come also thou heauenlie sweetnes, and let all bitternes of sinne flie farre frō me. Pardon me, and mercifully forgeue me, when I thinke in my prayer of any thinge, but of thee: for I confesse for truth, that in time past I haue vsed my selfe verie vnstable therein, for many times I am not there, where I stande or sit, but rather I am there, where my thoughtes leade me, for there am I where my thought is, and there as my thought is accustomed to be, there is that that I loue, and that ofte times commeth into my minde, that by
custome

cuſtome pleaſeth me beſt, and that moſt
deſireth me to thinke vpon. ✦Wherefore,
thou that art euerlaſtinge truth, ſayeſt:
Where as thy treaſure is, there is thy
heart. Wherefore, if I loue heauen, I
ſpeake gladlie of heauenlie thinges, and
of ſuch thinges as be of God, and that
pertaine moſt to his honoure, and to the
glorifyinge and worſhippinge of his holy
name. And if I loue the worlde, I ioye
anone at worldlie felicitie, and ſorowe
anone at his aduerſitie. If I loue the
fleſhe, I ymagine ofte times that pleaſeth the fleſhe, and if I loue my ſoule, I
delight muche to ſpeake and to heare of
thinges that be to my ſoule health. And
ſo whatſoeuer I loue of them, I gladlye
heare and ſpeake, and beare the images
of them ofte in my minde. Bleſſed is that
man that for thee (Lorde) forgetteth all
creatures, & learneth truelie to ouercome
him ſelfe, and with the feruour of ſpirite
crucifieth his fleſhe, ſo that in a cleane
and a pure conſcience he maye offer
his prayers to thee, and be worthy
to haue companye of bleſſed
Angels, all earthlie thinges
excluded from him, and
fullye ſet apart.
Amen.

Of the desire of euerlastinge liste, and of the great
rewardes that is promised to them that
stronglye fight agaynst sinne.

The 54.Chapter.

y sonne, when thou feelest
that a desire of euerlastinge
blisse is giuen vnto thee, ꝛ
thou couetest to go out of
the tabernacle of thy mortal
bodie, that thou might clearelie without shadowe beholde my clea-
renes, Open thine harte, and with al the
desires of thy soule, take that holie inspi-
ration, and yeelding most large thankes
to the high goodnes of God that so worthilie doth to thee, so beninglie visiteth
thee, so brenninglie stirreth thee, and so
mightelie beareth thee vp, that through
thine owne burden thou fall not downe
to earthilie likings, and thinke not, that
that desire commeth of thy selfe, or of
thine owne workinge, but rather that it
commeth of the gifte of grace, and of a
louelie beholdinge of God vpon thee,
that thou shouldest profite thereby in
meekenes and vertue, and that thou
shouldest also prepare thee to be readye
against another time for battels that are
to come, and the more surely to cleaue to
God with all the desire and affection of
thy hart, and to studie with all thy power
how thou mayest most purelie and moste
deuoutlie

deuoutlie serue him: and take heede of
this common prouerbe, The fire doth oft
burne, but the flame doth not ascende
without some smoke : So likewise the
desire of some men draweth to heauenlie
thinges, and yet they be not all free from
the smoke of carnall affections, and therfore they doe it not alwaye purelie for
the honour and loue of God, that they
aske so desirouslie of him. Suche ofte tymes is thy desire that thou shewest to be
so importune, for that desire is not cleane
and perfect that is mixte with thine
owne commoditie. Aske therefore not
that is delectable and profitable to thee,
but that is acceptable and honour to me:
for if thou do well, and iudge aright, thou
shalt preferre my ordinaunce, & my will,
before all thy desires, & before all thinges
that may be desired beside me. I knowe
well thy desire: Thou wouldest nowe be
in libertie of the glorie of the sonnes of
God: nowe the euerlastinge house, & the
heauenlie countrey full of ioye and glory
delighteth thee muche, but that time cōmeth not yet, for there is yet another
time to come, that is to saye, a time of
labour and of proufe. Thou desirest to be
fulfilled with the high goodnes in heauē,
but thou mayst not yet come therto. I am
the full rewarde of man, abide me till I
shall come, and thou shalt haue me to thy
rewarde. Thou art yet to be proued here

L b   vpon

upon earth, and make throughlye to be
assayed in many thinges, some comfort
shall be geuen to thee, but the fulnes
thereof shal not yet be graunted. Be thou
therefore comforted in me, and be thou
strong, as well in doeing as in sufferinge
thinges contrary to thy wil. It behoueth
thee to be clothed in thy blood, and to be
chaunged into a newe man, and thou
must ofte times doe that thou wouldest
not doe, and that thou wouldest doe thou
must forsake & leaue vndone. That shall
please other shall goe well forwarde, and
that shall please thee shal haue no speede:
that other men saye shall be well heard,
and that thou shalt saye, shall be set at
nought. Other shall aske, and haue their
askinge, thou shalte aske and be denied.
Other shal be great and haue great laude
and prayse of the people, and of thee no
worde shall be spoken. To other this office or that shall be committed, and thou
shalte be iudged vnprofitable in euery
thinge: for these thinges and other lyke,
nature will murmure and grudge, & thou
shalt haue a great battaile in thy selfe, if
thou beare them secrete in thy hart without complayning & missaying. Neuerthelesse, in suche thinges and other like my
faithfull seruauntes are wont to be proued, howe they can denie them selues,
and howe they can in all thinges breake
their owne wylles, and there is nothinge
that

that thou ſhalt neede ſo muche to ouer=
come thy ſelfe in, as to learne to be con=
tented not to be ſet anye price by in the
worlde, and to ſuffer ſuche thinges as be
moſte contratye to thy will, eſpeciallye
when ſuche thinges as in thy ſight ſeeme
vnprofitable, be commaunded to be done.
But (my ſonne) conſider well the pro=
fite and fruite of all theſe laboures, the
ſhorte ende, and the great rewarde, and
then thou ſhalt feele no greefe nor paine
in all thy laboures, but the moſt ſweeteſt
comfort of the holye ghoſt through thy
good will, and for that litle wil that thou
forſakeſt here, thou ſhalt alwaye haue thy
will in heauen, where thou ſhalt haue all
that thou canſt or mayeſt deſire. There
ſhalte thou haue full poſſeſſion of all
goodnes, withſout dread to loſe it. There
thy will ſhall be euer one with my will,
and it ſhall couete no ſtraunge nor pri=
uate thinges. There no man ſhall re=
ſiſte thee, no man ſhall complayne on
thee, no man ſhall let thee, nor no man
ſhall wythſtande thee, but all thinges
that thou canſt deſyre ſhall be there
preſent, and ſhall fulfill all the powers
of thy ſoule vnto the full. There ſhall I
yeelde glorye for reproſes, and a palle of
laude for thy heauines, and for the
loweſt place here, a ſeate in heauen
for euer. There ſhall appeare the fruite
of obedience, the labour of penaunce
ſhal

shall ioy, and the humble subiection shall be crowned gloriously. Bowe thee therefore meekelye nowe vnder euery mans hande, and force litle who saith this, or who commaundeth this to be done. But with all thy studie take heede, that whether thy prelate, or thy felowe, or anye other lower than thou, aske any thing of thee, or will any thing to be done by thee, that thou take it alwaye to the best, and with a glad will studie to fulfill it. Let this man seeke this thing, and another that, and let this man ioy in this thing, & another in that, whatsoeuer it be, and let them be lauded and praysed a thousande times, but ioye thou neither in this thinge nor in that, but onelye in thine owne contempt and despising, and in my will to be fulfilled, and whether it be by life or death, that I may alway be lauded and honoured in thee and by thee. Amen.

Howve a man that is desolate, ought to
offer hym selfe vvhollye to God.

The.55.Chapter.

LORDE holy father, be thou blessed now and euer, for as thou wilt so it is done, and that thou doest is alwaye well : let me thy poorest seruaunt and most vnworthy, ioye in thee, and not in my selfe, nor in nothinge els beside thee,

for

for thou Lorde art my gladnes, thou art
my hope, my crowne, my ioye, and all my
honor. What hath thy seruant but that
he hath of thee, and that without his desert? All things be thine, and I am poore,
and haue bene in trouble & in paine euer
from my youth, and my soule hath beene
in great heauines with weeping and teares, and sometime it hath bene troubled
in it selfe through manifolde passions,
that come of the world, and of the fleshe.
Wherefore Lorde, I desire that I maye
haue of thee the ioye of inwarde peace,
and I aske the rest of thy chosen childrē,
that be fedde and nourished of thee in
the light of heauenly comforts, but without thy helpe I can not come therto. If
thou Lorde geue peace, or if thou geue inwarde ioye, my soule shall be anone full of
heauenlye melodie, and be deuoute and
feruent in thy laudes and praysings: but
if thou withdrawe thy selfe from me, as
thou hast sometime done, then may not
thy seruant runne the waye of thy commaundementes, as he did first, but then
he is compelled to bowe his knees, and
knocke his brest, for it is not with him as
it was before, when the lanterne of thy
ghostlie presence shone vpon his heade,
and that he was defended vnder the shadowe of thy mercie from all perils and
daungers. O righteous father euer to be
prayled, the time is come that thou wilte
thy

thy seruaunt be praised, And righteousse
to it done, that I now shall suffer some=
what for thee:now is the hour come that
thou hast knowen from the beginninge,
that thy seruant for a time should out=
wardlie be set at naught, and inwardlie
to liue to thee,and that he shoulde a litle
be despised in the sight of the world,and
be broken with passions and sickenes,
that he might after rise with thee into a
newe light,and be clarified , and made
glorious in the kingdome of heauen. O
holie father, thou haste ordeyned it so to
be,and it is done as thou hast commaun=
ded:this is thy grace to thy freende, to
suffer, and to be troubled in this worlde
for thy loue, howe ofte so euer it be, of
what person soeuer it be , & in what ma=
ner soeuer thou suffer it to fall vnto him:
without thy counsayle & prouidence,nor
without cause nothinge is done vpon
earth. Oh , it is good to me,Lorde, that
thou hast meekened me,that I may ther=
by learne to knowe thy righteous iudge=
mentes , and put from me all maner of
presumption and highnes of minde. And
it is verie profitable to me , that confusion
hath couered my face,that I maye learne
thereby to seeke for helpe and succour to
thee rather thē to man.And I haue ther=
by learned to dreade thy secrete & terrible
iudgementes,which scourgest the righte=
ous mā with the sinner , but not without
equitie

equitie and iustice. I yeelde thankes to thee, that thou haste not spared my sins, but haste punished me with scourges of loue, and hast sent me sorowes and anguishes within, and without, so that there is no creature vnder heauen that may comfort me, but thou Lorde God the heauenlie leach of mans soule, which strikest and healest, and bringest a man nigh vnto bodilie death, and after restorest him to health againe, that he maye thereby learne to knowe the littlenes of his owne power, & the more fullie to trust in thee. Thy discipline is fallen vpon me, and thy rod of correctiõ hath taught me, & vnder that rodde I whollie submit me, strike my backe and bones as it shall please thee, & make me to bowe my croked will vnto thy will, make me a meeke & an humble disciple, as thou hast sometime done with me, that I may walke all after thy wil. To thee I commit my selfe, and all mine to be corrected, for better it is to be corrected by thee here, then in time to come. Thou knowest all thinges, & nothinge is hidde from thee that is in mans cõsciēce. Thou knowest thinges to come before they fall, & it is not nedefull that any man teache thee or warne thee of any thinge that is done vpõ the earth. Thou knowest what is speedefull for me, and howe much tribulation helpeth to purge the rest of sinne in me: do with

me

me after thy pleasure, and disdayne not
my sinfull life, to none so well knowen
as it is to thee. Graunt me Lorde that to
knowe, that is necessarie to be knowen:
that to loue, that is to be loued: that to
prayse, that highlie pleaseth thee: that to
regarde, that appeareth precious in thy
sight, and that to refuse that is vile before thee. Suffer me not to iudge after my
outwarde wits, nor to geue sentéce after
the hearinge of vncunninge men, but in
a true iudgement to discerne thinges visible and inuisible, and aboue all thinges
alway to searche and folowe thy will and
pleasure. The outwarde witnes of men
be ofte deceyued in their iudgementes,
And in likewise, the louers of the worlde
be deceyued through louinge onelie of
visible thinges. What is a man the better, for that he is taken better? truelie nothinge. For a deceitfull man deceyueth
an other, a vayne man deceyueth an other,
and a blinde & feeble creature deceyueth
an other when he exalteth him, and rather confoundeth him then prayseth
him. For why? howe muche soeuer a
man be in sight of God, so much he
is, and no more, sayth the meeke
Saint Fraunces, howe holye
and howe vertuous soeuer
he be taken in sight
of the people.

That

That it is good , that a man geue hym selfe to
meeke bodilye laboures, vvhen he feeleth
not hym selfe diſpoſed to high
vvorkes of deuotion.

The 56. Chapter.

y ſonne, thou mayeſt not alwaye ſtande in the high feruét
deſire of vertue, ne in the hi-
gheſt degree of contēplatiō,
but thou muſte of neceſſitie
through the corruption of the firſt ſinne
ſometime deſcende to lower thinges, and
againſt thy will, and with great tediousnes, to beare the burden of this corruptible body: for as longe as thou beareſt this
bodie of death, thou muſt neede feele
ſome tediouſnes and griefe of heart, and
thou ſhalt ofte times beweepe & mourne
the burden of thy fleſhlie feelinges, and
the contradictiō of thy body to thy ſoule,
for thou mayeſt not for the corruption
thereof perſeuer in ſpirituall ſtudies, and
in heauenlye contemplation as thou
wouldeſt doe, and then it is good to thee
to flie to meeke bodilie laboures, and to
exerciſe thy ſelfe in good outwarde workes, and in a ſtedfaſt hope and truſt to
abide my comminge, and my newe heauenlie viſitations, and to beare thy exile,
and the drines of thy hart patientlie, till
thou ſhalt be viſited by me agayne, and
be

to deliuered from all teutoulnes and vnquietnes of minde. When J ſhall come,
J ſhall make thee forget all thy former
laboures, and to haue inwarde reſt and
quietnes of ſoule. J ſhall alſo laye before
thee the floriſhing medowe of holy ſcrip-
ture, and thou ſhalte with great gladnes
of heart in a newe bleſſed feeling, fele the
very true vnderſtāding thereof, and then
quickly ſhalt thou runne the waye of my
commaundementes, and then ſhalt thou
ſaye in great ſpirituall gladnes. The paſſions of this worlde be not woorthy of thē
ſelues to bring vs to the ioy that ſhall be
ſhewed vs in the bliſſe of heauen, To the
which bring vs our Lorde Jeſus. Amen.

That a man ſhall not thinke him ſelfe, vvorthy
to haue comfort, but rather to haue
ſorovve and payne: and of the
profite of contrition.

The 57. Chapter.

LOrde, J am not woorthy to
haue thy conſolation, nor any
ſpirituall viſitatiō, and therefore thou doeſt righteouſly to
me, when thou leaueſt me
needy and deſolate: for though J might
weepe water of teares like to the Sea,
yet were J not woorthy to haue thy con-
ſolatiō, for J am woorthy to haue nothing
but

but forowe and paine, for I haue so greeuouslye and so ofte offended thee, and in
so many things greatly trespassed against
thee. Therefore I may well saye and confesse for truth, that I am not woorthy to
haue thy lesse consolation. But thou Lord
benigne and mercifull, that wilt not thy
workes doe perish, to shewe the greatnes
of thy goodnes in the vessels of thy mercy, aboue all my merites or desert, doest
vouchsafe sometime to comforte me thy
seruaunt more then I can thinke or de-
uise. Thy consolations be not like to mens
fables, for they be in them selues soothfast & true. But what haue I done Lorde,
that thou wilt vouchsafe to geue me any
heauenly consolation? I knowe not that
I haue done anye thing well as I should
haue done, but that I haue bene prone
and readie to sinne, and slowe to amendment. This is true, and I can not deny
it: for if I would deny it, thou shouldest
stand against me, and no man might defend me. What haue I then deserued,
but hell and euerlastinge fire? I confesse
for truth, that I am woorthy in this
worlde of shame and despite, and that it
becommeth not me to be conuersant with
deuout people. And though it be greeuous to me to say thus, yet (sith the truth
is so) I wil confesse the truth as it is, and
openlye will reproue my selfe of my defaultes, that I may the rather obteine of
thee

thee mercy & forgeuenes. But what maye
I then say Lorde, that thus am giltie and
full of confusion? truely I haue no mouth
nor tonge to speake, but onely this word:
I haue sinned Lorde, I haue sinned, haue
mercy on me, forgeue me, and forget my
trespasse, suffer me a litle, that I maye
weepe & waile my sinnes, or that I passe
hence to the lande of darknes couered
with the shadowe of death. And what
doest thou Lord aske most of such a wretched sinner, but that he be contrite, and
meeken him selfe for his sinne, for in true
contrition & meekenes of heart, is found
the very hope of forgeuenes of sinne, and
the troubled conscience is therby cleered,
and the grace before lost is recouered
agayne. Man also is thereby defended
fro the wrath to come, & almightie God,
and the penitente soule mete louinglie
together in holie kissinges of heauenlye
loue. A meeke contrition of heart is to
thee Lorde a right acceptable Sacrifice,
more sweetlie sauouringe in thy sight,
then burnynge incence. It is also the
precious oyntment, that thou wouldest
should be shed vpon thy blessed feete, for
a meeke and contrite heart thou neuer
despisest. This contrition is the place of
refuge, from the dreade and wrath of the
enemie, and therby is washed & clensed,
whatsoeuer is before misdone, or that
is defiled through sinne in any maner.

That

That grace vvill not be mixt vvith loue
of vvorldlye thinges.

The.58.Chapter.

Y sonne, grace is a precious
thing, and will not be mixte
with anye priuate loue, nor
with worldlye comfortes. It
behoueth thee therefore to
caste awaye all lettinges of
grace,if thou wilt haue the gratious gift
thereof. Chose therefore a secrete place,
and loue to be alone,and keepe thee from
hearinge of vayne tales and fables, and
offer to God deuout prayers, and praye
hartily,that thou mayest haue a contrite
hart,and a pure conscience.Thinke al the
world as naught,and preferre my seruice
before all other thinges, for thou mayest
not haue minde on me, and therwithall
delite thee in transitorie pleasures.It behoueth thee therefore to withdrawe thee
from thy deerest freendes, and from all
thine acquaintaunce,and to sequester thy
minde whollie fro the inordinate desire
of all worldlye comfort as muche as thou
mayest. Thus prayed Saint Peter, that
all Christien people might holde them
selues as strangers,and as pilgrimes vpõ
earth, for then they shoulde not set but
litle price by the comfort thereof.O howe
sure a trust shall it be to a man at his departinge out of this world, to feele inwardlie

uaecuie in his soule, that no movable loue, not yet the affection of no passinge or traitorie thinge hath any rule in him. But a weake feeble person newlie turned to God, may not so lightlie haue his hart seuered from earthlie likinge, nor the beastlie man knoweth not the freedome of a man that is inwardly turned to god. And therefore if a man will perfectlie be spirituall and ghostlie, he must aswell renounce strangers as kinsfolke, and speciallie before all other, that he be moste ware of him selfe, for if he ouercome him selfe perfectlie, he shall the sooner ouercome all other enimies. The moste noble and most perfecte victorie, is, a man to haue the victorie of him selfe. He therefore that holdeth him selfe so muche subiect, that the sensualitie obeyeth to reason, and reason in all thinges obeyeth to me, he is the true ouercommer of hym selfe, and the Lorde of the worlde. But if thou couet to come to that point, thou must beginne manfullie, and set thy axe to the roote of the tree, and fullie to cut awaye, and to destroye in thee all the inordinate inclination that thou haste to thy selfe, or to any priuate or materiall thinge, for of that vice that a man loueth him selfe inordinatlie, well nigh dependeth all that ought groundlie to be destroyed in man. And if that be truely ouercome, anone shall folowe great tranquilitie

litie and peace of conſcience. But foꝛaſmuch as there be but fewe that labour to
die to them ſelues, noꝛ to ouercome them
ſelues perfectlie, therefore they lye ſtill in
their fleſhlie feelinges and woꝛldlie com-
foꝛtes, and may in no wiſe riſe vp in ſpirite aboue them ſelues: foꝛ it behoueth
him that will be free in heart, & haue cõ-
têplatiõ of me, to moꝛtifie all his euill in-
clinations that he hath to him ſelfe, & to
the woꝛld, & not to be bounde to any creature by any inoꝛdinate oꝛ priuate ioue.

*Of the diuerſities and diuers mouinges be-
tvvene nature and grace.*

The 59. Chapter.

Y ſonne, take good heede of the
motions of nature and grace,
foꝛ they be verie ſubtil, and
much contrary the one to the
other, and hardlie may they be
knowen aſonder, but it be by a ghoſtly
man, that thꝛough ſpirituall grace is inwardlye lightned in ſoule. Euerye man
deſireth ſome goodnes, and pꝛetendeth
ſomewhat of goodnes in all his woꝛdes
and deedes, and therfore vnder pꝛetence
of goodnes many be deceaued. Nature is
wylie, and full of deceit, and dꝛaweth
many to her, whom ſhe often times ſna-
reth and deceyueth, & euer beholdeth her
owne wealth, as the ende of her woꝛke.
But

But grace walketh simplye, without be=
ing gyle, she declineth from all euill, she pre=
tendeth no gyle, but all thinges she doth
purelye for God, in whom finallye she
resteth. Nature will not gladlye dye, nor
gladlye be oppressed or ouercome, neither
will she gladlye be vnder other, ne be
kept in subiection: but grace studieth
howe she may be mortified to the world,
and to the flesh. She resisteth sensualitie,
she seeketh to be subiecte, she desireth to
be ouercome, she will not vse her owne li=
bertie: she loueth to be holden vnder holy
discipline, and coueteth not to haue lord=
ship ouer anye one creature, but to lyue
and to stande alway vnder the dreade of
God, and for his loue is alwaye readie to
bowe her selfe meekely to euery creature.
Nature laboureth for her owne profite
and aduantage, & muche beholdeth what
winning commeth to her by other. But
grace beholdeth not what is profitable
to her seife, but what is profytable to
manye. Nature receaueth gladlye ho=
nour and reuerence, but grace referreth
all honour and reuerence to God. Nature
dreadeth reprouinges and despising, but
grace ioyeth for the name of god to suffer
thē both, and take them when they some
as speciall giftes of God. Nature loueth
idlenes and fleshlie rest, but grace can
not be ydle without doeinge some good
deede, and therefore she seeketh gladlye
some

some profitable labours. Nature desireth
faire thinges and curious, and abhorreth
vile thinges and grosse: but grace delighteth in meke and simple thinges, she despiseth not harde thinges, nor refuseth
not to be clad in poore olde clothing and
simple garmentes. Nature beholdeth
gladlie thinges temporall, she ioyeth at
worldlie winninges, is heauie for worldlie leesinges, and anone is moued with a
sharpe word, but grace beholdeth things
euerlastinge, and trusteth not in thinges
temporall, nor is not troubled with the
losse of thē, nor she is not grieued with
a frowarde worde, for she hath layde her
treasure in God, and in ghostlie thinges
whiche may not perishe. Nature is couetous, & more gladlie taketh than geueth,
and loueth muche to haue propertie and
priuate thinges: but grace is pitifull and
liberall to the poore, she flieth singuler
profite, she is content with litle, and
iudgeth it more blessed to geue then to
take. Nature inclineth to the loue of
creatures, to the loue of the fleshe, and to
vanities and runnings about, and to see
newe thinges in the worlde: but grace
draweth a man to the loue of God, and
to the loue of vertues, she renounceth all
creatures, she flieth the world, she hateth
desires of the fleshe, restrayneth libertie
and wandringes about, and escheweth
asmuch as she may to be seene among re-
                    M   courle

courſe of people. Nature hath gladlye
ſome outwarde ſolace, wherein ſhe maye
fayſably delight in her outwarde wittes:
but grace ſeeketh onelie to be comforted
in God, and to delight her in his goodnes aboue all thinges. Nature doth all
thinges for her owne winninge and ſinguler profite, (ſhe may doe nothinge free,
but hopeth alwaye to haue like profite or
better, or laude or fauour of the people,
and coueteth much that her deedes and
workes be greatlie pondred and praiſed:
but grace ſeeketh no temporall thing, nor
none other reward for her hire, but onely
God, ſhe will no more of téporall goodes
then ſhall neede for the gettinge of the
goodes euerlaſtinge, and careth not for
the vayne prayſe of the worlde. Nature
loueth greatlie in many freendes & kinſ-
folkes, and is glorified much of a noble
place of birth, and of her noble bloud and
kinred ſhe loueth with mightie men: ſhe
flattereth riche men, and is merie with
them that ſhe thinketh like to her in noblenes of the worlde: but grace maketh a
man to loue his enemies, ſhe hath no pride in worldlie freendes, ſhe regardeth
not the noblenes of kynne, ne the houſe
of her father: but if the more vertue be
there, ſhe fauoureth more the poore then
the riche, ſhe hath more compaſſion of an
innocèt then of a mightie man: ſhe loueth
euer in truth, and not in falſehoode, and
always

alwaye comfoꝛteth good men moꝛe and
moꝛe to pꝛofite and growe in vertue and
goodnes, and to feeke daylie moꝛe higher
giftes of grace, that they may thꝛough
good vertuous woꝛkes be made like to
the fonne of God. Nature complayneth
anone foꝛ wantinge of a right litle thing
that fhe woulde haue, oꝛ foꝛ a litle woꝛldlie heauines, but grace beareth gladlie all
needines and wantinges of the woꝛlde.
Nature inclynethe all thinges to her
felfe, and to her owne pꝛofite as much as
fhe maye: fhe argueth foꝛ her felfe, and
ftriueth and fighteth foꝛ her felfe: but
grace rendꝛeth all thinges to God, of
whom all thinges doe flowe and fpꝛinge
oꝛiginallie. She afcribeth no goodnes to
her felfe, noꝛ pꝛefumeth of her felfe: fhe
ftriueth not, noꝛ pꝛeferreth her opinion
befoꝛe other mens, but in euery fentence
fhe fubmitteth her meeklie to the eternall
wifedome and iudgement of God. Nature coueteth to knowe and to here newe
fecret thinges, fhe will that her woꝛkes
be fhewed outwardlie, and will haue experience of manye thinges in the woꝛlde
by her outwarde wittes, fhe defyreth
alfo to be knowen, and to doe great
thinges in the woꝛlde, whereof laude
and pꝛayfinge maye folowe, but grace careth not foꝛ anye newe thinges,
noꝛ foꝛ anye curyous thinges what-
foeuer they be: foꝛ fhe knoweth well,
          ꝗ ij   that

that all suche vanities commeth of the
corruption of sinne, and that no newe
thinge maye longe endure vpon earth.
She teacheth also to restraine the outwarde wittes, and to eschewe all vayne
pleasure and outwarde shewinge, and
meekelie keepeth secrete thinges, that in
the worlde were greatlie to be meruayled
and praysed. And in euerie thinge, and in
euerie science she seeketh some spirituall
profite to her selfe, and laude and honour
to almightie God. She will not, that her
good deedes, nor her inwarde deuotion
be outwardly knowen, but most desireth,
that our Lorde be blessed in all his workes, which geueth all thinges freelie of
his high excellent charitie. This grace is
a light supernaturall, and a spirituall
gifte of God, and it is the proper marke
and token of elect people, and an earnest
pense of the euerlastinge life, for it rauis-
sheth a man fro loue of earthlie thinges,
to the loue of heauenlie thinges, and of
a fleshlie liuer maketh an heauenlie person: and the more that nature is oppressed and ouercome, the more
grace is geuen, and the soule
thorough newe gratious visitations is daylye refor-
med more and more
to the image
of God.

Of

Of the corruption of nature, and the vvor-
thynes of grace.

The 60. Chapter.

Lorde, which haste made me
to thine image and likenes,
graunt me this grace that
thou haste shewed to me to
be so great and so necessarye
to the health of my soule,
that I may ouercome this wretched nature which draweth me alwaye to sinne,
and to the losinge of mine owne soule. I
feele in my fleshe the lawe of sinne figh-
ting strongly against the lawe of my spirite, which leadeth me as a thral or bond-
man to obey to sensualitye in manye
thinges, and I may not resist the passios
therof, but if thy grace doe assist me therin. I haue therefore great neede of thy
grace, and that of the great aboundaunce
of thy grace, If I should ouercome this
wretched nature, which alwaye fro my
youth hath bene readie & prone to sinne.
For after that nature was vitiate & defiled by the sinne of the first man Adam,
the payne therof descended into all his
posteritie, so that, that nature which in
the first creatio was good & righteous, is
nowe taken for sinne and corruption, so
farre forth, that the motios that are now
lefte vnto nature, drawe man alwaye
vnto euill. And that is for this reason, for

M ij that

that the litle ſtrength and mouinge to goodnes, that yet remayneth in it, is as a litle ſparcle of fire, that is hid and ouer: hilled with aſhes, that is to ſaye, the naturall reaſon of man, which is all about belapped and ouerhilled with darkenes of ignoraunce, whiche neuertheleſſe hath power yet to iudge betwixt good and bad, and to ſhewe the diſtance and diuerſitie betwixt true and falſe. Howbeit that through weakenes of it ſelfe, it is not able to fulfill all that it approueth, nor hath not ſith the firſte ſinne of Adam the full light of truth, nor the ſweetnes of affections to God as it had firſte. Of this it commeth, moſt mercifull Lorde, that in my inwarde man that is in the reaſon of my ſoule, I delite me in thy lawes and in thy teachinges, knowinge that they are good, and righteous, and holie, and that all ſinne is euill, and to be fled and eſchewed: and yet in my outwarde man, that is to ſaye, in my fleſhelie felinge, I ſerue the lawe of ſinne, when I obeye rather to ſenſualitie then to reaſon. And of this it foloweth alſo, that I will good, but to perfourme it without thy grace I maye not for weakenes of my ſelfe. And ſometime I purpoſe to doe many good deedes, but for that grace wanteth, that ſhoulde helpe me, I goe backeward, and fayle in my doinge. I knowe the waye to perfection, and howe I ſhoulde do, I ſee

tt

it euidentlye, but for that I am so op=
pressed with the heauye burden of this
corrupt bodye of synne, I lye still, and
ryse not to perfection: O Lorde, howe
necessarye therefore is thy grace to me,
to beginne well, to continue well, and to
ende well, for without thee I maye no=
thinge doe that good is. O heauenlye
grace (without whom our merites are
nought woorth), nor the giftes of natu=
re nothinge to be pondred, neither craf=
tes or riches any thinge to be regarded,
nor beautie, strength, wit nor eloquen=
ce nothinge maye auayle) come thou
shortlye and helpe me. The gyftes of
nature be common to good men and
bad, but grace and loue are the giftes
of electe and chosen people, whereby
they be marked and made able and wor=
thy to haue the kingedome of heauen.
This grace is of suche worthynes, that
neyther the gyfte of prophecie, nor
the workinge of miracles, nor yet the
gyfte of cunninge and knowledge maye
nothinge auayle without it, ne yet
fayth, hope or other vertues be not
acceptable to thee without grace and
charitie. O blessed grace, that maketh
the poore in spirite to be ryche in ver=
tue, and hym that is ryche in worldlye
goodes, maketh meeke and lowe in heart,
come and descende into my soule, and
fulfill me with thy ghostlie comfortes,
M̃ iiij   that

that it fayle not, nor taynt nor weried
or daynes of it selfe. I beseche thee Lord,
that I may finde grace in thy fight, for
thy grace shal suffice to me, though I doe
wante that nature desireth. For although
I be tempted and vexed with troubles on
euery side, yet shall I not neede to drede,
whiles thy grace is with me: for she is my
strength, she is my comfort, and she is my
counsayle and helpe, she is stronger then
all mine enemies, and wiser then all the
wisest of this worlde. She is the maystres
of truth, the teacher in discipline, the
light of the hart, the comfort of trouble,
the driuer awaye of heauines, the auoy-
der of dreade, the nourisher of deuotion,
and the bringer of sweete teares and deuoute weepinges. What am I then without grace, but a drie stocke to caste
awaye? Graunt me therefore, that
thy grace maye preuent me and folowe me, and that It may make
me euer busie and diligent
in good workes vnto
my death. So
may it be.
Amen.

That

That vve ought to forsake our selfe, and to folovv
Christe by bearinge of hys Crosse.

The 61.Chapter.

My sonne, as much as thou canst go out fro thy selfe, and fro thine owne will, so much as thou mayest enter into me: and as to desire nothing outwardlie bringeth peace inwardlie into mans soule, so a man by an inwarde forsakinge of him selfe ioyneth him to God. I will therefore, that thou learne to haue a perfect forsaking, and a full resigning of thy selfe into my hands, without withsaying and complayninge, and that thou folowe me: for I am the waye, I am the truth, and I am the life. Without a waye no man maye go, and without truth no man maye knowe, and without life no man maye lyue. I am the waye which thou oughtest to goe, the truth which thou oughtest to beleue, & the life which thou shalt hope to haue. I am the waye that can not be defyled, the truth which can not be deceyued, and the life that neuer shall haue ende. I am the waye moste straite, the truth most perfect, and the life most soothfast. A blessed life, and a life vnmade that made all things. If thou dwell and abide in my waye, thou shalt knowe the truth, and truth shal deliuer thee, and thou shalt come to euerlastinge life. If

M v   thou

thou wilte come to that lyfe, kepe my co
mraundementes, If thou wilt knowe the
truth, beleeue my teachinges, If thou
wilt be perfect, sell all that thou haste, If
thou wilt be my Disciple, forsake thy
selfe, If thou wilt haue the blessed lyfe,
despise this present life, If thou wilt be
exalted in heauen, meeke thee here in
earth, And if thou wilt reigne with me,
beare the Crosse with me: for truely, only
the seruauntes of the Crosse shall finde
the life of blessednes, and of euerlastinge
light. O Lorde Iesu, forasmuche as thy
waye is narowe and straite, and is also
muche despised in the worlde, geue me
grace to beare gladlye the despisinges of
the worlde. There is no seruaunt greater
then his Lorde, nor any Disciple aboue
his master. Let thy seruaunt therefore be
exercised in thy wayes, for therein is the
health and the very perfection of lyfe:
whatsoeuer I reade or heare beside that
way, it refresheth me not, nor delighteth
me not fullye. My sonne, forasmuche as
thou knowest these thinges, & hast reade
them all, thou shalt be blessed if thou ful-
fil them. He that hath my commaundementes, and keepeth them, he it is that
loueth me, and I shall loue him, & I shall
shewe my selfe vnto him, and shall make
him sitte with me in the kingdome of my
father. Lorde as thou hast sayde and promised, so be it done to me, I haue taken
the

the Croffe of penaunce at thy hand, and
I fhall beare it vnto my death, as thou
haſte put it to me to doe. For the lyfe of
euery good man is the Croffe, and it is
alfo the way and leader to Paradiſe, and
nowe it is begonne, it is not lawfull for
me to go backe fro it, ne it is not behoue-
full for me to leaue it. Haue done therefore my welbeloued brethren, go we forth
together, Jefu fhall be with vs, for Jefu
we haue taken this Croffe, for Jefu let
vs perſeuer, and he fhal be our helpe, that
is our guyde and leader. Lo our kinge
goeth before vs , that fhall fyght for
vs , folowe we hym ſtronglye , dreade
we no perils , but be we readye to dye
ſtronglye with hym in battayle , that
we put no blot into our glorye, nor mi-
niſhe not our rewarde , by flyinge co-
wardlye awaye from the Croffe.

*That a man ſhall not be ouermuche caſt into
heauynes, though he happen to fall into
ſome defaultes.*

The.62.Chapter.

M y fonne, patience and meke-
nes in aduerſitie, pleaſe me
more, then much confolation
and deuotion in profperitie.
Why art thou fo heauy for
a litle worde fayde or done
againſt thee? yf it had bene more, thou
ſhoul-

shouldeſt not haue bene moued therwith, but let it nowe ouerpaſſe, it is not the firſt, and it ſhall not be the laſt if thou lyue longe. Thou art manfull inough as long as no aduerſitie falleth to thee, and thou canſt well giue counſaile, and well canſt thou comfort and ſtrengthen other with thy wordes: But when aduerſitie knocketh at thy doore, thou faileſt anone both of counſayle and ſtrength. Beholde well therefore thy great frayltie, which thou haſt daylie experience of in litle obiectes. Neuertheleſſe, it is for thy ghoſtly health that ſuche thinges and other like be ſuffered to come vnto the. Purpoſe thy ſelfe in thy harte to doe the beſt that lieth in thee, and then when ſuche tribulations ſhall happen to fall vnto thee, although it greeue thee, yet let it not whollie ouerthrow thee, nor let it not longe tarie with thee. And at the leaſt ſuffer it pacientlie, although thou maye not ſuffer it gladlie. Moreouer, though thou be loth to heare ſuche thinges, and that thou feele great indignation therat in thy hart, yet thruſt thy ſelfe downe lowe in thine owne ſight, and ſuffer no inordinate worde paſſe out of thy mouth, whereby any other might be hurt, and then all ſuch indignation ſhall be anone aſſuaged & ſoone appeaſed in thee. And then alſo that which before was taken to ſo great heauines to thee, ſhall anone
be

be made sweete & pleasaunt in thy sight.
For yet lyue I (sayth our Lozde)redie to
helpe thee, and to cōfozt thee, moze then
euer I did befoze , if thou wilt whollye
trust in me,and deuoutly call foz helpe to
me.Be quiet in hart,pzepare thy selfe yet
to moze sufferance. Foz it is not all lost
though thou feele thy selfe ofte troubled
oz greeuouslye tempted. Thinke thou art
a man,and not God, a fleshlye man, and
no Angell.Howe mayest thou alwayes be
in one state of vertue,when that wanted
to Angels in heauen and to the first man
in Paradise,the which stoode not longe?
I am he that rayse vp them that be sorowfull to health and comfozt,and those
that knowe their owne vnstablenes , I
lifte them vp to be stabled in the sight of
my Godhead foz euer.Lozde , blessed be
thy holie wozd.It is moze sweeter to my
mouth then honye combe. What should
I doe in all my troubles and heauines,if
thou diddest not sometime comfozt me
with thy wholsome and sweete wozdes?
Therefoze it shall not fozce what trouble
oz aduersitie I suffer here foz thee,so that
I maye in the ende come to the pozte of
euerlasting health. Geue me a good ende
and a blessed passage out of this wozlde:
 haue minde on me,my Lozde my God,
  and direct me by a straite and redy
   waye into thy kingdome,I
   beseech thee.Amen.

       That

The. 63. Chapter.

Y ſonne, beware to diſpute
of highe matters, & of the
ſecret iudgemēts of God,
why this man is ſo left &
forſaken of God, and why
this man is taken to ſo
great grace, why alſo one
man is ſo much troubled, and another ſo
greatly aduaunced. Theſe thinges ouerpaſſe all mans knowledge, for to ſerch
gods iudgement no mans reaſon maye
ſuffiſe, nor yet his diſputation. Therfore,
when the ghoſtly enemy ſtirreth thee to
ſuch thinges, or if any curious men aſke
of thee ſuche queſtions, anſwer with the
prophete Dauid, and ſay thus, Lord thou
art righteous, & thy iudgemēts are true,
and be iuſtified in them ſelfe, thy iudge-
ments are to be dread, & not to be diſcuſ-
ſed by mans wit, for they be to mans wit
incomprehenſible. Beware alſo that thou
ſearch not, nor reaſon not of the merites
of Saintes, which of them was holyer
then other, or which of them is higher in
heauen: Suche queſtions ofte times nou-
riſhe great ſtrifes and vnprofitable rea-
ſoninges, and proceede of pride & vaine-
glory, wherby enuy ſpringeth and diſſen-
tion: that is to ſaye, when one laboureth

to

to prefer this Saint, and another that.
And truely a desire to knowe such things
rather displeaseth Saints then pleaseth
them. For I (saith our Lord)am not God
of dissention and strife, but of vnitie and
peace, the which peace standeth rather in
true meekenes, than in exalting of them
selues. Some men be more stirred to loue
this Saint or that, and that with muche
greater affection, but truly that affection
is oft time more rather a manly affectio,
than a godlye. Am not I he that haue
made all Saints? yes truelye: and ouer
that I haue giuen thē grace, and I haue
geuen them glorye : I knowe all their
merites , I preuented them with the
sweetnes of my blessinges, I knewe my
elect and chosen people before the worlde
was made, I haue chosen them from the
worlde, they haue not chosen me, I called
them by my grace, I drewe them by my
mercy, I led them through temptations,
I sent them inwarde comfortes, I gaue
them perseueraunce , I crowned their
patience , I knowe the first man and the
laste, I loue them all with an inestimable
loue. Thus I am to be praysed in all my
Saintes, and aboue all thinges to be blessed and honoured in all ,and in euery of
them whom I haue so gloriouslye magnifyed and predestinate without anye
merites in them goeinge before. Therefore he that despyseth the leaste of my
                              Saintes

Saintes, doth no honour to the greatest,
for, I haue made both the lesse and the
more, and he that dispraiseth any of my
Saintes, he dispraiseth me and other of
my Saintes in the kingdome of heauen,
for they be all one, fasse vnited and knit
together in one sure bonde of perfect
charitie. They feele all one thinge, and
they will all one thinge, and they loue
altogether all into one thinge, and they
loue me muche more then them selues, or
their own merites, for they be rapt aboue
themselues, and be drawen from their
owne loue, and whollie be turned into
my loue, in the which they rest by eternal
fruition. There is nothinge that maye
turne them from my loue, nor that may
thrust them downe out of their glorie, for
they be full of eternall trueth, and burne
inwardlie in soule with fyre of euerlastinge charitie, that neuer shall be quen-
ched. Let all them cease therefore that be
carnall and beastly, and that can not loue
but priuate loue, to searche the state of
my blessed Saintes in heauen, for they
put awaye, and adde to their merites as
they fauour, and not after the pleasure of
the eternall truth of God. In many folkes is great ignoraunce, but moste speciallie in them that haue so litle light of
ghostlie vnderstanding, that they can not
loue any person with a cleane loue. Many
also be moued by a naturall affection, or
by

by a worldly frendship to loue this saint
or that, and as they imagine in earthly
thinges, so they imagine of heauenlye
thinges, but there is a distaunce incom-
parable betwixt thinges which imperfect
men imagine by naturall reason, and
which men truelye illumined with grace
beholde by heauenlye contemplation.
Beware therefore, my sonne, to treate
curiously of suche thinges, for they passe
thy knowledge, and endeuour thy selfe,
that thou mayest be worthy to be nubred
with the least Saint that shall come to
heaué. And if percase a man might knowe
who were holyer, or who should be taken
greater in the kingdome of heauen, what
shoulde that knowledge auayle him, but
if he would therby the more meeke him
selfe, and the more ryse thereby, into the
laude and praysinge of my name? truelie
nothinge. Therefore he is much more acceptable to God that thinketh on the
greatnes of his sinnes, and of the littlenes of his vertues, and howe farre he is
from the perfectió of the least Saint that
is in heaué, then he that argueth of their
greatnes, or of their litlenes, or blessednes of life, forgettinge them selfe. It is
better also with deuout prayers, & with
weepinges and teares meekelie to praye
to Saintes, and to call to them for helpe,
then vaynelie to searche for their perfection. They be verie well contented with
the

the loue that they haue, if men woulde
refrayne themselues from suche vayne
argumentes. They glozifie not themselues of their merites, ne they ascribe no
goodnes to themselues, but they referre
all goodnes to me, for they knowe well
that I of my infinite goodnes and charitie haue geuen all vnto them.And they
be so muche fulfilled with loue of the
godhead,and with ouerpassing ioye,that
no glozie maye want in them, nor anye
felicitie. And the higher that they be in
heauen, the meeker be they in them selues, and the moze nighe and the moze
louing to me. Therefore it is written in
the Apocalips, that Saintes in heauen
layde their crownes befoze God, and fell
proftrate on their faces befoze the meeke
lambe,that is Iesu, and they wozship-
ped him as their Lozde God, that is and
shalbe lyuing euermoze without ending.
Amen. Manye searche who is highest in
heauen, that knowe not whether they
shall be wozthy to be numbzed with the
leaft that shall come thither: for it is a
great thinge to be the leaft in heauen,
where all be great, foz all that shall come
thither shall be called the sonnes of God,
and so shall they be in deede:the left there
shall be counted foz a thousande, and a
sinner of a hundzed yere shall be set at
naught When the Apostles asked amōg
them selues, who shoulde be greatest in
the

the kingdome of heauen,they heard this
answer of Chriſt:but ye(ſayde he)be con=
uerted from your ſinne , and be made
meeke as litle childzen , ye maye not en=
ter into the kyngdome of heauen. He
therefore that meeketh him ſelfe as this
litle childe,he ſhalbe greateſt in the king=
dome of heauen. Woe then be to them
that diſdayne to meeke them ſelues with
litle childzen, for the meeke part of hea=
uen will not ſuffer them to enter into it:
wo alſo be vnto the proude riche men
that haue their côſolation here,for when
the good poorze men ſhall enter into the
kingdome of God,they ſhall ſtande wee=
pinge and waylinge without. Joye ye
then,ye that be meeke and poorze
in ſpirite, for yours is the
kingdome of God,ſo that
ye walke and houlde
your iorney aſſu=
redlye in the
waye of
truth.

That

The 64. Chapter.

O Lorde, what is the trust that I haue in this life? or what is my moste solace of all thinges vnder heauen? Is it not thou, my Lorde God, whose mercy is without measure? where hath it beene well with me without thee? or when hath it not beene well with me, thou being present? I had leuer be poore with thee, then rich without thee, I had leuer be with thee as a pilgrime in this world, then without thee to be in heauen, for where thou art, ther is heauē, and where thou art not, there is both death and hell. Thou arte to me all that I desire, and therefore it behoueth me to sigh to thee, to crie to thee, & hartily to praye to thee. I haue nothinge to trust in that maye helpe me in my necessities, but onelye thee, for thou art my hope, thou art my trust, thou art my comforte, and thou arte my moste faithfull helper in euerye neede. Man seeketh that is his, but thou seekest my health and profite, and turnest all thinges into the best for me, for if thou sende temptations and other aduersities, thou ordeinest all to my profite, for thou art wont by a thousande wayes to proue thy chosen people. In whiche proufe

proufe thou art no lesse to be lauded and
praysed, than if thou haddest fulfilled the
with heauenlie comfortes. In thee Lorde
therefore I put my trust, and in thee I
beare patientlye all my aduersities, for I
finde nothinge without thee but vnstable-
blenes and follie, for I see well, that the
multitude of worldlye freendes profiteth
not, nor that stronge helpers nothinge
maye auayle, ne wise counsayler geue
profitable counsayle, ne cunninge of doctours gyue consolation, ne ryches dely-
uer in tyme of neede, ne secrete place any
thinge defende, yf thou Lorde doe not
assist, helpe, comforte, counsail, informe,
and defend. For all thinges that seeme to
be ordeined to mans solace in this world,
if thou be absent, be right nought worth,
nor maye not bring to man anye true felicitie, for thou art the ende, Lorde, of all
good thinges, the highnes of lyfe, and the
profounde wisedome of all things that is
in heauen and in earth. Wherfore to
trust in thee aboue all thinges, is the
greatest comfort to al thy seruauntes. To
thee therefore I lifte mine eyes, and in
thee onely I put my trust, my Lorde my
God, the father of mercy, blesse thou, and
halowe thou my soule with thy heauenlie blessinges, that it may be thy dwelling
place, and the seate of thy eternall glorie,
so that nothinge be founde in me at any
tyme, that maye offende the eye of thy
maiestie

maieste. Beholde me (Lorde) after the
greatnes of thy goodnes, and of thy manyfolde mercies, and graciouslye heare
the prayer of me thy poorest seruaunt,
outlawed, and farre exiled into the countrey of the shadowe of death, defend and
keepe me amonge the manyfolde perils
and daungers of this corruptible lyfe,
and direct me through thy grace
by the waye of peace, into the
countrey of euerlastinge
clearnes with-
out ending.
Amen.

Finis.

Hereafter

Hereafter foloweth the fourth Booke of
the folowinge of Chrifte, which treateth mofte fpeciallye of the
Sacrament of the aultare.

Prologue.

 Ome to me (faith our Lozde)
all ye that labour and be charged, and I fhall geue vnto you
refection. And the breade that
I fhall geue vnto you, fhall be
my flefh foz the lyfe of the wozlde. Take
                                      it

it and eate it, for it is my bodye, that for
you shall be geuen in sacrifice, doe ye this
in remembrance of me, for who so eateth
my fleshe, and drinketh my bloud, he shal
dwell in me, and I in him. These wordes
that I haue sayde to you be spirite and
lyfe.

*VVith hovve great reuerence Chrifte
is to be receaued.*

The firste Chapter.

MY Lorde Iesu Chrifte, eternall truth, these wordes
aforesayde be thy wordes, al-
beit they were not sayde in
one selfe time, nor written in
one selfe place. And for that they be thy
wordes, I will thankefully and faithfull-
lie accept them. They be thy wordes, and
thou haste spoken them, and they be now
myne also: for thou haste sayde them for
my health. I will gladlye receyue them
of thy mouth, to the end they maye be the
better sowen and planted in mine heart.
Thy wordes of so great pietie, full of
sweetnes and loue, greatly excite me. But
Lorde, my sinnes feare me greatlie, and
my conscience not pure to receaue so great
a misterie, draweth me sore abacke. The
sweetnes of thy wordes prouoketh me,
but the multitude of mine offeces charge
me verie sore. Thou commaundest that I
shall

shall come vnto thee faythfullie, if I will haue part with thee, & receaue the nourishinge of immortalitie, and couete to obteyne the glorie and life eternall. Thou sayest Lorde, come ye to me that labour and be charged, and I shall refreshe you. O howe sweete, and howe amyable a worde is it in the eare of a sinner, that thou Lorde God wilt bidde me, that am so poore and needie to the Communion of thy moste holie bodie? But what am I Lorde, that I dare presume to come to thee? Loe heauē and earth may not comprehende thee, and thou sayest, come ye al to me. What meaneth this moste meeke worthynes, and this louelie and frendly biddinge? howe shall I dare come vnto thee, which knowe not that I haue done any thinge wel? Howe shall I bringe thee into mine house, which so ofte haue offēded before thy face? Angels and Archangels honor thee, & righteous men dreade thee, And thou sayest yet, Come ye all vnto me: but that thou Lorde haddest sayde it, who woulde beleue it to be true? And but thou haste commaunded it, who durst attempt to go vnto it? Noe that iust man laboured an hundred yere to make the shippe, to the end he might be saued with a fewe of his people. Howe maye I prepare me then in an houre to receaue thee with due reuerence, that art maker and Creatour of all the worlde? Moyses thy ser-

N

feruant? and great familier and foreſaine feruinge made the arke or timber not corruptible, whiche he couered with right pure golde, and put in it the tables of the lawe. And I a corrupt creature, how ſhall I ſo lightlie dare receaue thee, that art maker of the lawe, & geuer of grace and lyfe vnto all creatures? The wiſe Salomon, kinge of Iſrael, edified a meruelous temple to the prayſinge of thy name in the ſpace of ſeuen yeres, and by eight dayes halowed the feaſt of the dedication of the ſame: he offred a thouſande peaciable hoſtes, and put the arke of God in the place made readie for it with great melodie of clarions and trumpettes. Howe dare I then that am moſte poore amonge other creatures receaue thee into mine houſe, who ſcarcelie haue well ſpent one houre of time, or one halfe hower of my life? O my good Lorde howe muche ſtudied they to pleaſe thee, and howe litle is it that I doe? Howe litle time take I, when I diſpoſe me to be houſeled? ſeldome am I gathered together in thee, and more ſeldome am I purged fro hauinge my mind ouermuch on worldlie thinges. And certainly, no vnprofitable thoughts ought to come into the holie preſence of thy Godhead, nor no creatures ought there to haue place, for I ſhall not receaue an Angel, but the Lorde of Angels into my heart. Neuertheleſſe, there is great
diffe=

difference betwene the arke of God with his reliques, and thy most pure & precious bodie, with his vertues, which are mo then can be spoken: and betwene the Sacrifice of the olde lawe, that was but a figure of the newe lawe, & the true hoste of thy precious bodie, whiche is the accomplishement of all the olde sacrifice. Why then am I not more inflamed to come to thee, why do I not prepare my selfe with greater diligēce to receaue this holie and blessed Sacramēt, sith the holy auncient fathers, the patriarches & prophetes, Kinges and Princes, with all the people, haue shewed so great affectiō towardes thy seruice in time passed. The moste deuout & blessed Kinge the Kynge Dauid, went before the arke of God, and honoured it with all his strength, alwaye remembringe the great benefites before geuē vnto the fathers: he made Organes of diuers maners, & also Psalmes, which he ordeyned to be songe, and he him selfe sang them with great gladnes, and ofte times with his harpe, he beinge fulfilled with the grace of the holie ghost, taught the people of Israel to laude and prayse God with all their heart, and dayly with their mouth to blesse him, & preache his goodnes. And yf there were shewed then so great deuotion and remembraunce of laude and praysinge to God, before the arke of the olde testament: howe muche

reuerence and deuotion, ought we then howe to haue in the presence of this holy Sacrament, and in the receauinge of the moste excellent bodye of our Lorde Iesu Christe? Many runne to diuers places to visite reliques of Saintes, and meruayle greatlye when they heare of their blessed deedes, they see great buyldinges of temples, and beholde howe their bones and holie reliques be couered with silke, and lapped in golde: and loe thou my Lorde God , thou arte present here with me vpon the Aultar, the moste holie Saint of Saintes, maker of all thinges, and Lorde of Angels. Ofte times there is great curiositie and vanitie in the sight of suche thinges, and litle fruite and amendemēt is had thereby, and that speciallie, where there is so light recourse and waueringe, without anye contrition goinge before. But thou my Lorde God, my Lorde Iesus Christ, god and man, art here wholle present in the Sacrament of the Aultare, where the fruit of euerlastinge health is had plenteouslie, as ofte as thou art worthilie and deuoutlie receaued. But if that shall be done fruitfullie, there maye be no lightnes, curiositie, nor sensualitie: but stedfast fayth, deuoute hope , and pure charitie. O God inuisible, maker of all the worlde: howe maruayloustye doest thou with vs, howe sweetelie, and howe gracioustie disposest thou all thinges to
thy

thy chosen people, to whom thou offerest thy selfe to be taken in this glozious Sacrament? Certainlie it surmounteth all vnderstandinge, and it draweth the hartes, and kindleth the affection of all deuout men. The true faythfull people that dispose all their life to amendement, receaue ofte times through this glozious Sacrament great grace and deuotion, and great loue of vertue. O meruaylous and secretlie hid is the grace of this Sacrament, the which faythfull people of Christ doe onelie knowe: for infidels, and they that liue in sinne, maye haue thereof no maner of experience. In this Sacrament spirituall grace is geuen, and the vertue that was lost in their soule is repayred, and the beautie that was deformed through sinne, returneth agayne: and the grace of this Sacrament sometime is so much, that of the fulnes of deuotion that commeth thereby, not onelie the minde, but also the feeble bodye recouer their former strength. But verilye, it is greatlie to be sorowed, that we be so slowe and negligent, and that we be stirred with no moze affection to receyue Christ then we be, for in him standeth all merite and hope of them that shall be saued. He is our health and our redemption, he is the comfortour of all that liue in this woe, and the eternall rest of all Saintes in heauen. And it is also

N iij　　　　greatly

greatly to be sorowed, that so many take
so litle heede of this high misterie, which
gladdeth the heauen, and preserueth all
the world. Alas the blindnes and hardnes
of mans hart, that taketh no greater
heede to so noble a gifte, but by the dayly
vsing thereof is negligent, and taketh
litle heede thereto. If this blessed Sacrament were ministred onelie in one place,
& consecrate but by one priest in the world,
with how great desire, thinkest thou, the
people would runne to that place, and to
that Priest, that they myght see there
these heauenlie misteries? Nowe there be
manye priestes, and Christe is offred in
many places, that the grace and loue of
God to man maye appeare so muche the
more, as the holie communion is spreade
the more abrode throughout the worlde,
thankinges be to thee therefore, my Lord
Jesu, that thou vouchsafe to refresh vs
poore outlawes with thy precious blood
and to stir vs with the wordes of thine
owne mouth to receiue this holie
misterie, sayinge, come ye all
to me that labour and
be charged, and I
shall refresh you.

That

That the great goodnes and charitie of God is geuen to man in this blessed Sacrament.

The second Chapter.

My Lorde Iesu, trustinge in thy great goodnes & mercye I come to the, as a sicke man to him that shall heale him, and as he that is hungrye & thirstie to the fountayne of life, that is needie, to the Kinge of heauen, as a seruaunt to his Lord, a creature to his creator, and as a desolate perso to his meeke and blessed comfortour. But howe is it that thou commest to me? who am I that thou wilt geue thy selfe vnto me? howe dare I a sinner appeare before thee? and howe is it that thou wilt vouchsafe to come to so simple a creature? Thou knowest thy seruant, and seest well that he hath no goodnes of him selfe, whereby thou shouldest geue this grace vnto him. I confesse therefore mine owne vnworthines, and I knowledge thy goodnes, I prayse thy pietie, and yeelde thee thankings for thy great charitie. Verily thou doest all this for thine owne goodnes, & not for my merites, that thy goodnes may therby the more appeare, & thy charitie the more largelie be shewed, and thy meekenes the more highlie be commēded. Therefore because this pleaseth thee,

N. iiij.   and

and thou hast commaunded that it shoulde
thus be done, thy goodnes and therein
pleaseth me: and woulde to God that
mine iniquities resisted me not. O my
Lorde Iesu, howe great reuerence and
thankinges, with perpetuall praysinges
of thy name, ought to be geuen thee for
the receyuinge of thy holie bodie, whose
dignitie no man is able to expresse? But
what shall I thinke in this communion,
and in goeinge to my Lorde God, whom
I can not worship as I ought to doe, and
yet I desire to receyue him deuoutly. But
what may I think better or more health-
full to me, then whollie to meeke my selfe
before thee, exaltinge thy infinite goodnes farre aboue me. I laude thee my Lord
God, and shall exalt thee euerlastinglie,
I despise my selfe, and submit me to thee,
and sorowe greatlie the deepenes of mine
iniquitie. Thou arte the Saint of all
Saints, and I am the filth of all sinners,
and yet thou enclinest thy selfe to me,
that am not worthye to looke towarde
thee. Thou commest to me, thou wilt be
with me, thou biddest me to thy feast,
thou wilt geue me this heauenly meate,
and this Angelles foode to eate, which
is playnlye none other but thy selfe that
art the liuely bread which descendest from
heauen, and geuest lyfe to the worlde.
Beholde Lorde from whence all this loue
proceedeth, and howe great goodnes shineth

neth vpon vs,and howe great thankes &
prayses are due to thee therfore. O howe
heithful and howe profitable a counsayle
was it whē thou ordeinedst this glorious
Sacrament:and how sweete and ioyous
a feast was it when thou gauest thy selfe
as meat to be eaten? O Lorde howe mer-
uailous is thy worke, howe mightie is
thy vertue, and howe farre vnspeakable
is thy trueth? By thy worde all thinges
were made,and all thinges were done as
thou hast commaunded. It is a meruaylous thinge & worthy to be beleeued,and
farre aboue the vnderstandinge of man,
that thou Lorde that art God and very
man,art wholly conteyned vnder a litle
likenes of bread and wine,and art eaten
without consuminge,of him that taketh
thee : and that thou that art Lorde of all
thinges,and that needest nothing in this
world, wouldest by this glorious Sacrament dwell in vs,kepe thou mine heart &
my body immaculate, that in a glad and
a pure conscience I may ofte times cele-
brate thy misteries, and receiue them to
my euerlastinge health,which thou haste
ordeined most speciallye to thy honour &
perpetuall memory. O my soule be thou
mery and glad for so noble a gift , and so
singuler a cōfort left to thee in this vale
of misery,for as ofte as thou remembrest
this mistery,& takest the body of Christe,
so ofte thou workest the worke of thy re-

R v   dēption

demption, and art made partaker of all
the merites of Christ. Truely the charitie
of Christ is neuer minished, & the great=
nes of his mercy is neuer consumed, and
therefore thou oughtest alwaye with a
newe renewing of minde to dispose thee
to it, and with a well aduised and a deepe
consideration to thinke on this great
mysterie of health. It shoulde seeme to
thee as newe, and as pleasaunt a ioy and
comfort when thou singest masse, or hea=
rest it, as if Christe the same daye first en=
tred into the wombe of the virgin, and
were made man, or if he the same daye
suffered and dyed vppon the Crosse, for
the health of mankinde.

That it is very profitable ofte to be houseled.

The. 3. Chapter.

ORde I come to the to thede
that it maye be weil with me
through thy gifte, and that
I maye ioye at the holy feast
that thou of thy great good=
nes haste made redy for me. In thee is all
that I may or shoulde desire, for thou art
my health & my redemption, my hope, my
strength, my honour and glorie. Make me
thy seruant this daye mery and glad in
thee, for I haue lifte my soule vnto thee,
nowe I desire deuoutlie and reuerentlie
to receiue thee into mine house, that I
may

may deserue with zeale to be blessed of thee, and to be accompanied amonge the children of Abraham. My soule coueteth to receiue thy body, my hart desireth to be vnited with thee, betake thy selfe to me Lord and it sufficeth, for without thee there is no comfort, nor without thee I may not be, nor without thy visitation I may not liue, and therefore it behoueth me ofte times to goe to thee, and for my health to receiue thee, leste happilye if I should be defrauded from that heauenlie meat I should faile in the waye. So thou sayedst thy selfe, moste mercifull Iesu, as thou were preaching to the people, & healedst them of their sicknesses: I will not let the returne into their houses fasting, lest they fayle by the waye. Doe with me therefore in like maner, that hast left thy selfe in this glorious Sacrament for the comfort of all faithfull people. Thou art onely the true refection of the soule, and he that worthily eateth thee shall be partaker and heire of eternal glorie: it is necessarie to me that so oft do offende, so soone waxe dull and slowe, that by ofte prayers and confessions I may renewe my selfe, purifie my selfe, and kindle my selfe to quicknes & feruour of spirite, lest happily by long abstaining I might fall from that holy purpose: for the wittes of man and woman be from their youth proude and readie to euil, and but this heauenly medi-

ne Medicine do helpe, man maye alwaye
fall to worse and worse, therefore this
holy communion draweth a man trom
euill, and comforteth him in goodnes. If
I nowe be ofte times so negligent and
slouthfull when I am cōmaunded, what
should I be if I receiued not that blessed
medicine nor sought not for that great
helpe? And though I be not euery daye
apte nor disposed to receyue my Creator:
neuerthelesse I shall take heede to receyue him in times conuenient, so that I
maye be partaker of so great a grace, for
it is one of the moste principall consolations to a faithfull soule, that is to saye,
that as long as he is as a pilgrime in
this mortall bodye, that he ofte remember his Lorde God, and receyue him that
is his onely beloued aboue all thinges. It
is a maruellous goodnes of the great pitie that thou Lorde haste against vs, that
thou Creatour and geuer of lyfe to all
spirites, vouchestsafe to come to a poore
creature, and with thy godhead & man-
hood to refresh his hunger and neede. O
happie is that man, and blessed is that
soule that deserueth deuoutlie to receiue
his Lorde God, and in that receiuinge to
be fulfilled with a spirituall ioy. O howe
great a Lorde doth he receiue? howe welbeloued a gest doth he bringe into his
house? howe ioyous a felowe doth he receiue? howe faithfull a freende doth he
accept

accept? howe noble a ſpouſe doth he im=
brace that receiueth thee? For thou art
onelie to be beloued before all other, and
aboue all thinges. Let heauen and earth,
and all the ornamentes of them be ſtill in
thy preſence, for whatſoeuer they haue
worthy laude or praiſe, they haue that of
the larges of thy gift: and yet they maye
not be lyke to the honour and glorie of
thy name, of whoſe wiſedome there is no
number nor meaſure.

That many commodities be geuen to them,
that deuoutly receaue this holye
Sacrament.

The 4. Chapter.

My Lorde God, preuent thy
ſeruant with the bleſſinges
of thy ſweetenes, that he
may deſerue to go reuerent=
ly and deuoutly to this high
Sacrament. Stirre vp my
hart into a full beholdinge of thee, and
deliuer me from the great ſlouth and
ydlenes that I haue bene in in time paſ=
ſed: biſite me in thy goodnes, and geue
me grace to taſte inwardlie in my ſoule,
the ſweetnes that is hid ſecretlie in this
bleſſed Sacramēt, as in a moſt plenteous
fountaine. Illumine alſo mine eyes to ſee
and beholde ſo great a miſterie, & ſtreng=
then

then me, that I maye alwaye faythfullie
and undoubtedly beleeue it: for it is thy
operation, and not the power of man, thy
holie institutiō, and not mans inuention.
And therefore to take and to vnderstand
these thinges, no man is sufficient of him
selfe, and they also ouerpasse the subtility
of all Angels and heauenlye spirites.
What may I then moste vnworthy sinner, earth and ashes searche and talke of
so high a secret, but onelye that in simplenes of hart, in a good stable fayth, and
by thy commaundement I come to thee
with meeke hope and reuerence, and beleue verily, that thou art here present in
this Sacrament God and man? Thou
wilt therefore, that I shall receaue thee,
and knit my selfe to thee in perfecte charitie. Wherefore I aske thee mercy, and
desire, that thou geue me thy special grace, that I maye from henceforth be fully
molten, and relented into thee, flowe in
thy loue, and neuer after to intermit my
selfe with any other comfort. This moste
high and moste worthy Sacrament is the
life of the soule and body, the medicine of
all spirituall sicknes, wherby all vices be
cured, passions refrayned, temptations
ouercome and diminished: the greater
grace is sent, vertue increased, and faith
stablished, hope strengthed, and charitie
kindled and spread abroade. Thou haste
geuen, and ofte times geuest manye great
g025es

giftes by this Sacrament to thy beloued
seruantes that deuoutly receaue thee, for
thou thereby art the stronge vpholder of
my soule, the repairer of all the infirmi=
ties of man, and the geuer of all inward
consolation, and of comfort in tribulation:
and from thee deepnes of their owne de=
tection thou raysest them againe into a
strong hope of thy preseruation, and re=
newest them, and lightest them inward=
lie with a newe grace, so that they that
felte them selues before receauing of that
blessed Sacrament, heauy and without
affection, after when they haue recea=
ued it, haue founde them selues chan=
ged into a great ghostly feruour. And all
this thou doest to thy elect people of thy
great goodnes, that they may see and
knowe openlye by experience, that they
haue nothing of them selues, but that all
grace and goodnes that they haue, they
haue receaued of thee, for of them selues
they be colde, dull and vndeuoute, and
by thee they be made feruent, quicke in
spirite, and deuout folowers of thy will:
who maye go meekly to the fountaine of
sweetnes, but that he shall bringe awaye
with him great plentie of sweetnes? or
who may stande by a great fyre, but he
shall feele great heate thereof? and thou
Lorde arte the fountaine of all sweet=
nes, and the fyre alwayes brenning, and
neuer faylinge, and therefore, though. I
                                        maye

maye not drawe the fulnes of that fountaine, nor drinke thereof to the full, I
shall neuerthelesse put my mouth to the
hole of the heauenlie pipe, that I maye
take some litle droppe thereof to refresye
my thirst,so that I be not all dried away.
And though I be not all heauenlye and
brenninge in charitie, as the Seraphins
and Cherubins be, neuerthelesse I shall
endeuoz me to set my selfe to deuotion,
and to prepare mine heart, that I maye
get some litle sparcle of the brenninge of
heauenlie life, through the meeke rece-
uing of this liuely Sacramēt:and whatsoeuer wanteth in me, I beseeche thee my
Lozde Iesu,most holie & blessed,that thou
beninglye and gratiouslie supplie in me:
for thou haste vouchedsafe to call all to
thee, saying:Come ye all to me that labour and be charged, and I shall refreshe
you. I labour in the sweate of my bodie,
and am tormented with the sorowe of
mine heart, and charged with sinnes,
trauayled with temptations, intriked
and oppressed with many euill passions,
and there is none that may helpe,or that
maye deliuer me, ne that maye make me
safe, but thou Lozde God my onely Sauiour, to whome I commit me and all
mine, that thou kepe me, and lead me
into life euerlastinge:accept me and take
me into the laude & glozye of thy name,
that haste ozdeyned to me thy bodie and
                                    bloud

bloud to be my meate and drinke: and graunt me Lorde, I beseech thee, that by the ofte receauinge of thy high misterie, the feruour of deuotion maye daylie increase in me.

Of the vvorthines of the Sacrament of the Aultar, and of the state of priesthood.

The. 5. Chapter.

IF thou haddest the puritie of Angels, and the holines of S. John Baptist, thou shouldest not for that be worthie to receaue nor touche this holy Sacrament: for it is not graunted for the merites of man, that a man shoulde consecrate and touche the Sacrament of Christe, and take to his meate the breade of Angels. It is a great misterie, and it is a great dignitie of priests, to whome it is graunted, that is not graunted to Angels, for priests onely that be duely ordeined in the Church, haue power to singe Masse, and to consecrate the bodye of Christ: for a priest is the minister of God, vsinge the worde of consecration, by the commaundement and ordinance of God: and God is there the principall doer, and the inuisible worker, to whom is subiect all that he willeth, and all obeyeth to that he commaundeth. Thou oughtest therefore more to beleeue almightie God

in

in this moste excellent Sacrament, then thine owne will, or any other visible toke or signe. And therefore with breade and reuerēce it is to go to this blessed worke. Take heede then diligentlie, and see from whēce this mistery and seruice commeth that is geuen vnto thee by the touchinge of the handes of the bishop. Thou arte nowe made a priest, and art consecrate to sing Masse. Take heede therefore, that thou faithfullye and deuoutlye offer thy sacrifice to God in due time, and that thou keepe thy selfe without reproufe, thou haste not made thy burden more light, but thou arte nowe bounde in a straiter bonde of discipline, and of muche more high perfection then thou were before. A priest ought to be adorned with all vertues, and to geue other example of good life: his conuersation shoulde not be with the common people, nor in the common waye of the worlde, but with Angels in heauen, or with perfect men in earth, that be best disposed to serue God. A priest also clothed in holye vestimentes beareth the place of Christ, that he should humblie and meekly praye to our Lorde for him selfe, & for all the people: he hath before him and behinde him the signe of the Crosse of Christ, that he shoulde diligently remember his passion: he beareth before him the Crosse, that he maye diligently behould & see the steppes of Christ,

and

and study feruentlye to folow them, and behinde him also he is signed with the Crosse, that he should gladly and meekly suffer all aduersities for the loue of God: he beareth the Crosse before him, that he shoulde bewayle his owne sinnes, and he beareth it behinde hym, that he maye through compassion beweepe the sinnes of other, and knowe him selfe to be set as a meane betwene God and al the people, and not to cease of prayer and holye oblation, til he maye deserue of almighty God mercy & grace. When a priest saith Masse, he honoreth God, he maketh Angels glad, he edifieth the Churche, he helpeth the people that be a liue, and geueth rest to them that be deade, and maketh him selfe partaker of all good dedes.

Of the invvarde remembraunce and exercise that a man ought to haue afore the receauinge of the bodye of Christe.

The 6. Chapter.

LORDE, when I thinke of thy worthines, and of my great filthines, I tremble stronglie, and am cōfounded in my selfe: for if I receaue thee not, I flie the eternall life: and if I vnworthylie receaue thee, I runne into thy wrath. What shall I then do my good Lorde, my helper, my protectour, comforter, and right sure Counsailer in all my necessities

ties? Teache me (good Lorde) the right
waye, and purpose vnto me some readie
exercise conuenable to the receauinge of
this holye misterie, for it is necessarye
vnto me, & greatlie profitable to knowe,
howe deuoutlie and reuerentlie I ought
to prepare mine heart to receaue it, or to
consecrate so great and so goodlie a Sacrifice as it is.

*Of the discussing of our ovvne conscience, and
of the purpose of amendment.*

The 7. Chapter.

IT behoueth thee aboue all
thinges with soueraigne reuerence and profounde meeknes of hart, and with full
fayth, and humble intent (to
the honour of God) to cele-
brate, take and receaue this holie Sacrament, examine diligentlie thy conscience
by true contrition and meeke confession,
and make it cleane after thy power, so
that thou know nothing that greueth or
biteth thy conscience, or that may let thee
to go frelie vnto it: haue displeasure of
all thy sinnes in generall, & for thy daylie
excesses and offences haue sighinges and
sorowinges more speciall. And if the time
will suffer it, confesse vnto God in secrete
of thine heart the miseries of all thy
passions, weepe and sorowe, that thou
art

art yet so carnall and worldly, so vnmor-
tified from thy passions, so full of motiõs
of concupiscences, so vnware, and so euill
ordred in thy outward wits, so oft wrapped in vayne phantasies, so muche inclined to outwarde and worldlie thinges,
so negligent to inwarde thinges, so redie
to laughinge and dissolution, so harde to
weepinge and compunction, so readie to
easie thinges, and to that that is likinge
to the fleshe: so slowe to penance & seruor
of spirite, so curious to heare newe thinges, and to see fayre thinges, so lothe to
meeke and abiect thinges, so couetous to
haue muche, so scarse to geue, so glad to
holde, so vnaduised in speakinge, so in-
continent to be still, so euill ordred in maners, so importune in deedes, so greedie
vpon meate, so deafe to the word of God,
so quicke to rest, so slowe to laboure, so
attentiue to fables, so sleepye to holye
vigils, so hastie to thende, so vnstable to
take heede to the waye to the ende, so
negligent in the seruice of God, so dull
and so vndeuout to go to Masse, so drye
in thy housell, so soone fallen at large to
outwarde thinges, so seldome gathered
together to inwarde thinges, so soone
moued to anger and wrath, so lightlye
stirred to the displeasure of other, so readie to iudge, so rigorous to reproue, so
glad in prosperitie, so feeble in aduersitie,
so ofte purposinge many good thinges,
                                                    and

and so seldome bringinge them to effecte.
And when thou haste thus confessed and
bewept all these defaults and such other
like in thee, with great sorowe and displeasure of thine owne fraylenes, set thee
then in a full purpose to amende thy life,
and to profite alwaye from better to better, and then with a full resigninge and a
wholle will offer thy selfe into the honour of my name in the Aulter of thy
hart, as sacrifice to me, that is to saye,
faythfullie committinge to me both thy
bodie and soule, so that thou mayest be
worthye to offer to me this high sacrifice, and to receyue healthfullie the Sacrament of my holie bodie, for there is no
oblation more worthie, nor satiffaction
greater to put awaye sinne, then a man
to offer him selfe purelie and whollie to
God, with the offeringe of the bodie of
Christ in masse and in holie communion.
If a man doe that in him is, and is truelie penitent as ofte as he commeth to me
for grace and forgiuenes, I am the
Lorde that sayth, I will not the
death of a sinner, but rather that
he be conuerted to liue, and I
shall no more remember his
sinnes, but they all shall
be forgeuen and pardo-
ned vnto hym.

Ff

*Of the oblation of Chriſte on the Croſſe, and
of a full forſakinge of our ſelfe.*

The 8.Chapter.

Ur Loꝛde Ieſus ſayth to his
ſeruant thus: As I hanginge
all naked with mine armes
ſpꝛead abꝛoad vpon the croſſe,
offered my ſelfe to God the
father foꝛ thy ſinnes, ſo that nothinge
remayned in me, but that all went in ſa=
crifice to pleaſe my Father, and to appea=
ſe his wꝛath agaynſt mankinde: ſo thou
oughteſt to offer thy ſelfe freelie to God
as muche as thou mayeſt, in a pure and
holie oblation daylie in the Maſſe with
all thy power and affection. What re=
quire I moꝛe of thee, then that thou
ſhouldeſt ſtudie whollie to reſigne thy
ſelfe vnto me? foꝛ whatſoeuer thou geueſt
beſide thy ſelfe I regarde it not, foꝛ I
looke not foꝛ thy giftes, but foꝛ thee. Foꝛ
as it ſhoulde not ſuffiſe to thee to haue
all thinges beſide me, ſo it maye not plea=
ſe me whatſoeuer thou geue beſide thy
ſelfe. Offer thy ſelfe to me, and geue thy
ſelfe all to God, and thy oblation ſhall
be acceptable. Lo I offered my ſelfe whol=
lye to my father foꝛ thee, and I gaue my
bodye and bloude to thy meate, that
I ſhoulde be all whollie thine, and
thou mine. But if thou haue a truſt in thy
ſelfe, and doeſt not freelye offer thee to
my

my will, thy oblation is not pleasinll, and there shall be betwene us no perfect vnitie. Therefore a free offeringe of thy selfe into the handes of God, must go before all thy workes, if thou wilte obteine grace and the true libertie. Therefore it is that so fewe be inwardlie illuminate and free, because they can not wholye forsake them selfe (for my words be true) but a man renounce him selfe he may not be my disciple. Offer thy selfe fullie to me with all thine affection and loue. Amen.

That vve ought to offer our selfe and all ours to God, and to praye for all people.

The 9. Chapter.

LOrde all thinges be thine that be in heauen & earth. I desire to offer my selfe to thee in a free and perpetual oblation, so that I may perpetuallie be with thee. Lord in simplenes of hart I offer me this daye to thee to be thy seruant in the seruice & sacrifice of laude perpetuall, accept me with this oblation of thy precious bodye which I this daye offer to thee in the presence of thy holie Angels that be here present inuisible, that it maye be to my health, and to the health of all the people. And Lorde I offer to thee all my sinnes and offences that I haue committed before

fore thee and thy holie Angels fro the
daye that I might first offende vnto this
daye, that thou vouchesafe through thy
great charitie to put away all my sinnes,
& to clense my cōscience of all mine offen=
ces, and restore to me agayne the grace
that I through sinne haue lost, and that
thou forgeue me all thinges past, and re=
ceyue me mercifullie into a blessed kissing
of peace and forgeuenes. What may I
do then but meekelie cōfesse and bewaile
my sinnes, and continuallie aske mercye
of thee: forgeue me mercifull Lorde I be=
seeche thee, for all my sinnes displeale me
muche, and I will neuer commit them
againe, but sorow for them, readie to doe
penance and satisfactiō after my power.
Forgeue me Lorde, forgeue me my sinnes
for thy holie name, saue my soule that
thou hast redeemed with thy precious
bloode. I commit my selfe whollie vnto
thy mercie, I resigne me whollie into
thy handes, doe with me after thy good=
nes, and not after my malice and wret=
chednes. I offer also to thee all my good
deedes, though they be verie fewe and
imperfect, that thou amende them, and
sanctifie them, and make them likinge
and acceptable to thee, and alwaye make
them better and better, and that thou
bringe me, though I be a slowe and an
vnprofitable person, to a blessed and a
laudable ende. I offer also to thee all the
D   desires

desires of deuout persons, the necessitie of mine dungeoners, succenders, brother, suster, and of all my louers, and of all them that for thy loue haue done good to me or to any other, & that haue desired & asked me to praye, or to doe sacrifice for them or for their freendes, whether they be a-liue or deade, that they maye the rather feele the helpe of thy grace, and the gifte of thy heauenlie consolation, thy protec-tion from all perils, and the deliuerance from all payne, and that they so beinge deliuered from all euils, may in spirituall gladnes yeelde to thee high laude and praysinges. I offer to thee also my prayer and my peaceable offeringe, for all them that haue in any thinge hindred me, or made me heauy, or that haue done me any hurt or greeue: and for all them also whom I haue at anye time made heauy, troubled, greued, or slaundered, in worde or deede, wittinglye or ignorantlye, that thou forgeue vs altogether our sinnes and offences againft thee, and of eche of vs againft other, and that thou Lorde take fro our heartes all suspition and indignation, wrath, variance, and whatsoeuer may let charitie, or diminish fraternall loue, that eche of vs shoulde haue to other: haue mercie Lorde, haue mercie on all them that aske thee mercie, and geue grace to them that haue neede, and make vs to ftande in suche case, that we

we be worthye to haue thy grace, and
finallye to come to the lyfe euerlastinge.
Amen.

*That the holye Communion is not light-
lye to be forborne.*

The.10.Chapter.

IT behoueth thee to runne
ofte to the fountayne of grace and mercye, and to the
fountaine of all goodnes and
puritie, that thou mayest be
healed from thy passiōs and
vices, and be made more stronge agaynst
all the temptations and deceytfull crafte
of our enemie. The fiende knowinge the
greatest fruit, and highest remedie to be
in receauinge of this blessed Sacrament,
inforceth him by all the wayes that he
can, to let and withdrawe all faythfull
and deuout people from it as muche as
he can: and therefore some men, whē they
dispose them selues to it, haue more greater temptations then they had before: for
as it is written in Job, the wicked spirit
commeth amonge the children of God,
that he maye by his olde malice and wickednes trouble them, or make them ouermuch fearefull and perplexed, so that he
maye diminishe their affection, or take
awaye their fayth, if happilie he maye
thereby make them eyther vtterlye to
O ij   ceasse

ceasse from beinge houseled, or els that
they goe to it with litle deuotion. But it
is not any thing to care for al his craftes
and phantasies, howe vyle and vgglye
soeuer they be, but all phantasies are to
be throwen agayne at is owne head, and
he so far to be despised, that for all his
assaults and commotions that he can stirre
vp, the holy communion be not omitted.
Sometime ouer much curiousnes to haue
deuotion, or ouer great doubt of making
confession, letteth muche this holye purpose. Doe therefore after the counsayle of
wise men, and put awaye all doubtfulnes
and scrupulousnes, for they let the grace
of God, and destroy whollie the deuotion
of the minde. Also it is not good that for
any litle trouble or griefe, that thou leaue
this holie worke, but go lightlie and be
confessed and forgeue gladlye all that
haue offended thee. And if thou haue offé-
ded any other, meekelie aske of them for-
geueues, and God shall right mercifully
forgeue thee. What profiteth it longe to
tarie from confession, or to deferre this
holie Communion? Purge thee first, and
quickelie cast out thy venim, and haste
thee after to take the medicine, and thou
shalt feele more profite thereby, then yf
thou tariedst longer for it. If thou deferre
it to daye for this thinge or that, to morowe may happen to come a greater, and
so thou mayest be let longe from thy good
                                    purpose

purpose, and be made afterwarde more
vnapt vnto it. Therfore as soone as thou
canst, discharge thy selfe from suche heauines and dulnes of minde, and fro all
slouth, for it nothing profiteth long to
be anguished, long to go with trouble, &
to sequester him selfe for suche dayly ob-
stacles, fro the diuine misteries: but it
doeth great hurt, and comonly bringeth
in greath slouth, and lacke of deuotion.
But alas for sorowe, some slouthfull and
dissolute persons gladlye seeke causes to
tarye from confession, and so defer the
longer this holye Communion: and that
they doe, to the intent that they shoulde
not be bounde to geue them selues to any
more sure kepinge of them selues in time
to come, then they haue done before. But
alas, howe litle charitie, and slender deuotion haue they that so lightly leaue of
so holie a thing, & howe happie is he, and
howe acceptable to God that so liueth,
and that so keepeth his conscience in such
cleannes, that he is euerie daye readie, &
hath good affection to be housled, if it
were lawfull vnto him, & that he might
doe it without note or slaunder? He that
sometime abstaineth of meekenes, or for
any other lawfull impediment, is to be
praysed for his reuerence, but yf it be
through slouthfulnes, he ought to quicken him selfe, and to doe that in him is,
and our Lorde shall strengthen his desire

for his good will, for to a good will our
Lorde hath alwaye a speciall respect, and
when he is lawfullie let, he shall haue a
good will and a meeke intent to it, and
so he shall not want the fruite of the Sacrament. And verilie euerie deuout man
maye euerye daye, and euerye houre go
healthfullie, and without prohibition
vnto the spirituall Communion of Christe,
that is to saye, in remembringe of his
passion, and neuerthelesse, in certaine
dayes and times he is bounde to receaue
Sacramentally the bodie of his Redemer
with a great reuerēce: and rather to pre-
tende therein the laude and honour of
God, then his owne consolation. For so
ofte a man is housled misticallye and
inuisibly, as he remembreth deuoutly the
misterie of the incarnation of Christ, and
his passion, and is thereby kindled into
his loue. He that doeth prepare him selfe
for none other cause, but because the feast
is comminge, or the custome compelleth
him therto, he shall commonlie be vnready
to it. Blessed is he therefore, that as ofte
as he sayth Masse, or is housled, offereth
him selfe vnto our Lorde in holie Sacrifice. Be not in sayinge Masse ouer longe,
nor ouer short, but keepe the good common waye, as they doe with whom thou
liuest: for thou oughtest not to do that
shoulde greeue other, or make them tedious, but to keepe the common waye,
                                        after

after the ordinance of the holie fathers, and rather to confirme thy selfe to that that shall be profitable to other, then to folowe thine owne deuotion, or priuate pleasure.

That the bodye of Chriſte and holye Scrip-
ture, are moſte neceſſarye for the
health of mans ſoule.

The.11.Chapter.

Moſte ſweeteſt Ieſu, howe great ſweetenes is it to a deuout ſoule, when he is fedde with thee at thy heauenlie feaſt, where there is none other meate brought forth to eate, but thou his onely beloued, and that art moſt deſirable to him, aboue all the deſires of his heart. And verilie it ſhoulde be ſweete and pleaſaunt to me, by an inwarde and meeke affection, to weepe before thee, and with the bleſſed woman Marie Magdalene, to waſhe thy feete with the teares of mine eyes. But where is that deuotion? where is that plenteous ſheddinge out of holie teares? Certainlie all my heart ought to brenne, and to weepe for ioye in the ſight of thee, and of thy holye Angels: for I haue thee verilye preſent with me, though thou be hid vnder another likeneſſe, for to behold

D iiij   thee

thee in thy proper and diuine cleerenes,
mine eyes might not beare it, neither all
the worlde might sustteyne to see thee in
the cleerenes and glorye of thy maiestie.
Therefore thou greatly helpest my weaknes, in that thou hidest thy selfe vnder
this blessed Sacrament. I haue him verily, & worship him, whom Angels worship
in heauen, but I onely in faith, and they
in open sight, and in thine owne likenes
without any couerture. It behoueth me
to be content in the light of true faith,
and therein to walke till the day of euerlasting cleerenes shall appeare, and that
the shadowe of figures shall go awaye.
When that that is perfect shall come, all
vse of Sacramentes shall ceasse, for they
that be blessed in the heauēly glorie, haue
no neede of this Sacramental medicine:
for they ioye without end in the presence
of God, beholding his glory face to face, &
so transsformed fro cleerenes to cleerenes of
the godhead, they tast the glorye of the
sonne of God made man, as he was in his
godhead fro the beginninge, and shall be
euerlasting. When I remember all these
maruailous comfortes, whatsoeuer solace
I haue in this world, though it be spiritual, it is greeuous and tedious vnto me,
for as longe as I see not my Lorde openlie in his glorie, I set it at naught al that
I see and heare in this world. Lord, thou
art my witnes, that nothing may cōfort
me

me, nor any creature maye quiet me, but
thou my Lorde God, whom I desire to
see and beholde eternally: but that is not
possible for me to doe, as longe as I shall
be in this mortall life. Wherefore it behoueth me to keepe my selfe in great patience, and to submit my selfe to thee in
euery thinge that I desire, for thy holye
Saintes that nowe ioy with thee, abode
in good fayth & patience all whiles they
liued here the comming of thy glory. That
they beleeued, I beleeue, that they hoped
to haue, I hope to haue, and thither as
they by thy grace be come, I trust to come, and till then I shall walke in faith, &
take comfort of the examples of the sayde
holy Saints. I haue also holie bookes for
my solace, as a spirituall glasse to looke
vpon, & aboue all these I haue for a singuler remedie thy holye bodye. I perceue
wel, that two thinges be much necessarie
vnto me in this worlde, without which
this miserable lyfe should be to me as importable: for as long as I shall be in this
body, I confesse my selfe to haue neede of
two things, that is to say, of meat & light.
These two hast thou geuen vnto me, that
is to saye, thy holy body to the refreshing
of my bodye and soule, and thou haste set
thy word as a lanterne before my feete,
to shewe me the waye that I shall go.
Without these two I may not wel liue,
for the worde of God is the light of my

O v   soule

foule, and this Sacrament is the breade
of my lyfe. These two may alfo be called
the two tables, fet here & there in the fpi-
ritual treafure of holy Church: The one is
the table of the holy Aultar, hauinge this
holie bread, that is the precious bodie of
Chrift: The other is the table of the lawes
of God, conteining the holie doctrine of
the lawe of God, and inftructing man in
the right fayth, and in the true beliefe,
leadinge him into the inwarde fecrettes
that be called Sancta Sanctorum, where
the inwarde fecrettes of Scripture be
hid and conteyned. I yeelde thankinges
to thee my Lorde Iefu, the brightnes of
the eternal light, for this table of holie
doctrine the which thou haft miniftred to
vs by thy feruauntes, Prophetes, & Apo-
ftles, and other doctours: and thankings
alfo be to thee the creator & redeemer of
mankinde, that thou to fhewe to all the
worlde the greatnes of thy charitie, pre-
paredft a great fupper, in the which thou
fetteft not forth the Lambe figured in the
olde lawe, but thy holy body and bloude
to be eaten, gladding thereby in that holy
feaft all faithfull people, and geuing them
to drinke of thy chalice of health, in the
which be conteyned all the delightes of
Paradife, where Angels eate with vs
with much more plenteous fweetenes. O
howe great and howe honourable is the
office of Prieftes, to whom is geuē power
to

to consecrate with the holye wordes of
consecration, the Lorde of all maiestie, to
blesse him with their lippes, to holde him
in their handes, to receiue him into their
mouthes, and to minister him to other. O
howe cleane shoulde the handes be, howe
pure a mouth, howe holye a bodye, and
howe vndefiled shoulde be the heart of a
Priest, to whom so ofte entreth the authour of al cleannes? Truely there ought
to procede from the mouth of a priest
that so ofte receaueth the Sacrament of
Christes bodie, no worde but that is holy,
honest, and profitable, his eyes should be
full simple and chaste, that vse to behold
the bodie of Christe, & his handes shoulde
be full pure, & lifte vp into heauen, which
vse to touche the Creatour of heauen and
earth: and therefore it is speciallye sayde
in the lawe to Priestes, be ye holye, for I
your Lord God am holy. O God almightie, thy grace be with vs, and helpe vs
that haue receiued the office of priesthood
that we may serue thee worthely and deuoutly in all puritie, and in a good conscience. And though we maye not liue in
so great innocecie as we ought to do, yet
geue vs grace at the least, that we maye
weepe and sorowe the euils that we haue
done, so that in spirituall meeknes,
and in full purpose of a good will
we may serue thee here-
after. Amen.

                              That

That he that shall be houseled ought to prepare hym selfe therto before with
great diligence.

The. 12. Chapter.

I Am the louer of al puritie, and
the liberall geuer of al holines.
I seeke a cleane heart, & there
is my restinge place, make ready for me a great chamber stra-
wed, that is thyne hart, and I with my
Disciples shall keepe mine Easter with
thee. If thou wilte that I shall come to
thee, and dwell with thee, clense thee of
all the olde filth of sinne, and clense also
the habitacle of thyne heart, and make it
pleasaunt and fayre. Exclude the worlde,
and all the clamorous noyse of sinne, and
sit solitarie, as a sparowe in an house ea-
singe, and thinke vpon all thy offences
with great bitternes of hart, for a true
louer will prepare to his beloued freende
the best and the fayrest place that he can,
for in that is knowen the loue and affection of him that receyueth his freende.
But neuerthelesse, I knowe that thou
mayest not of thy selfe suffise to make
this preparinge fullie, as it ought to be
in euerie point, though thou went about
it a wholle yere together, and haddest
none other thing in thy minde to thinke
vpon, but of my mercie and grace onely:
Thou

Thou art suffred to go vnto my table, as
if a poore man were called to the dinner
of a riche man, and he had none other
thinge to geue him againe, but onelie to
humble him selfe, and thanke him for it:
doe that in thee is, with thy best diligēce,
and doe it not onelie of custome, nor of
necessitie onely, for that thou art bounde
to it, but with dreade and reuerence and
great affection take the bodie of thy beloued Lorde God, that so louinglie vou-
chethsafe to come vnto thee. I am he that
hath called thee, I haue commaunded
that this thinge shoulde be done, I shall
supplie that wanteth in thee. Come therfore and receaue me, & when I geue thee
the grace of deuotion, yeelde thankes to
me therefore, not for that thou art worthy to haue it, but for that I haue shewed
my mercy louinglye to thee. And if thou
haue not the grace of deuotion through
receauinge of this Sacrament, but that
thou feelest thy selfe more drye, and more
vndeuout then thou were before, yet cō-
tinue still in thy prayer, wayle, weepe, &
and call for grace, and ceasse not, til thou
mayest receaue some litle drop of this
helthfull grace of deuotion. Thou haste
neede of me, and not I of thee, ne thou
commest not to sanctifie me, but I come
to sanctifie thee, and to make thee better
then thou were before. Thou commest to
be sanctified, and be vnited vnto me, and
that

that thou mayeſt receaue a newe grace,
and be kindled a newe to amendement.
Do not forget this grace, but alway with
all thy diligence prepare thine heart, and
bringe thy beloued vnto thee: and it behoueth thee not onelye to prepare thy
ſelfe vnto deuotion before thou ſhalt be
houſled, but alſo, to keepe thy ſelfe therein diligentlye after the receauinge of the
Sacrament. And there is no leſſe keeping
requiſite after, then a deuout preparatiõ
is needefull before: for a good keepinge
after is the beſt preparation to receaue
newe grace hereafter, and a man ſhall be
the more vndiſpoſed thereto, if he anone,
after he hath receaued the Sacrament,
geue him ſelfe to outward ſolace. Beware
of much ſpeakinge, abide in ſome ſecrete
place, and kepe thee with thy Lorde God,
for thou haſt him that all the worlde may
not take from thee. I am he, to whom
thou muſt geue all, ſo that fro henceforth
thou liue not in thy ſelfe, but onely in me.

*That a deuout ſoule ſhoulde greatlye deſire
vvith all his heart to be vnited to Chriſte
in this bleſſed Sacrament.*

The. 13 Chapter.

Who ſhal graũt vnto me (Lord
that I maye finde thee onelie,
and opẽ all mine heart to thee,
and haue thee, as mine heart
deſireth

defireth, fo that no man maye deceaue me, no2 any creature moue me no2 d2awe me backe, but that thou onelie fpeake to me, and J to thee as a louer is wont to fpeake to his beloued, and a freende with his beloued freende? That is it that J p2aye fo2, that is it that J defire, that J may be whollie bnited to thee, and that J maye withd2aw my hart fro all things create, and th2ough the holie cõmunion, and ofte faying Maffe, to fauo2 and tafte eternall thinges. Ah Lo2de God, when fhall J be all bnited to thee, and whollie be molten into thy loue, fo that J wholly fo2get my felfe? Be thou in me, and J in thee: and graunt, that we maye fo abide alwaye together in one. Uerilie, thou art my beloued, elect and chofen befo2e all other, in whom my foule coueteth to abide all dayes of his life. Thou art the Lo2de of peace, in whom is the foueraine peace and true reft, without whom is labour and fo2owe, and infinite miferye. Uerilie thou art the head God, and thy counfayle is not with wicked people, but with meeke men, and fimple in heart. O howe fecrete and howe benigne is thy holy fpirite, which to the intẽt thou woldeft fhewe to thy chofen people thy fwetnes, hafte vouchedfafe to refrefhe them with the moft fwete b2ead that defcẽdeth from heauen Uerilie there is none other nation fo great, that hath their goddes

fo

in nigh vnto them, as thou Lorde God
art to all thy faithfull people, to whom
for their dayly solace, and to rayse their
heartes into the loue of heauenly things,
thou geuest thy selfe as meat and drinke.
O what people be there, that be so noble
as the christien men are? or what creature
vnder heauen is so muche beloued as the
deuout christien soule, into whom God
entreth, and feedeth her with his owne
glorious flesh and bloude? O inestimable
grace, O meruaillous worthines, O loue
without measure, singulerly shewed vnto
man: but what shall I yeelde againe to
God for all this grace and high charitie?
Truelie there is nothing more acceptable
to him, then that I whollye geue mine
heart, and inwardly ioyne my selfe vnto
him, & then shall all mine inward partes
ioye in him, when my soule is perfectlie
vnited vnto him. Then shall he say to me,
If thou wilte be with me, I will be with
thee: And I shall answere to him againe,
and say, Uouchesafe Lorde to abide with
me, and I will gladly abide with thee, for
that is all my desire, that mine heart
maye be fast knit vnto thee
without departinge.
Amen.

*Of the brenninge desire that some deuoute
persons haue had to the body of Christe.*

The 14. Chapter.

Owe great multitude of sweet=
nes is it Lorde that thou hast hid
for them that dreade thee? But
what is it that for them that loue
thee? Uerilie, when I remember me of
manye deuout persons that haue come to
this holie Sacrament with so great fer=
uoure of deuotiõ, I am then many times
astonied and cõfounded in my selfe, that
I go vnto thy aultar, and to the table of
thy holy communion so coldely, and with
so litle feruour, and that I abide still so
drie, and without any affection of hart,
and that I am not so whollie kindled be=
fore thee my Lorde God, nor so stronglie
drawen thereby in affection to thee as
manie deuout persons haue beene, the
which of the great desire that they haue
had to this holie communion, and for a
feeleable loue of hart that they haue had
therto, might not restrayne them from
weping, but effectuously with the mouth
of their heart and bodie together, opened
their mouthes to thee Lorde that art the
liuelie fountaine, because they coulde not
otherwise aswage, ne tempt their hũger,
but that they tooke thy holie body, which
they did with great ioye and spirituall
gredines. Truelie the great brenninge
　　　　　　　　　　　　　　fayth

ealth of them is a probable argument of
thy holy presence, and they allo knowe
verily their Lorde in breaking of breade,
whole heartes fo ftronglye brenneth in
them by the prefence of their Lorde Jefu,
facramentalive then walking with them.
But verily, fuch affection and deuotion,
and fo ftronge feruour and loue be ofte
time far from me. Be thou therefore moft
fwete and benigne Lorde Jefu, mercifull
and meeke vnto me, and graunt me thy
poore feruaunt, that I maye feele fometime fome litle part of the harty affection
of thy loue in this holy Communion, that
my fayth maye the more recouer and
amende, & mine hope through thy goodnes be the more perfect, and my charitie
being once perfectly kindled, and hauing
experience of the heauenlye Manna, doe
neuer fayle. Thy mercy (Lorde) is ftronge
ynough to graunt to me this grace, that
I fo muche defire : and when the time of
thy pleafure fhall come, beninglye to vi-
fite me with the fpirit of a brenninge feruour to thee. And though I doe not brenne in fo great defire as fuche fpeciall deuout perfons haue done, yet neuertheleffe, I haue defired the grace to be inflamed with that brenninge defire,
praying and defiring, that I maye
be made partaker of all fuch thy
feruent louers, and to be num-
bred in their holy companye.

That

That the grace of deuotion is gotten thorough meekenes, and forsakinge of our selfe.

The 15.Chapter.

It behoueth thee abidinglie to seeke the grace of deuotion, and without ceassing to aske it, patientlie and faithfullie to abide it, thankefullie to receaue it, meekelie to keepe it, studiouslie to worke with it, and whollie to committ to God the time and maner of his heauenlie visitation, till his pleasure shall be to come vnto thee: and principallie thou oughtest to meeke thee, when thou feelest but litle inward deuotion, but thou shalt not be ouermuche caste downe therfore, nor inordinatlie be heauie, for our Lorde geueth many times in a short moment, that he denied longe time before: he geueth also sometime in the ende, that in the beginninge of the prayer he deferred to graunt. If grace shoulde alwayes anone be graunted, and shoulde anone be present, after the will of the asker, it shoulde not be well able to be borne by a weake and feeble person, and therefore in a good hope and meeke patience the grace of deuotion is to be abiden and taried for, and thou oughtest to impute it to thy selfe and to thine owne sinnes, when grace is not geuen thee, or that it is secretlie taken from thee. Sometime it is but a litle thinge
that

that letteth grace or hideth it awaye,
if it maye be called litle, and not rather
great, that letteth and prohibiteth so
good a thinge, but whether it be litle or
great, if thou remoue it, and perfectlye
ouercome it, it shall be graunted vnto
thee that thou desirest, and forthwith as
thou betakest thy selfe with all thine hart
to God, and desirest neither this thinge
nor that for thine owne pleasure, but
whollye puttest thy will to his will, thou
shalt finde thy selfe vnited to him, and
set in a great inwarde peace, for nothing
shall sauour so well to thee, nor so muche
please thee, as that the will and pleasure
of God be fullie done in thee. Whoso-
euer therefore in a pure simple harte
lifteth his intent vp to God, and voyde
him selfe from all inordinate loue and
displeasure of any worldlye thinge, shall
be more apte to receiue grace, and shall be
best worthy to haue the gift of deuotion.
For there our Lorde geueth his blessinge
where he findeth the vessels empty and
voide. And the more perfectlye a man can
renounce him selfe & all worldly things, &
can by despising of him selfe the more die
to him selfe, so much the sooner grace shal
come, and shall the more plenteouslie enter into him, and the higher shall lifte vp
his hart into God. Then his harte shall
see and abounde, and shall maruelle and
be delated in him selfe, for the hande of

our

our Lord is with him, and he hath wholly put him into his hande for ever. Lo, so
shall a man be blessed that seeketh God
with all his hart, and taketh not his soule
in vaine. Suche a man in receiuinge this
holye Sacrament deserueth great grace
of the vniting in God, for he looketh not
to his owne deuotion and consolation,
but to the glorie and honour of God.

That vve shoulde open all our necessities
to Christe, and aske his grace.

The 16.Chapter.

MOste sweete Lorde, whom I
desire deuoutly to receiue, thou
knowest the infirmitie and necessitie that I am in, in howe
many sinnes and vices I lye,
howe ofte I am greeued, tempted, troubled, and defiled, I come to thee for remedie, and I make my prayer to thee for
comfort, & I speake to him that knoweth
all thinges, to whom all my secrete and
inward thoughtes be manifest and open,
and the which onelye mayest perfectlye
counsayle me & helpe me. Thou knowest
what I neede to haue, and howe poore I
am in vertue. Lo I stande before thee
poore & naked, askinge and desiringe thy
grace. Refresh me therefore thy poorest
seruaunt, begginge for spirituall foode,
kindle my hart with the fyre of thy loue,
                                    and

and illumine my blindnes with the cle=
rewes of thy pzouided: turne all wozldlye
thinges into bitternes to me , and all
greeuous thinges & contrarious thinges
into patience , and all create thinges
into despisinge, and into forgettinge of
them. Lifte vp myne harte to thee into
heauen, and suffer me not liue vaynlie,
nor to erre in this wozlde. Thou Lozde
from henceforth shalt be sweete to me for
euer, for thou art onelye my meate and
dzinke, my loue, my ioye, my sweetnes,
and all my goodnes: woulde God that
thou wouldest kindle me, enflame me,
and turne me wholye into thee , that I
maye be made one spirite with thee by
grace of inward vniting, and meltinge of
burning loue into thee: suffer me not to
depart from thee fadinge and dzye, but
wozke with me mercifullye, as thou haste
ofte times marueillouslye wrought with
thy beloued seruauntes in tyme paste.
What maruaile were it if I were all in=
flamed into thee, and fayled in my selfe,
sith thou art the fyre alwaye burning,
and neuer fayling, the loue puri=
fying the hartes, and light=
ning the vnderstanding
of all creatures.

Of the burninge loue and great affection that
vve shoulde haue to receyne Chryste.

The 17.Chapter.

With high deuotiõ and bur=
ninge loue,and with all fer=
uour and affection of the
hart,I desire to receiue thee
Lord,as many Saintes and
deuout persõs haue desired
thee in their communiõ.; & that most spe=
ciallie pleased thee in the holines of their
life,& were in most burninge deuotion to
thee.O my Lorde God,my loue eternall,
all my goodnes and felicitie without en=
dinge:I couet to receyue thee with as
great desire,& as due reuerẽce as any ho=
lie man euer did,or might do:& though I
be vnworthie to haue such feelinge in de=
uotiõ as they had,yet neuerthelesse I of=
fer to thee the whole affection of my hart
as vetille as if I onelie had all the bur=
ninge & flaminge desires that they had,&
ouer that,all that a meeke minde maye
imagine & desire,I giue and offer to thee
with high reuerẽce & worship,& inwarde
feruour:& I desire to reserue nothinge to
my selfe,but me and all mine I offer to
thee in sacrifice freely and most liberally.
And also my Lorde God , my creatour
and redeemer,with such affection , reue=
rence,laude and honour:with such than=
kes, dignitie and loue , and with suche
fayth

tayth, hope and puritie, I desire to receaue thee this daye, as thy most holie and glorious mother the virgin Marye desired and receaued thee, when sho meekely and deuoutlie answered the Angel that shewed her the misterie of thy incarnation, and sayde: Ecce ancilla domini, fiat secundum verbum tuum, that is to saye, Loe, I am the hand mayd of God, be it done to me after thy worde: and as thy blessed precursour Saint John the Baptist, moste excellent of all Saintes, was glad, and ioyed in great ioye in the holie ghost through thy presence, when he was yet in his mothers wombe, And after when he saw thee walkinge amonge the people, verie meekelie, and with deuout affection he sayde: The freend of a spouse that standeth and heareth, ioyeth with great ioye to heare the voyce of the spouse: and so couete I in great and holie desires to be inflamed, and to present my selfe to thee with all mine heart, and also I offer and yeelde to thee all the laudes of deuout heartes, the brenninge affectiõs, excessiue thoughtes, spirituall illuminations, and heauenlie visions, with all vertues and praysinges, done, or to be done by any creature, in heauẽ or in earth for me, and for all them that be cõmitted to my prayer, that thou mayest be worthilie lauded and glorified for euer. Accept Lorde God my minde, and the desires of the manifolde laudes and

and bleſſinges,that by me are to thee due
of right,after the multitude of thy greatnes, more then can be ſpoken. And all
theſe I yelde to thee, and deſire to yelde
to thee euerye daye,and euerye moment,
and with all my deſire and affection
meekelye exhort and praye all heauenlye
ſpirites and all faythfull people, to yelde
with me thankinges and laudes to thee.
And I beſeeche thee that all people, tri-
bes and tonges maye magnifie thy holye
and moſte ſweete name with great ioye
and brenning deuotion,and that all they
that reuerentlie and deuoutlye miniſter
this moſte high Sacrament, or with full
faith receyue it, maye thereby deſerue to
finde before thee thy grace and mercy:
and when they haue obteyned the deuotion that they deſired, and be ſpiri-
tuallye vnited to thee , and be thereby
well comforted and maruelouſlye
refreſhed,and be departed from
thy heauenly table,that they
will haue me poore
ſinner in their re-
membraunce.
Amen.

B   That

That a man shall not be a curious searcher of
this holye Sacrament, but a meeke folovver
of Christe, subduinge alvvaye his
reason to fayth.

The 18.Chapter.

Hou muſt beware of a cu-
rious, and an vnproſitable
ſearching of this moſte profounde Sacrament, if thou
wilt not be drowned in the
great depth of doubtfulnes,
for he that is the ſearcher of Gods ma-
ieſtie ſhall be anone thruſt out of glorie.
God is of power to worke muche more
then man may vnderſtand, neuertheleſſe
a meeke and an humble ſearchinge of the
truth, readie alwaye to be taught, and to
walke after the teachinges of holye fathers, is ſufferable. Bleſſed is the ſimpli-
citie that leaueth the waye of harde queſtions, and goeth in the playne and ſtedfaſt waye of the commaundementes of
God. Manye haue loſt their deuotion, be-
cauſe they woulde ſearch higher thinges
then perteineth to thẽ. Faith and a good
life is aſked of thee, and not the highnes
of vnderſtanding, nor the depenes of the
miſteries of God. If thou maye not vn-
derſtãd nor take ſuch thinges as be within thee, howe maieſt thou then compre-
hend those thinges that be aboue thee?
Sub-

Submit thy selfe therefore meekelie to
God, and submit also thy reason to
faith, and the light of knowledge and
true vnderstandinge shall be geuen vnto
thee, as it shalbe moste profitable and necessary for thee. Some be greuously tempted of the fayth, and of the Sacrament,
but that is not to be reputed to them, but
rather to the enemye: therefore care not
for him, nor dispute not with thy thoub-
tes, nor aunswere not to the doubtes
that thine enemie shall laye vnto thee,
but beleue the wordes of God, and beleue
his Saintes & Prophetes, and the wicked
enemye shall anone flee awaye fro thee.
And it is ofte times much profitable, that
the seruaunt of God shoulde feele and
susteine suche doubtes for their more
proufe: and comonly the enemy tempteth
not vnfaithfull people & sinners, whom
he hath sure possessio of, but he tempteth
& vereth in diuers maners the faithfull
and deuout persons. Go therefore with a
pure and vndoubted faith, and with an
humble reuerence procede to this Sacrament, and whatsoeuer thou canst not vnderstand, commit it faithfullye to God,
for God will not deceaue thee, but he
shall be deceaued that trusteth ouermuch
to him selfe. God walketh with the simple persons, he openeth him selfe, and
sheweth him selfe to meeke persons. He
geueth vnderstanding to them which are

more in spirite, he openeth the wit to pure and cleane mindes, and hideth his grace from curious men and proude men. Mans reason is feeble and weake, and anone maye be deceyued, but faith is stable and true, and can not be deceyued, therefore all reason and all naturall workinge must folowe faith without further reasoning: for faith and loue in this most holy and moste excellent Sacrament surmount and worke high in secrete maner aboue all reason. O the eternal God, and the Lorde of infinite power doth great thinges in heauen & in earth, that maye not be serched, for if the workes of God were suche that they might be lightlye vnderstanded by mans reason, they were not so marueylous and so inestimable as they be.

Here endeth the fourth booke of the folowinge of Christe, the whiche fourth booke treateth moste principallye of the blessed Sacrament of the Aultar.

HERE BEGINNETH A GODLY

Treatise, and it is called a notable Lesson, otherwise it is called the golden Epistle.

Iesu fili Dauid miserere mei.
O mater Dei memento mei

The exposition of the name of this lytle Booke.

Right good and wholsome Lesson, profitable vnto all Christians, ascribed vnto S. Bernard, and put among his workes, I thynke by some vertuous man, that woulde it shoulde thereby haue the more authoritie, and

P ij   the

the father of loads, and better be borne
awaye: for doubtlesse, it is a good matter,
and edificatiue vnto all them that haue
zeale and care vnto soule health, and de=
sire of saluation. It is called in the Title
(Notabile documentum) that is to saye. A
notable lesson: And some do call it the
golden Epistle. It foloweth immediatlie
after a litle worke called Formula honestæ
vitæ, the forme and maner of an honest
life, or of honest liuing.

IF you intend to please God,
and woulde obtaine grace to
fulfill the same, two thinges
be vnto you very necessarye.
The first, you must withdrawe
your minde from all worldlie and tran=
sitorie thinges, in such maner, as though
you cared not whether any such thinges
were in this worlde or no. The seconde
is, that you geue and applye your selfe so
wholie to God, and haue your selfe in
such a wayte, that you neuer doe, saye, or
thinke, that you know, suppose, or beleue
shoulde offende or displease God, for by
this meane you maye soonest and moste
readily obtayne and winne his fauor and
grace. In all thinges esteeme and accōpt
your selfe moste vile and moste simple,
and as verie naught, in respect and re=
garde of vertue: and thinke, suppose and
beleeue, that all persons be good and bet=
ter

ter then you be, for ſo ſhall you muche
pleaſe our Lorde. Whatſoeuer you ſee,
or ſeeme to perceaue in anye perſon, or
yet heare of any chriſtian, take you none
occaſion therein, but rather aſcribe and
applie you all vnto the beſt, and thinke or
ſuppoſe all is done or ſayd for a good in=
tent or purpoſe, though it ſeeme contra=
rie: for mans ſuſpition and light iudge=
mentes be ſoone and lightlie deceaued or
begiled. Deſpiſe no perſon willinglye, nor
euer ſpeake euill of any perſon, though it
were neuer ſo true that you ſaye. For it
is not lawfull to ſhew in confeſſion the
vice or default of any perſon, except you
might not otherwiſe ſhewe and declare
your owne offence. Speake litle or no=
thing vnto your proper & ſelfe laude or
prayſe, though it were true, and vnto
your familier felowe or faythfull frende,
but ſtudie to keepe ſecret and priuie your
vertue, rather then your vice: yet were it
a cruell deede for any perſons to defame
them ſelfe. Be more glad to geue your
eare and hearing vnto the prayſe, rather
then vnto the diſprayſe of any perſon,
and euer beware aſwell of hearinge as
ſpeakinge of detraction: and when you
ſpeake, take good deliberation, and haue
fewe wordes, and let thoſe be true and
good, ſadlie ſet and wiſelie ordred. If any
wordes be ſpoken vnto you of vice or va=
nitie, as ſoone as ye may, breake of, and

P iiij　　　　leaue

leaue that talke or communication. And
euer returne, and apply your selfe vnto
some appointed good and godlie occupation, bodilie or ghostlie. If anye todayne
chaunce fall or happen vnto you, or vnto
any of yours, leane not to lightlie there-
vnto, or care muche therefore. If it be of
prosperitie, reioyce not muche therein, or
be euer glad thereof: If it be aduersitie,
be not ouercast or ouerthrowen therwith,
or brought to sorowe or sadnes, thanke
God of all, and set litle thereby. Repute
all thinges transitorie as of litie price or
valure. Geue euer most thought and care
vnto those thinges, that may profite and
promote the soule. Flye and auoyde the
persons and places of muche speeche, for
better it is to keepe silence, then to speake.
Keepe the times and places of silence pre-
ciselie, so that you speake not without
reasonable & vnfained cause. The times
of silence in religion be these. From colla-
tion vnto Masse be ended after the houre
of tierce: from the first grace in the fratour vnto the end of the later grace. And
from the beginninge of euensonge, vnto
grace be ended after supper, or els(Bene-
dicite) after the common beuer. The places of silence be the church and the claus-
tre, the fratour and the dortour. If you
be slaundred, and do take occasion at the
fault or offence of any person, then loke
well vpon your selfe; whether you be in
the

the fame default fometime your felfe, and
then haue compaffion vpon your brother
or fifter. If there be none fuche default in
you, thinke verily, and beleue there maye
be, and then do as (in like cafe) you would
be done vnto. And thus, as in a glaffe ye
maye fee and beholde your felfe. Grudge
not, ne complaine vpon any perfon for
any maner caufe, except you fee and perceaue by large coniecture, that you may
profite and edify thereby. Neither denie,
nor affirme your minde or opinion ftiffye
or extremelie, but that your affirmation,
denegation, or doubt be euer powdred
with falte, that is to faye, wifedome dif-
cretion and patience. Vfe not in any wife
to mocke, checke, or fcorne, ne yet to
laugh or fmile but right feldome. And
that alwaye to fhew reuerence or louing
maner, light countenance or loofe behauiour becõmeth not a fadde perfon. Let
your communication be fhort, and with
fewe perfons, alway of vertue, learning,
or good and Chriftian edification, and
euer with fuch warines, that no perfon
in thinges doubtfull may take any authoritie of your wordes or fentence. Let
all your paftime be fpent in bodilie labours, good and profitable, or els godlie
in ftudie, or that paffeth all, in holie and
deuout prayer, fo that the hart and mind
be occupied with the fame you fpeake.
And when you praye for any certain per-

fons, remember their begree, eſtate and
condition ſfrō a forme and order ſ ſyour
prayer, this maye be a good and ceadye
waye,to folowe the order of the ſixe gra-
maticall caſes : The nominatiue, the ge-
nitiue,the datiue,the accuſatiue, the vocatiue, and the ablatiue.The nominatiue, that is, firſte to praye for your ſelfe,
that you maye haue ghoſtly ſtrength and
conſtancie, that you fall not into any
deadlye offence by frayltie, and that you
maye haue right knowledge of God by
faith,and of your ſelfe by due conſidera-
tion of your eſtate and condition,and of
the lawes of God for your conduct and
countenance:and thirdly,that you maye
haue grace and good will, accordinge to
the ſame ſtrength and knowledge, and
that hauinge vnto God a reuerēt dreade,
you neuer offende in thought, worde or
deede,but that you may euer loue him for
him ſelfe,& all his creatures in due order
for him,and in him.The ſecōde is the ge-
nitiue caſe.Then muſt you praye for your
genitors,your progenitours and parēts,
that is to ſaye,your fathers and mothers
ſpirituall and carnall, as your ghoſtlye
fathers or ſpirituall ſouuerains , your
godfathers, your godmothers, your na-
tural father and mother,your graundfa-
thers and graundmothers,your brothers
and ſiſters,and all your kin.In the third
place is the datiue caſe. There muſt you
pray

praye for benefactours, good doers, of whom you haue receaued any maner of giftes spirituall or temporall, vnto the welth of your soule or bodie. In the fourth place is the accusatiue case, where you shoulde praye for your enemyes, such persons as by any meanes haue anoyed, hurt, or greeued you, either ghostly or bodilie, that is to saye, in your soule or maners by anye suggestion, intisinge, euill counsaile, or euill example. In your fame or good name by detraction, backbiting, or slaundering, or yet by familier companie. For a person commonlie is reputed and supposed to be of such condition, as they be, with whom he hath conuersatiō and companie. And for them that hurt your bodie, either by strokes, or by anye other occasion haue hindred the state and health thereof. And lykewise of your worldlie goodes or possessions. For all these maner of enemies must you praye, that our Lord God would forgeue them as you doe, and as you forgeuen woulde be, and that they may come to right charitie and peace. The fifth case is called vocatiue, that is to saye, the calling case, where you conuenientlie maye call, crie, and pray vnto our Lorde for all maner of persons that be out of the state of grace, either by infidelitie, as Turkes, Sarazens, and suche other: or els by errour, as all maner of heretikes : or els by anye
deadly

deadly sinne oz offence to God. Pzaye foz
all theie matter oz persons, that they may
come vnto the right waye of their salua=
tion. In the sirte and last place is the
ablatiue case, where thou must pzaye foz
al them that be taken out of this life, and
that died oz passed the same life in chari=
tie, and that nowe haue neede of pzayer.
In the which you maye keepe a fozme of
the same ozder that is befoze, that is to
say: In steede of the nominatiue, where
you pzayed foz your selfe, you may nowe
pzaye foz all those that doe bide in pai=
ne foz anye default oz offence done by
your example oz occasion: and foz the ge=
nitiue in the second place, foz your pa=
rentes and all your kinne departed this
life. And in the thirde place foz the dati=
ue, pzaye foz your benefactours passed.
And foz the accusatiue in the fourth pla=
ce, you maye pzaye foz them that liue in
payne, foz any occasion oz ensample that
they gaue vnto you. And in the fifte place
foz the vocatiue, pzaye foz all them that
haue greatest paines in purgatozie, and
least helpe here by the suffrage of pzayers.
And foz the ablatiue in the sirte and laste
place, pzay foz all soules in generall. And
that you may be the moze apte to pzaye,
call thzee thinges ofte times to remem=
bzance, that is to saye, what you haue
bene, what you be, and what you shall be.
First, by reason of your bodie, you were
con=

conceaued of the moſte filthie abhomina=
ble matter of man, ſhameful to be ſpoken,
farre more bile then the ſlutche or ſlime
of the earth, and after borne in a ſinfull
ſoule, & purged onely by grace. And nowe
(as vnto the bodie) you be a muckheape
or dunghill of filth, more byle then any
vpon earth, if you remember what doth
iſſue daylie, and come forth out of the
meates of your bodie. And your ſoule is
daylie in ſome ſinne, or (at the leaſt) full
like to be. What you ſhall be as vnto
your bodie, you maye ſee in experience,
wormes meate, and earth againe. And
what ſhall become of your ſoule, no man
in this world can aſſure you. To remem=
ber then the ioyes of heauen, and paines
of hell, and that both be infinite, endles,
and without rebate, but both euer encre=
ſinge and neuer ceaſing, neuer haue eaſe
nor reſt, but euer continue & euerlaſtinge.
To remember then, I ſaye, theſe thinges
may greatly moue you to haue your ſelfe
in a good awayte, and to ſtudie howe you
may auoyd the one, & obteyne the other.
Remember ſpecially howe great a loſſe it
is to looſe heauen, and howe vncomfor=
table gaines to winne helle, and howe
ſoone and howe lightlie either of them
may be gotten or loſt. When any thinge
then of aduerſitie, hurt, or diſpleaſure
happen vnto you thinke the or imagine,
that if you were in hell, you ſhould haue
                                                    the

the same displeasure and manye worse.
And so to auoyde those, you shall here the
better suffer, and for our Lorde, the more
patientlie beare all these that nowe be
present, or any that may come hereafter.
And in like maner, if any good prosperitie or pleasure happen vnto you, thinke
then that if you were in heauen, you
should haue that pleasure and many mo
excellent ioyes. And so for the feruent desire of those ioyes, you shall set litle by
any worldlie comfort or pleasure. A good
contemplation therefore may it be vnto
you in feastes of holie Saintes, to thinke
and record howe great paines they suffered here for the loue of our Lorde, and
howe short these were, and howe soone
passed: and then againe how marueylous
reward they had therefore in ioye and
blisse euerlastinge. So the troubles and
tormentes of good persons be soone and
shortlie gone and ended, and the ioyes
and pleasures of sinful persons doe soone
fade and flie for euer. The good persons
for their troubles suffered here vppon
earth, doe get and win eternall and euerlasting glorie, which the euill persons doe
lose. And contrarie, these euill and sinfull
persons for their ioy and pleasures here,
do receiue by exchaunge eternall and
euerlastinge shame & rebuke, with paine
and wo vnspeakeable. When oeuer the
you be disposed to sluggishnesse, or to be
drowsie

drowſie, remiſſe in prayers, oz dull in
deuotion, then take this litle wozke, oz
els ſome other good Treatiſe, and read
therin, and euer note well the contentes
thereof, and what is meant thereby. And
if you be not thereby deliuered oz eaſed
thereof, then ſhift vnto ſome other wozke
oz occupation, ſo that euer you auoyde
ydlenes, and all vaine paſtimes, which in
dede is loſſe of time. And then remember,
that thoſe that nowe bide in paine, either
in hell, oz yet in purgatozie, foz ſuche ti=
mes ſo paſſed oz loſt, had rather then all
the wozld haue ſuch time to redeme their
paines by, as you maye haue if you will.
Time then vnto al perſons wel occupied,
is verie pzecious and deare. Beware well
therefoze, howe you ſpend it, oz paſſe it,
foz you can neuer reuoke it noz call it
backe. If the time paſſe you by trouble &
veration, thinke they be happie and gra=
cious, that be paſt this wzetched life, and
nowe in bliſſe, foz they ſhall neuer haue
any ſuche miſerie. And when you feele a
comfozt oz conſolation ſpirituall, thanke
God thereof, & thinke the damned ſoules
ſhall neuer haue any ſuche pleaſure. And
thus let this be foz your exerciſe in the
datiue. At night when you go to reſt, firſt
make accompt with your ſelfe, and re=
member howe you haue ſpent oz paſſed
the daye and time that was geuen you to
be vſed in vertue, and howe you haue be=
ſtowed

nowed your thoughtes , your wordes, &
your workes. And if you finde any great
thing amiſſe, geue the whole laude and
praiſe vnto our Lorde God. And if you
perceaue cōtrarie, that you haue miſpent
any part thereof, be ſorie therefore, and
beſeech our Lorde of mercy & forgeuenes,
and promiſe, and verilie purpoſe to make
amendes the next daye. And if you haue
oportunitie thervpon, it ſhall be full conuenient for you to be cōfeſſed on the next
morow, and ſpecially, if the matter done,
ſaide or thought by deliberate conſent, vo
greuouſlie weigh & worke with a grudge
in your conſcience, then woulde I aduiſe
you neuer to eate nor drinke , till ye be
diſcharged thereof, if you maye conuenientlie get a goſtlie father. Nowe for a
concluſion of this worke, put before you,
as by caſe or ymagination two large
Cities, one full of trouble, turmoyle and
miſerie, & let that be hel. The other Citie
ful of ioy, gladnes, comfort and pleaſure,
and let that be heauen. Loke wel on them
both , for in both be many dwellers and
great companye. Then caſt and thinke
within your ſelfe, what thing here might
ſo pleaſe you , that you ſhoulde choſe the
worſe citie, or what thing ſhould diſpleaſe you on the other part , whereby you
ſhoulde withdrawe your ſelfe from that
vertue that might conuey and bring you
vnto the other citie. And when you haue

ſtudied

ftudied well-herevpon,and can nothinge
finde,I dare well affure you,if you keepe
well the precepts and counfailes of this
litle leffon,you fhall find the right way,
for the holie ghofte will inftruct & teache
you, where you be not fufficient of your
felues,fo you indeuor and geue diligence
to beare awaye and folowe that here is
taught. Reade it euerie weake once or
twife, or oftener if you will. And where
you profite,geue the thankes,laude,and
prayfe vnto our Lorde God , and mofte
fweete Sautour Iefu Chrifte, who fende
you his mercie and grace , that alwaye
liueth God worlde without ende.Amen.

This leffon was brought vnto me in
Englifhe of an olde tranflation,rough and
rude , with requeft to amende it. I thought
leffe labour to write new the whole,which
I haue done accordinge to the meaning of
the authour,though not worde for worde:
and in diuers places added fome thinges
folowinge vpon the fame , to make the
matter more fentétious and full.I befeeche
you take all vnto the beft , and praye for
the olde wretched brother of Sion, Ri-
chard VVhitforde.

A spirituall glasse

Reade distinctlie, praye deuoutlie, sigh deepelie, suffer
paciętlie, meeke you lowlye,
geue no sentence hastelie,
speake but rathe, and that
truelie, preuęt your speache
discretly, do your deedes in charitie, tęp-
tations resiste stronglie, breake his heade
shortlie, weepe bitterlie, haue compassion
tenderlie, doe good workes buslie, loue
perseuerantlie, loue hartelie, loue faythfullie, loue God alonelie, and all other
for hym charitablie, loue in aduersitie,
loue in prosperitie, thinke alway of loue,
for loue is none other but God him selfe.
Thus to loue bringeth the louer to loue
without ende. Amen.

THE RVLES OF A CHRISTIAN
lyfe, made by Iohn Picus the elder
Erle of Mirandula.

Irst, if to man or woman the waye of vertue doth seeme harde or painefull, bycause we must nedes fight againſt the fleſhe, diuell, and the worlde, let him or hir call to remembraunce, that whatſoeuer life they will choſe accordinge to the worlde, many aduerſities, incommodities, muche heauines and labour are to be ſuffred.

Moreouer let them haue in remembraunce, that in wealth and worldlye poſſeſſions is muche and longe contencion, laborious alſo, and therwith vnfruitfull, wherein trauaile is the concluſion or ende of labour, and finallye paine euerlaſting, if thoſe thinges be not well ordered and charitablie diſpoſed.

Remembre alſo, that it is very foliſhenes, to thinke to come vnto heauen by any other meane than by the ſayed battaile, conſideringe that our heade and maiſter Chriſte did not aſcende vnto heauen but by his paſſion: And the ſeruaunt ought not to be in better eſtate or condicion than his mayſter or ſoueraine.

Furthermore conſider that this battayle

taile ought not to be grudged at, but to
be deſired and wiſhed to? , all though
thereof no price or rewarde myght en-
ſue or happen, but onelie that thereby we
might be comfourmed or ioyned to Chriſt
our God & maiſter. Wherefore as often
as in reſiſtinge any temptacion thou doeſt
withſtande any of thy ſences or wittes,
thinke vnto what part of Chriſtes paſſiō
thou mayeſt applie thy ſelfe or make thy
ſelfe like: As reſiſtinge glotonie, whiles
thou doeſt puniſhe thy taſt or appetite:
remembre that Chriſte receyued in his
drinke, ayſell mixte with the gall of a
beaſte, a drinke moſt vnſauerie and loth-
ſome.

Whan thou withdraweſt thy hand
from vnlawfull takinge or keepinge of
any thinge, which liketh thine appetite,
remembre Chriſtes handes as they were
faſte nayled vnto the tree of the Croſſe.
And reſiſtinge of pride, thinke on hym,
who beinge verie God almightie, for thy
ſake receyued the fourme of a ſubiecte,
and humbled hym ſelfe vnto the moſte
vile and reprochefull death of the Croſſe.
And whan thou arte tempted with wrath:
Remembre that he, whiche was God,
and of all men the moſt iuſt or righteous,
whan he behelde him ſelfe mocked, ſpitte
on, ſcourged, and puniſhed with all diſ-
pites and rebukes, and ſet on the Croſſe
amonge errant theues, as if he hym ſelfe
were

were a falſe harlot,he not withſtandinge
ſhewed neuer token of indignation , or
that he were greeued , but ſufferinge all
thinges with wonderfull pacience , aun-
ſwered all men moſte gentillie. In this
wiſe , if thou peruſe all thinges one after
an other, thou mayeſt finde , that there
is no paſſion or trouble , that ſhall not
make the in ſome parte conformable or
lyke vnto Chriſte.

Alſo put not thy truſte in mans helpe,
but in the onelie vertue of Chriſte Ieſu,
which ſayed:Truſt well,for I haue vainquiſhed the worlde.And in an other place
he ſayth : The prince of this worlde is
caſte out therof. Wherfore lette vs truſt
by his onelie vertue , to vainquiſhe the
worlde , and to ſubdue the diuell. And
therefore ought we to aſke his helpe by
our owne prayers and by the prayers of
his bleſſed Sainctes.

Remembre alſo,that as ſone as thou
haſt vainquiſhed one temptacion,alwaye
an other is to be loked for : The diuell
goeth alwaye about and ſeeketh for hym
whom he would deuoure. Wherefore we
ought to ſerue diligentlie and be euer in
feare , and to ſaye with the prophete: I
will ſtande alwaye at my defence.

Take heede moreouer,that not onely
thou be not vainquiſhed of the diuell,
that tempteth the,but alſo that thou vainquiſhe and ouercome him.And that is not
onelye

onelle whan thou doest no sinne, but also whan of that thinge wherein he tempted thee, thou takest occasion for to her good. As if he offreth to the some good acte to be done to the intent that thereby thou mayest fall into vainglorie : forthwith thou thinkynge it, not to be thy deede or worke, but the benefite or rewarde of God, humble thou thy selfe, and iudge the to be vnkinde vnto God in respecte of his manifolde benefites.

As often as thou doest fight, fight as in hope to vainquishe, and to haue at the last perpetuall peace. For that paraduenture God of his abundant grace shall gyue vnto the, and the diuell beinge confused of thy victorie, shall retourne no more againe. But yet whan thou haste vainquished, beare thy selfe so as if thou shouldest fight againe shortelie. Thus alwaye in bataile, thou muste thinke on victorie : & after victorie, thou must prepare the to batalle immediatlie againe.

Although thou feelest thy selfe well armed and readie, yet flee (not withstandinge) all occasions to sinne. For as the wise man saith: Who loueth perille, shal therein perishe.

In all temptacions resist the beginninge, and beate the Children of Babilon against the stone, whiche stone is Christe, and the children be euill thoughtes and imaginacions. For in longe continuynge
of

of sinne, seldome worketh any medicine
or remedie.

Remembre, that although in the saied
conflict of temptacion the bataile semeth
to be verie daungerous: yet consider how
muche sweter it is to vainquishe temp=
tacion, than to felowe sinne, whereto
she inclineth the, whereof the ende is re=
pentaunce. And herein many be foule de=
ceiued, whiche compare not the swetenes
of victorie to the swetenes of sinne, but
onelye compareth bataile to pleasure.
Notwithstandinge a man or woman,
whiche hath a thousande times knowen
what it is to gyue place to temptacion,
shoulde ones assaie, what it is to vain=
quishe temptacion.

If thou be tempted thinke thou not
therefore that God hath forsaken the, or
that he setteth but littell by the, or that
thou arte not in the sight of God, good
or perfecte: but remēbre, that after Saint
Paule had seene God, as he was in his
diuinitie, and suche secreate misteries as
be not lawfull for any man to speake or
rehercec, he for all that suffred temptacion
of the flesh, wherewith God suffred him
to be tempted, leaft he shoulde be assaul=
ted with pride. Wherein a man ought to
consider, that Saint Paule, whiche was
the pure vessell of election, and rapt into
the thirde heauen, was not withstãdinge
in perill to be proude of his vertues, as
he

he fayth of him felfe. ⸿ Wherfore noone a
temptacious man or woman ought to
athe the moste strongste agaynst the tep-
tacion of pride, since pride is the rote of
all mischiefe, agaynst the whtch the onelie
remedie is to thinke alwaye that God
humbled him selfe for vs vnto the Crosse.
And moreouer that death hath so humbled vs whether we will or no, that our
bodies shall be the meate of wormes lothsome and venimouse.

FINIS,